DECISION ON EUROPE

An Explanation of the Common Market

by

Derek H. Hene

JORDAN & SONS LTD

London 1970

SBN 85308 005 4

First published in 1970
by Jordan and Sons Limited
190 Fleet Street
London EC4

Printed in Great Britain by
Western Printing Services Ltd
Bristol

Bound by Mansell London N1

Decision on Europe

For P.F.S. and A.

Publisher's Note

Some of the material in this book derives
from the author's earlier book, now out of print,
What the Common Market Really Means.

Contents

Preface and Acknowledgments

'To join or not to join' is one of the most important and also one of the most difficult problems facing Britain today. The problem itself can only be solved in the first instance by the Government when they decide their future policies *vis-à-vis* the Community of Europe. The people of Britain—through their Members of Parliament, letters to the Press, editorials, public speeches and in factories and pubs will continue to provide the 'climate', the background to the official action.

When the British Prime Minister decided to leave Britain's application lying 'on the table', he in fact took an irrevocable step. That second application for full membership in 1967 was a decisive step for Europe. The present stalemate is now likely to be resolved – one way or another. But the decision is almost certain to be final as far as this problem is concerned. It seems most improbable that Britain will ever again turn away from Europe and just as unlikely that Europe will keep Britain out much longer now that France has a new President. Postponement of membership has not made the alignment between the Community and Britain any easier and probably the effects of joining will be exacerbated for both parties, because the Community has integrated further. In the meantime, the British Government may be able to do quite a lot to soften the blow. When linking two spacecraft it is essential to ensure that they are travelling at the same speed, in the same direction and on parallel courses. The same conditions are required when it is intended to forge a link between nations after centuries of separate existence.

After many years of involvement in many ways with those problems, it is my belief that even now, twelve years after the creation of the Common Market as we know it today, the reasoning, purposes and activities of the new Europe are not fully understood by many people in Britain. On the other hand, there can be no doubt that there is a wide and intense interest in these matters, on the part of people of all age-groups (but mostly among the younger generation), and in all walks of life.

Somehow or other the Channel, having proved to be a magnificent moat in 1939/40, behind which the armed forces from many countries were able to prepare themselves for the liberation of the European Continent from a New Order imposed by force, has prevented the 'Community Spirit' from crossing westward to the British Isles. No matter what the Government and the protagonists of the 'pro' and 'anti' market factions were saying in Britain, the people themselves remained politely interested but essentially uninformed.

This strange example of a major failure of communication two years ago seemed to me to justify the production of a book to bridge this gap. In the course of the preparatory work I began to realize how rapidly the literature on the subject had multiplied, all over the world. There were weighty textbooks and learned expositions, studies of all kinds and tomes of statistics. Also there was a veritable flood of partisan books and pamphlets, every one of them fervently seeking to convince the reader of the merits of some cause or other. In Britain, there were clarion calls to resist the sirens from the other side of the Channel, as well as strident counterblasts from the pro-market brigades. In the face of this literary whirlpool, I could not but ask myself whether yet another volume could justifiably be added to such a formidable list.

The principal reason which made me decide to persevere was that there seemed to be no book at all written for the ordinary man or woman with average interest in the subject, but without special training or experience, which was reasonably comprehensive, easy to understand, unbiased, not unduly lengthy and up-to-date. I tried to fill this apparent 'vacancy' in the Market literature. It was at that time my earnest hope that the problems connected with the Community of Europe, their possible solutions and the consequences likely to follow would have become a little clearer and more real for some of the readers of that book. I hoped that at any rate I might have managed to stimulate some other person sufficiently for him (or her) to improve upon this effort to bring home to the people of Britain the essential problems of the 'Common Market'.

I do not know whether this hope was ever fulfilled. The spate of literature became a mere trickle; interest in the Common Market began to die away. The percentage of 'Don't know' replies to the pollsters' inquiries grew, and so did the number of 'anti-Marketeers'. Only recently, following a change of political climate in France, has there been a re-awakening of interest in Europe.

At that stage I decided to re-model my previous book, take a new look at the developments across the Channel and try once more to explain the problems and the implications as fairly as possible. It is a contentious subject, likely to arouse deep emotions in many people. I have set out my personal views in a few separate Notes, at the very end of this book, which in itself, I hope, represents an impartial analysis of this unique attempt at European unification.

Two years ago I expressed my sincere thanks to the many people in Brussels, Luxembourg, Strasbourg, London and elsewhere who responded to every call for help most magnificently. I derived much help from the many discussions, interviews, attendances at sittings and other occasions when those concerned almost 'fell over themselves' in their endeavour to provide me with the material and the facts I was seeking. I then expressed my very special thanks to the Official Spokesmen of the three Commissions in Brussels and Luxembourg, of the Ministerial Councils, the European Parliament and the European Court, and last but not least to the ever helpful and efficient library staff of the Information Office of the European Community in London for their provision of information and literature to keep me up-to-date in dealing with an ever-changing Community in the modern world.

Once again my thanks are due to all the above, for their continued advice and assistance. It is revealing and encouraging to observe the many and varied developments behind the deceptively calm façade of the European Community. A fascinating piece of unrehearsed evidence of good will was the relief so patently noticeable in Brussels after the retirement of President de Gaulle. For me, it was relief tempered with more than a soupçon of sadness, at the passing of a shadow cast over the Community by a man who had once been very great indeed.

April 1970   D.H.H.

Step by Step

1946 (19 Sep.)   Winston Churchill, at Zurich University: 'We must create a kind of United States of Europe'.
1947 (29 Oct.)   'Benelux' established.
1948 (16 Apl.)   Convention for European Economic Co-operation (O.E.E.C.) signed.
1949 (5 May)   Statute of Council of Europe signed.
1950 (9 May)   Schuman Declaration: Proposal to pool French and German coal and steel production.
1951 (18 Apl.)   E.C.S.C. Treaty signed in Paris.
1952 (27 May)   E.D.C. Treaty signed in Paris.
      (10 Aug.)   E.C.S.C. starts work.
1953 (10 Feb.)   E.C.S.C. coal, iron ore and scrap 'common markets' operative.
1954 (30 Aug.)   E.D.C. Treaty for a Defence Community rejected in Paris.
      (21 Dec.)   U.K. and E.C.S.C. sign Association Agreement.
1955 (1 June)   Messina Conference begins.
1956 (26 June)   Negotiations for the 'Rome Treaties' begin in Brussels.
1957 (25 Mar.)   E.E.C. and Euratom Treaties signed in Rome.
1958 (1 Jan.)   'Rome Treaties' in force.
1959 (20 Nov.)   E.F.T.A. Convention signed.
1960 (3 May)   E.F.T.A. Convention in force.
1961 (1 July)   Finland becomes an Associate of E.F.T.A.
      (9 July)   Greece becomes an Associate member of E.E.C.

	(18 July)	Bonn Declaration on political union.
	(10 Aug.)	U.K. applies for membership of E.E.C.
1962	(15 May)	Fouchet Plan for a Political Community fails.
1963	(14 Jan.)	U.K. application for membership of E.E.C. fails.
	(1 July)	Yaoundé Agreement signed between 18 African States and E.E.C.
	(12 Sep.)	Turkey becomes an Associate member of E.E.C.
1964	(27 Oct.)	Belgian Senate approves 'three wise men' Plan for political integration devised by M. Spaak.
	(31 Dec.)	Equal pay applicable in the Community.
1965	(8 Apl.)	Treaty establishing a single Council and a single Commission signed at Brussels.
	(5 July)	France begins to boycott the Community over introduction of majority voting and her delegates do not attend for 7 months.
1966	(1 Jan.)	Third and last 'stage' of E.E.C. begins.
	(12 May)	Common Agricultural Policy agreed.
	(16 July)	Nigeria signs Association Agreement with E.E.C.
1967	(16 Jan.)	British Prime Minister begins his Tour of Community with a view to reapplication for membership.
	(9 Feb.)	Decision taken to introduce 'Euro-tax' in 1970.
	(2 May)	Britain re-applies for membership. Denmark and Ireland also apply.
	(29 Sep.)	Preliminary Opinion submitted by Commission *re* application for membership by U.K., Ireland, Denmark and Norway.
	(19 Dec.)	Ministerial Council declines to consider 4 applications from E.F.T.A. members, and Sweden's letter, but all five remain 'on the Council's agenda'.
1968	(19 Jan.)	Nigeria ratifies Association Agreement.
	(1 July)	Removal of customs duties in E.E.C.

(1 July)   Introduction of full customs union in the Community and operation of the C.E.T.

(5 Oct.)   Harmel Plan announced for E.E.C.-British co-operation in certain fields.

(20 Nov.) French monetary crisis. Foreign exchange markets closed.

(4 Dec.)   Commission approves French controls subject to permanent review.

1969 (3 Jan.)   E.E.C. becomes world's largest trader: 30 per cent of all exports, 27 per cent of all imports.

(28 Apl.) President de Gaulle resigns.

(1 Oct.)   Commission publishes a revised 'Opinion' dealing with problem of 'enlarged' Community.

(1–2 Dec.) Hague Conference of Premiers of the Six. Candidate nations to be considered after Agriculture Policy settlement.

(22 Dec.) Agreement reached on farming policy and how to finance it.

(31 Dec.) Transition period (laid down in Treaty of Rome) ends after twelve years.

1970 (10 Feb.) British White Paper: An Economic Assessment.

Terminology

A number of expressions not in common usage or which have acquired a special meaning in 'Community language' have been employed in this book. These expressions are in current use in Brussels and Luxembourg and occur constantly in official publications. The explanations set out hereunder are intended as a guide to the reader and not as 'definitions' in the strict legal sense.

ASSOCIATION
As regards a European state, a special bilateral arrangement with the Community, possibly leading to full membership in due course.

As regards a non-European state, arrangements of a permanent nature under Articles 131–136 of the E.E.C. Treaty.

COMMON MARKET
A popular term referring to the European Economic Community, but often applied to the entire European Community.

COMMON POLICY
Complete alignment, usually by stages, of objectives, planning, and execution pertaining to a specific branch of national life, such as agriculture or transport, usually in accordance with the Treaties of Paris or Rome.

COMMUNITY LAW
The body of law built up by Directives, Decisions and Regulations and to some extent by interpretative judgments of the

European Court. Community Law takes precedence over national law in the member-states where there is a conflict.

CONFEDERATION
A rather loose form of Federation. The member-states retain a fairly considerable measure of self-government but share one central administration for limited purposes of unified direction in such matters as Foreign Policy or Defence. Sometimes the individual states within a Confederation retain the right to secede in certain circumstances.

CONSULTATION
A process, usually laid down in a Treaty, Protocol or Agreement, by which two or more bodies or organizations within the European Community should or must discuss certain problems or propositions, before a final decision is reached.

CO-OPERATION
Arrangements between sovereign states to assist each other, without compulsion, and subject to termination by unilateral action.

CO-ORDINATION
Arrangements to bring into line national plans or policies, but only in general terms or for the purpose of achieving a common objective.

DECISION
A written statement by the Council(s) or Commission(s), addressed to a Government of a member-state, a company or an individual within a member-state. It will bind the addressee in accordance with its terms, but is not of general applicability except by way of guidance.

DIALOGUE (OR TRIALOGUE)
Discussion (or peaceful confrontation) between two or three of the Institutions of the Community prior to a final decision being reached, in order to clear the air by hearing the views of all sides. A dialogue involves the Commission and the Council, and a trialogue involves the Parliament as well.

DIRECTIVE
A written document addressed by the Ministerial Council(s) or the Commission(s), to one or more of the member-states. The member-state is then obliged to achieve the result specified in the Directive, but details of procedure are left to the discretion of the national authorities.

EURO- . . .
A prefix frequently applied to existing or proposed European projects, such as Euro-patents, Eurovision, etc.

FEDERALIZATION
The process of combination between sovereign or independent states for the purpose of establishing a common central governmental agency.

FEDERATION
Collective administration of formerly independent states by a single government which is placed in charge of all common policies *vis-à-vis* the outside world.

HARMONIZATION
The process in the Community of 'aligning' policies or laws within a member-state to those in some or all of the other member-states, in accordance with Community objectives and principles.

IMPLEMENTATION
The process of carrying out a measure, a law, a policy, a plan, etc., as laid down in one of the Treaties or in a Regulation.

INITIATION OF POLICY
One of the principal tasks of the Commission(s): after exhaustive preliminary discussions a policy is 'initiated' when it is laid before the Council(s) for action.

INSTITUTIONS
The four principal organizations created by the Treaties of Paris and Rome: the European Parliament, the European Court, the Council(s) of Ministers and the Commission(s) (and the High Authority).

INTEGRATION
The procedure of bringing about much closer relations between states than co-operation. Normally achieved in the Economic Community by setting up supra-national committees, boards or institutions to assume control over specific sectors of the economies of the member-states.

INTERNATIONAL
A term applicable to a body composed of representatives of member-states of the Community or of sovereign nations generally, or to measures emanating therefrom.

OPINION (OR RECOMMENDATION)
Written statements by the Council(s) or Commission(s) of considerable guidance value, but without binding force.

REGULATION
A legal enactment issued by the Council(s) or Commission(s), which under the Treaty is automatically and generally applicable in every member-state. No legislative action within the member-states is required to accord the force of law to a Regulation.

SUPRA-NATIONAL
A term applicable to a body placed above the national governments of the member-states or their departments, or to measures emanating from such bodies.

UNIFICATION
Similar to integration but without necessarily involving the establishment of common administrative control. Implies complete fusion at all essential levels.

UNITY
The ultimate objective of unification. Implies a single governmental and administrative system, and full integration at higher levels.

VETO
The right (usually under a Treaty or Agreement) of a member-state or its representative to hold up the passing of a measure, a law, etc., for which unanimity is required, even by means of solitary opposition thereto.

WEIGHTING OF VOTES
The system by which multiple votes are accorded to the representatives of member-states on the Council and on certain Committees, in order to give expression to the respective numbers of population, territorial sizes, financial powers and other aspects of comparative national standing of the several member-states.

Abbreviations

(Abbreviations have been avoided as far as possible. The following, which are in official use, have been used throughout the text.)

Benelux	Association of BElgium, NEtherlands and LUXembourg.
C.A.P.	Common Agricultural Policy.
E.C.S.C.	European Coal and Steel Community.
E.D.C.	European Defence Community.
E.D.F.	European Development Fund.
E.E.C.	European Economic Community.
E.F.T.A.	European Free Trade Association.
E.I.B.	European Investment Bank.
E.L.D.O.	European Launcher Development Organization.
E.P.C.	European Political Community.
E.S.R.O.	European Space Research Organization.
Euratom	European Atomic Energy Community.
G.A.T.T.	General Agreement on Tariffs and Trade.
N.A.F.T.A.	North Atlantic Free Trade Area.
N.A.T.O.	North Atlantic Treaty Organization.
O.E.E.C.	Organization for European Economic Cooperation.
S.E.T.I.S.	Société Européenne pour l'Etude et l'Intégration des Systèmes spatiaux.
U.K.A.E.A.	United Kingdom Atomic Energy Authority.
U.N.	United Nations.
T.V.A.	Value added tax.
W.E.U.	Western European Union.

CHAPTER I

Background

To most men Europe has always meant little more than a densely populated Continent off Asia. Its peoples have gone their separate ways for centuries. The haphazard settlements of wandering tribes, the vagaries of battle fortunes and the endless search for fertile fields combined to produce the establishment of ethnic groups in the more hospitable regions which offered protection and sustenance. Wide rivers and high mountain ranges divided the settlers into isolated 'compartments'.

As the centuries passed and the population expanded, some of these peoples (through contact with earlier civilizations) developed more rapidly than others who lived in greater seclusion. Their newly acquired culture, wealth and power enabled these peoples to take henceforth a leading part in the forward march of humanity towards a better and richer life. During these formative eras some of the nations of Europe were responsible for a great deal of progressive thought and action. Simultaneously, however, their perpetual warring with each other for the ultimate leadership was the cause of unending bloodshed and misery. Thus the European nations gave to mankind hope as well as despair, progress as well as perdition.

For centuries these wars between the European peoples blotted the pages of history with ugly stains of scarlet and put the brakes on the social and economic progress of their peoples. Throughout the era of Roman rule and during the ensuing centuries when the Church maintained her spiritual and temporal hold over much of the Continent, the principal events recorded in the annals of history were those relating to wars, conquests and suppression. Yet the thought that more sustained progress could be achieved under peaceful conditions had occurred to many statesmen and philosophers. But those high-minded plans were clearly Utopian – no practicable method of producing order out of chaos without force was devised. It was considered impossible seriously to appeal to fraternization among the ignorant masses. No attempt to ensure peace by force was likely to have lasting effects. No ruler could hope to escape the vengeful desires of those kings and princes whom he had relegated to subordinate roles. All agreed that it was madness to destroy in a few lawless years the precious progress of the preceding decades. Numerous writers of those times expressed in words what the multitudes could only feel – problems which even today are not finally solved: if Europe was to remain the cultural mainspring of mankind, if the high living standards of her peoples were to be maintained, they simply could not afford the waste and expense of recurring warfare. Co-operation by consent being impossible, temporary unity by force from above seemed to be the only solution. Neither the rule of Rome as the old Empire broke up and slowly decayed, nor the application of force masked by the velvet cloak of Faith during the long era of the Holy Roman Empire, provided a satisfactory answer. Under the specious and largely ineffective cover of universal power the cauldrons continued to bubble and boil over. From one end of the Continent to the other the peoples of Europe went to war at least once during every generation and sometimes much more frequently. It was during that period quite the fashion to write and talk loftily of world states and the rule of law, but the writers were dreamers and the talkers merely talked.

The Empire of Charlemagne dissolved in seas of blood and territorial division. European 'unity' through force had failed once again. When the Peace of Westphalia was signed in 1648, the Continent made a pretty picture, but only for those who delight in coloured maps. A maze of frontiers, natural and artificial, now divided not only peoples but small provinces and cities from one another. The Empire had been but a shadow under Charles II. The heritage was nationalism gone mad.

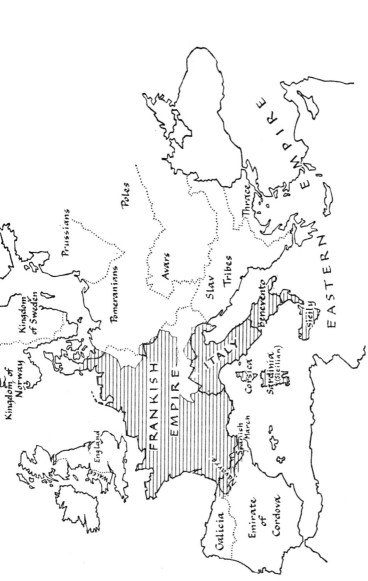

The Frankish Empire extended over a large section of the present Community area. Italy was still divided into several small states. This was the nearest approach to political unification in the territories which are now Western Europe until the present time. 'L'effondrement d'un empire et la naissance d'une Europe' (Joseph Calmette, Paris, 1941).

The shaded portion indicates the area now occupied by the six member-states of the Common Market.

MAP B: EUROPE IN 1648

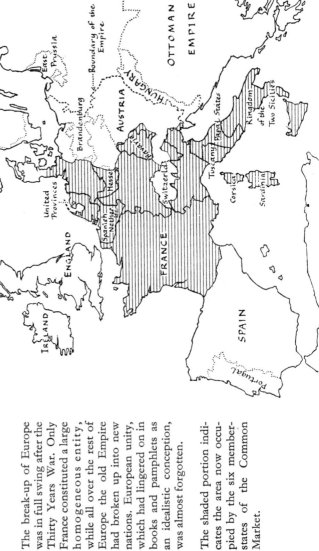

The break-up of Europe was in full swing after the Thirty Years War. Only France constituted a large homogeneous entity, while all over the rest of Europe the old Empire had broken up into new nations. European unity, which had lingered on in books and pamphlets as an idealistic conception, was almost forgotten.

The shaded portion indicates the area now occupied by the six member-states of the Common Market.

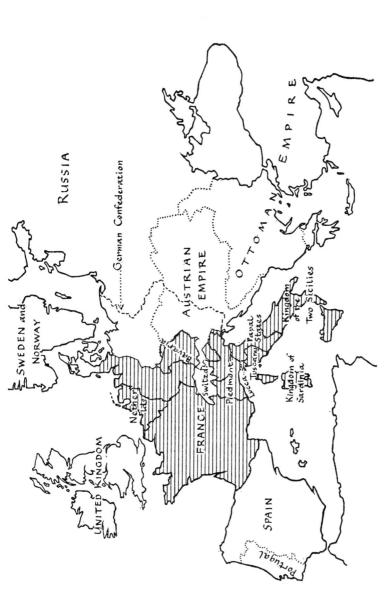

Some of the German territories were beginning to rival France as territorially important units, and the Austrian Empire embraced much of Central and Eastern Europe. There were now fewer 'splinter' states in Europe. In 1876 Bismarck was to say: 'Qui parle Europe a tort'.

The shaded portion indicates the area now occupied by the six member-states of the Common Market.

Now the few remaining large nations began to struggle for the leadership. Europe alternated between attempts to subjugate her peoples by force, first by one nation then by another. In the end, at the conclusion of the Napoleonic bids for supreme power, the Congress of Vienna offered a brief chance for some kind of wider and divided control. The rise of Prussia, her resignation from the German Bund, and the destruction of the last remnants of the old Empires, however, directly led to the creation of a number of larger and more powerful nation-states.

The seeds of the World Wars were sown when the leaders of Europe could not find statesmen more liberal than Metternich or less brutal than Bismarck to solve their most vital problems. The concert of Europe lacked the essential harmonies which alone can provide pleasant music, and the balance of power proved to be far too precarious for peace. The scales of a balance are not a safe foundation for an edifice built to endure.

During the strangely uneasy days until the outbreak of the First World War, so oddly referred to as the Good Old Days by some, national aggrandisement was generally considered preferable to co-operation between the nations of Europe. Even the liberal uprisings of 1848 and the decade following, the widespread feeling of revulsion engendered by Bismarck's attacks on Prussia's neighbours, and the atmosphere of anxiety, due to the periodic clashes and quarrels between the Great Powers, produced no more potent reaction than slightly hysterical pamphlets and rather incomprehensible poetry. The nation-states of Europe had become supreme; the division of the Continent was more or less permanent. Amidst a welter of uniforms, flags, formalities and protocol the nations took up their respective positions behind the gaily coloured frontier booms. The scene was set for Europe's first civil war on a grand scale.

Almost forgotten among the battle-cries are the few positive achievements of those days which have persisted into the present era: the creation of the International Postal Union, and, much later, the setting up of an International Court at the Hague. However, it was not by writing letters nor by recourse to law that the nations of Europe were to attempt the solution of their problems. Many of the protagonists of peaceful co-operation were hardly attractive figures. It was easy to label most of them as cosmopolitan driftwood, romancers and dreamers. When their cries become too insistent one could even call them traitors.

It is strange that European unification was regarded as an unattainable ideal or a foolish fancy for so long. There, right in the middle of the Continent, was the little Republic of Switzerland, where nationals (in the wider sense) of three powerful nation-states lived in peaceful harmony within a single federal state. And across the Atlantic refugees from Europe, immigrants from every state, were beginning to build a new and powerful nation. They had come together through the vicissitudes of common misery – perhaps such pressure from outside was, and possibly still is, the best stimulant for peaceful relations between different nationalities.

The European Powers, or rather their respective leaders, wasted no time on such idle thoughts. The fruits of colonization and industrialization were making them rich beyond their wildest dreams. There was enough for all: let every nation fend for itself and heaven help those who would fall by the wayside. The *bon ton* of international amity was preserved by occasional state visits of monarchs and presidents. In an age of increasing affluence among ever wider sectors of the people hardly anybody felt any need for co-operation, let alone for integration between the nations of Europe.

In July, 1914, the veneer of polite pretences cracked beyond repair. All hell broke loose; scores of long-dormant grievances came alive and the latent hatreds and rivalries burst like so many purulent blisters.

The entire globe was eventually involved in this struggle which had begun as yet another attempt to resolve Europe's problems by force. For more than four years the battles raged, and among the millions who died or were maimed there were many from far-off countries who had been drawn into this conflict by virtue of kinship or treaty obligation. The failures of the past had proved very costly, and they had to be paid for by blood and tears. At long last, in the winter of 1918 a grey and shaken world greeted an uneasy but nonetheless welcome

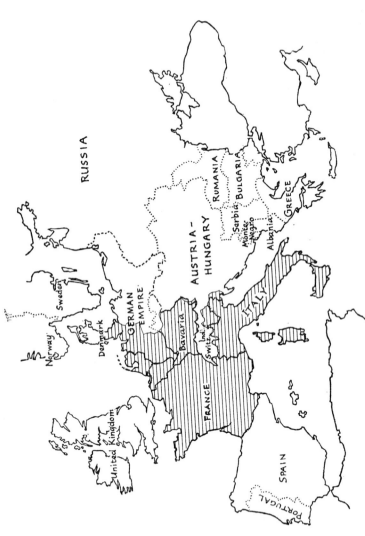

MAP D: EUROPE IN 1914

The new nation-states were poised for war. France, Germany, Italy and the Austro-Hungarian Empire had emerged as the four Continental bastions of power. The twentieth century began as the Century of Imperialism.

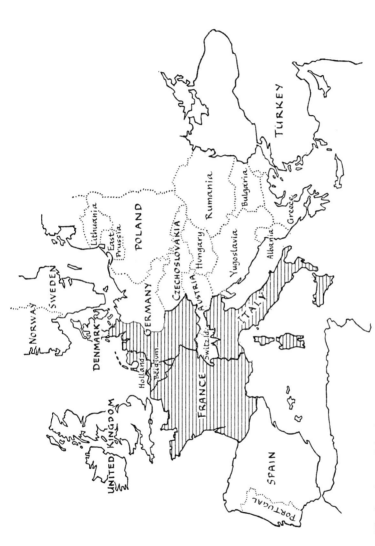

The break-up of the Austrian Empire had added several small states to the Central and Eastern scene. Now only France, Germany and Italy remained as major Continental powers. A few years later Europe had to be liberated from outside, by Britain, America and Russia.

The shaded portion indicates the area now occupied by the six member-states of the Common Market.

MAP F: EUROPE IN 1970

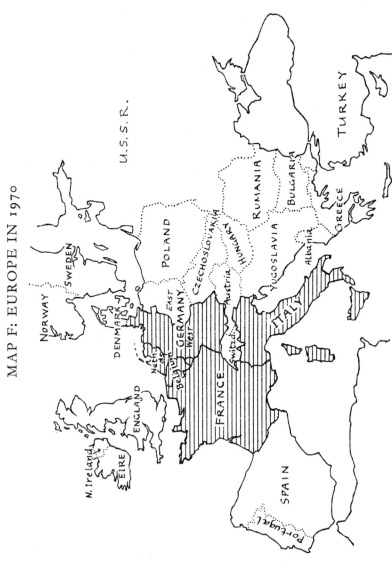

The division of Germany has added a new Eastern 'state', but Western Germany is still comparable in size to France and Italy. The nation-states of Europe have become fairly stabilized as a comparison between maps E, D and F will show, but they are still a long way from achieving the degree of political union of the 9th century (map A).

armistice. The Treaty of Versailles solved few problems, but left the vanquished despairing of the present but nurturing hopes of revenge for the days to come.

The spasmodic booms and depressions, the feeling that Europe as a whole was beginning to loosen her grip on world affairs, and the understandable wish to stem the tide of competition from overseas, had some slight effect on governmental policies although much less than might have been anticipated. The League of Nations indulged in verbal fisticuffs and there was little positive news from Geneva. Some of the more far-sighted Foreign Ministers raised their voices in support of greater European collaboration, but in vain. Men like Briand and Stresemann were quite unable to overcome the aftermath of the recent war. Organizations like Count Coudenhove-Kalergi's 'Paneuropa Union' faltered in their struggle for support. They could not compete with the private armies, dressed in shirts of many colours, and all promising their supporters total ultimate victory. The victors had no common policy at all and the losers only one: revenge.

Against a background of rising mass-unemployment and economic recession, the unintelligible squabbles in various elegant resorts about the distribution of the spoils of war sounded more and more unrealistic. As one loan succeeded another, each in turn followed by the inevitable moratorium when the borrowers could not repay, as inflation increased and in some cases got wholly out of control, it became obvious that there was only one single practicable remedy: re-armament. As there was no glory in peace, recourse to war seemed the only available alternative. It sounds incredible now, but the expenditure of a mere fraction on effective conciliation measures of what was spent to prepare for war, might have avoided the subsequent catastrophe. The losers were by now absorbing their unemployed millions into the armed forces, via their private armies. The victors, who felt it was not easy to arouse much enthusiasm in defence of the Treaty of Versailles, somewhat sluggishly abandoned their disarmament programme and began to rearm themselves. The one-sided Treaty provided little material for national enthusiasm, but soon the vain-glorious and seemingly insane claims by the erstwhile losers to world power and universal supremacy provided the democracies with ample reasons for worry and concentrated efforts. Once again Europe split into two camps for war: the dictators with ambitions for complete supremacy against the democracies who were now – rather late – proclaiming their willingness to fight to the death for the freedom of Man. In fact it was their very existence which was at stake. Provocation quickly gave way to aggression and within a few months Europe was at war again.

A year later the German armies, with Italian support in Europe and Japanese aid in the Far East, had subjugated every major European power with the exception of Britain. They then turned against their uneasy Russian allies, Japan attacked the U.S.A., and once again the European nations had succeeded in embroiling the whole world in their disputes. This time the annihilation of the hostile forces was no longer the sole objective. Genocide and total destruction of the civilian population and their homes and workshops were added as 'permissible' targets. These endeavours were highly successful: millions lost their lives, more millions were maimed and entire cities were laid waste. Europe's industry was partially wrecked and wholly disorganized. The blood-bath ended with the first use of nuclear weapons, whose destructive effects surpassed anything hitherto dreamed of. Eminent scientists could now claim, with justification, that it was at long last possible to destroy the whole of Europe within an hour or less.

It took some little time before the dazed peoples and their respective leaders were able to think more or less clearly again. As the lights went on again in 1945/46 the statesmen of Europe regretfully observed that there had been many changes. While the bombs were raining down on the cities of Europe, the old colonial empires had begun to disintegrate. The nations of Europe had neither the men nor the materials to halt this process. They had lost millions of lives, they had wrecked their industrial strongholds and now they were losing their sources of raw materials and their military bases as well.

The home-coming soldiers, sailors and airmen, and the impatient civilians, were not very interested in grand schemes for international friendship. They wanted food, homes and rest. They were fed up with generals and politicians and desired above all to be left alone to do as they wished. Then, in September 1946, Europe's greatest statesman, Winston Churchill, addressing a meeting in Zürich after his rejection by the British electorate, called for 'a kind of United Europe'. This clarion call is now best remembered for what Churchill did not say, namely whether Britain was to be within or without such a scheme. That question will never be answered.

During the next four years more and more voices were raised in favour of some kind of European reorganization. But what was meant by 'European'? Marshal Stalin's Russia was certainly not interested, nor were his newly acquired satellites allowed to contemplate the possibilities of such an escape route. The Iron Curtain descended across Europe and added to the difficulties of that unhappy Continent. More than half a dozen of her nations were now cut off from the rest – yet another loss of potential.

But at this stage oppression developed into a blessing in disguise. With Russia, under Stalin's suspicious control, transferring her hatred of Germany almost instantaneously to her recent allies in Europe, it seemed that the usual interim period between one European War and the next would now be further reduced to a mere half-decade. The frontiers of 1939 had been largely re-established, except to undo a number of German conquests. There was a strange atmosphere of '*déjà vu*' about; it was rather like 1919 all over again. The futility of reparations, the artificial frontiers, the endless arguments among the victors – only this time reinforced by the clamour of the 'emergent' nations in other Continents. The thought occurred to some that possibly Europe could not afford the luxury of one blood-bath per generation any longer. And at last there came a call for positive action out of the fatuous squabbles among the ruins: On 9th May 1950, at the famous old Quai d'Orsay in Paris, the French Foreign Minister read to a distinguished audience a Declaration proposing the pooling of the entire coal and steel resources of France and Germany.

Such a proposal from a victor to the vanquished only five years after the end of hostilities was an unheard-of event. If the scheme worked it would be virtually impossible for these two nations to fight each other again. Now M. Schuman invited all the other democratically governed nations of Europe to join his scheme. As it stood, the Declaration had been very largely drafted by another great European, M. Jean Monnet, and it bore his imprint in many ways. None of the later Treaties have so far repeated the brave avowal of supra-national control of that Declaration of 1950. It also proclaimed unequivocally the need for reconciliation between France and Germany and the creation of a Federation of Europe, the United States of Europe. Germany, Italy, Belgium, the Netherlands and Luxembourg accepted the invitation. The concept of the 'Six' was born. The recently returned British Labour Government was 'reluctantly unable to accept'.

On 18th April 1951, the European Coal and Steel Community Treaty was signed. Its High Authority was found quarters in Luxembourg, where it was provided with a modest Law Court of its own, with a small Assembly of delegates and an international civil service to administer its affairs. It was an odd setup for an international organization with such a limited, though vital, task. Fortunately, the planners had two objectives beyond mere industrial mergers: the elimination of another European war by merging their nations' essential raw materials, and the testing of a system of supra-national administration, designed for more extensive use in Europe if it worked properly. Europe was under very great pressure from outside. The world's have-not's were aligning themselves against the have's. The U.S.A. and Western Europe controlled about nine-tenths of the riches of the world, while their peoples' living standards were wholly out of proportion compared with their numbers and territorial possessions.

Having given much to the world to make it a better place to live in, they had not failed to reward themselves more than adequately. All this was now at risk.

It was for these reasons and in the face of very great danger, six years after the end of the Second World War, that six European nations, every one of which had suffered invasion and defeat through that war, decided to merge their entire coal and steel industries under the control of a supra-national authority. It was the end of an era. It was also the test of a new approach.

CHAPTER II

Beginnings of Union

(1) CONTROL OVER COAL AND STEEL

The new Coal and Steel Community was formally launched on 9th May 1952. Its headquarters were established in the former Railway Offices in the Place de Metz at Luxembourg where they have remained to this day. It was from this neutral centre that it was decided to operate Europe's first 'custom-built' organization, a supra-national control system with a rather sophisticated ancillary apparatus. Its primary objective was the administration of the merged coal and steel industries of the Six, including control over a number of derivative products.

The difficulties encountered during the early stages are even now of more than merely historical interest, as they show clearly the man-made obstacles in the way of 'harmonization' and 'integration' of competitive interests. Although the objectives of E.C.S.C. were limited, the Authority was soon involved in violent conflicts. Its efforts were opposed to the creation of the very atmosphere under which the two industries over which it exercised control enjoyed maximum prosperity, namely mutual suspicion and consequent armament.

This was a moral dilemma. In the view of economists the Authority was also taking grave risks by upsetting the price rings and production arrangements which guaranteed a steady level of wages and employment even during periodic recessions. In 1952 the steel production in Europe was rising to meet increased demand, while on the other hand the consumption of coal was adversely affected by the transfer to the use of oil in many sectors of industry as well as for domestic purposes.

Under these circumstances it seemed sensible to concentrate the Authority's work as regards integration on the steel industry, whereas concerning coal it devoted most of its efforts to the supervision and control of prices and profits, without causing major upheavals. The labour forces in the mines were shrinking all over the world, and the Authority set to work to reduce the available manpower fairly by cutting down on intake, arranging for premature retirement and limiting actual redundancies as much as possible. Large sums were raised by industrial levies and made available to mitigate hardship. Sixty million dollars were spent on re-training and re-adjustment, low interest loans (2 per cent) were arranged to alleviate loss of earnings and more than 100,000 homes were provided for the labour force as reduced to meet the revised requirements.

Meanwhile the integration of the steel industry proceeded according to plan. In both industries E.C.S.C. was responsible for the progressive abolition of customs duties, quantitative restrictions and dual pricing arrangements for coal, steel, iron and scrap. The many and often ingenious devices by means of which customers within the producer country managed to secure preferential treatment as to price, delivery dates, quality or quantity over customers in the other five member-states, were abolished by stages and prohibited throughout the area under the control of the High Authority.

Gradually these measures resulted in fairer competition through the establishment of 'consumer equality'. After this plateau had been achieved, surprisingly little resistance was offered from within the industries to an agreement concerning the introduction of a 'harmonized' common external tariff, applicable to all the dealings in respect of both the industries between any of the Six and the outside world.

The Authority delegated the actual supervision to ensure compliance with its decrees and rules to a Consultative Committee, and in the event of a dispute, the matter was referred to its own independent Tribunal, a small international Court with compulsory jurisdiction within its limited field. It was an ambitious arrangement for a comparatively small organization, and in effect resembled a miniature 'United Europe'. As we now know, its six founder members have remained the member-states of the Community, while both its Court and Assembly have been adapted for rather wider and more important tasks. It is curious how the somewhat fortuitous composition of E.C.S.C. in 1951 eventually led to the split between the nations of Western Europe in the Sixties.

Some of the principal features of the E.C.S.C. Organization continue to play an important part in the European Community. The High Authority itself was and still is, for the time being, independent of the member-states politically as well as financially. It is financed by a levy directly imposed on the two industries. Under Art. 50 of the E.C.S.C. Treaty, this condition of maximum independence was one of the crucial test features of the early days. If it was impossible to operate this specialized Community without dependence on national control, clearly there was little hope for a more broadly-based Organization.

The E.C.S.C.'s large and important Consultative Committee of 51 members formed the link between the industries and the Authority. It was composed of representatives of all sides of the industries, as well as of distributors and users of its principal products. In attendance were four observers from the Council of Ministers, to ensure a permanent link with this vital body and through it, with the six Governments. The system of obligatory discussion, under which the High Authority must 'discuss' matters of policy with the Committee, which was first laid down in the E.C.S.C. Treaty, was eventually introduced into the Rome Treaties. It is one way of ensuring that all matters concerning policy, administration and enforcement of regulations are dealt with under conditions which allow for comment by those most concerned in practice. Consultation of this type is obligatory, but compliance with any recommendations received is discretionary.

The Community's Assembly and its Court proved successful. This system of four specialized and closely linked Institutions was in due course adapted to become a blue-print for the new Europe. In many details it was more grandly conceived and more definitely designed along supra-national lines than either of the two later Communities. But then the background was rather different in the early Fifties, when there was much real apprehension of another war. During the next few years the general situation improved and the threatening clouds receded. When the Treaties of Rome were drafted supra-national provisions were no longer welcomed quite so enthusiastically by some of the member-states.

In 1953, the little common markets began to operate, coal and iron in February, scrap in March and steel in May. Inter-community trade increased briskly. The commercial stimulation due to reduced tariffs and simplified procedures combined to make the introduction of the various measures under the Treaty a most successful operation. The High Authority came in on a favourable flood tide and proceeded ahead on the crest of the wave of success. There was little industrial opposition and the planners were justified by the success of their scheme. The green light was switched on in Luxembourg: it was 'Go' for further Community introductions.

(2) CONTROL OVER DEFENCE

Waves of success are liable to break on rocky shores. Heartened by the successful launching of E.C.S.C., the leaders of the Six at once proceeded to their next target, the development of an integrated European Defence Policy by means of another Community, charged this time with the overall control of the member-states' armed forces. The European Defence Community (E.D.C.) was designed in keeping with the Schuman blue-print for E.C.S.C. The Treaty was ready in 1953, drafted in accordance with the established 'Community' principles and adapted for military and defence purposes generally. The assembled statesmen were so carried away by the possibilities of their Grand Design that they even agreed on a basic plan for a European Political Community. At that stage they did not appreciate that they were setting too hot a pace. It seems that one specialized Community must be more or less fully established and operative before the member-states are ready for the creation of another. Similarly, it seems difficult to initiate the implementation of a new Common Policy under, say, the E.E.C. Rome Treaty, until a previously agreed major Common Policy has

THE BASIC COMMUNITY SYSTEM
*as exemplified by the original organization of E.C.S.C. under
the Treaty of Paris, 18th April, 1951.*

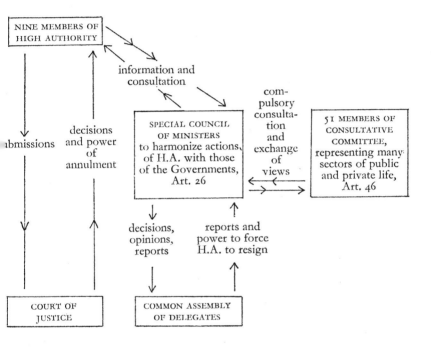

either been largely implemented or temporarily shelved. One step at a time.

As it happened, the introduction of political integration even as a matter for discussion was received with apprehension by many French politicians. The French Press and large sectors of the public considered that this might be the thin end of a very dangerous wedge. Furthermore, the establishment of E.D.C. would undoubtedly facilitate political unification. France had only very recently emerged from a most unhappy war. Her newly organized forces were considered by many of her citizens too precious to be merged with the forces of other nations however friendly. The French Government was not willing to risk foreign supervision and shared control of its armed forces after years of occupation. In the agonizing conflict between the quest for peace and the need for security (a conflict which many may consider rather unrealistic), the traditionalists were victorious. The Treaty was easily passed through the Assemblies of France's five partners. Then, in the summer of 1953, it reached the French National Assembly. After a heated discussion, in August 1953, that body by an adverse vote of 319 to 264 refused to ratify it. In desperation Jean Monnet organized an Action Committee to prevent such setbacks on future occasions. Eventually, by way of the Western European Union and N.A.T.O., France was persuaded to contribute troops and material to the common defence of Europe. But the death of E.D.C. had its after-effects, as it were, beyond the grave, and France has now largely opted out of N.A.T.O. and other European defence arrangements. The planners then lowered their sights and faced reality disenchanted but undismayed. For some months to come their principal concern was the preservation of E.C.S.C. and in this they succeeded.

(3) WHAT NOW?

Ten years after the end of the Second World War, the Six were in a difficult position. Their colonial possessions were disappearing, raw materials were becoming difficult to obtain and certainly were costing much more, Russia and America were sharing the leadership among the nations, each heading a camp of satellites and allies. Britain had been unable to follow up her splendid stand in the war by an equally successful peace – the costs of a nuclear armoury and the expenditure required of a top rank power by way of loans to the poorer nations, prestige development programmes, etc., were proving too high for a country which had spent so much of her reserves to win the war. On top of all this, her weary population was for the time being more interested in improving social conditions at home than in co-operating with those countries who had either fought against her, or had suffered years of occupation following military defeat. Thus the United Kingdom, having opted out of the Big Three arrangement, was not willing to do more than maintain association ties with E.C.S.C. As far as the Six were concerned the early hopes based on the success of the Coal and Steel Community were beginning to evaporate a little. No further recruits were lining up, and France had forcefully demonstrated her fundamental opposition to further integration in matters of defence. If not by way of Common Security then through Common Trade: the solution of the problem lay in the approach through the national economies. There were good reasons to expect a wider response to a call for economic integration than in respect of just coal and steel.

At Messina, on 1st June 1955, the representatives of the Six formally declared their intention to persist with their efforts towards European unity on a more general basis, in the face of French doubts. They announced that their aim was to 'maintain Europe's place in the world, to restore her influence and prestige, and to ensure a continuous rise in the living standards of her peoples'. A Committee was set up, under the chairmanship of another of the great European statesmen, M. Paul-Henri Spaak, to examine the possibilities of a wider economic union and the joint development of atomic energy for peaceful purposes.

At that time there were in existence three European organizations which might have been used as prototypes for economic integration: the European Movement, the Council of Europe and E.C.S.C. The Movement had been founded at the Hague in 1948 to sponsor political integration. It had been active in the formulation of the Schuman Plan but had not done much effective work since then. The Council, set up at Strasbourg in 1949, was quite unsuitable for practical integration work. It was a forum which enabled its eighteen members, including the United Kingdom, to propound schemes for social, scientific and cultural activities. Its Committee of Foreign Ministers, assisted by a Consultative Assembly of 144 members and a Joint Committee of both these bodies, provided splendid opportunities for the exchange of views and the promulgation of activities of many kinds. In those fields its record over the years had been rather impressive, but the Six felt that its composition would not allow for positive integration of elaborate structures such as the member-states' entire economic systems. All the members of the Council were in general agreement that it would be a good thing to exchange orchestras, organize football competitions or encourage tourism, but there was little common ground between many of them concerning the problems now facing the men who had set up E.C.S.C.

In the end it was decided to carry on from the point reached when the Common Defence Policy failed to get off the ground. In May 1956 the Spaak Committee recommended the drafting of two Treaties, one to establish a European Economic Community (E.E.C. or the 'Common Market'), and the other to set up a European Atomic Energy Community (Euratom). It was decided to start discussion of both drafts in Brussels at the end of June. In the vicinity of the Belgian capital and in several other of the capitals of the Six, the experts conferred, and two Treaties were drafted, two Communities set up. But although many invitations were extended, including one to the United Kingdom, there were no new recruits for the time being.

For the Six, for Britain and for the rest of Europe this was indeed a crucial moment of decision. Political and military union had proved too ambitious for those who agreed with the French concept of the New Europe. No other nation outside the charmed circle of the Six seemed to be interested in further integration plans. So the Six decided to proceed step by step for the purpose of implementing the new Treaties as they had done in the case of E.C.S.C. Political unity was off the agenda for the time being and Britain was not even loosely associating herself with the plans for a Common Economic Policy, as she had done in connection with the Coal and Steel Community.

CHAPTER III

The E.E.C. Treaty of Rome

(1) NOT AN EASY BIRTH

Rather appropriately the two Rome Treaties were ready to welcome the light of day nine months after the scheme had been conceived and the Spaak Committee set up. On 25th March 1957, twelve senior delegates from the Six, including all the Prime Ministers, signed the Treaties on the Capitol Hill in Rome.

It had been a difficult task. There had been many conflicts on points of principle: to what extent were the new Communities to be independent of the six national Governments; how and in which respects were the Commissions to be answerable to national legislatures or even to the new Community Parliament; were the new Institutions to be supra-national in all respects and was their authority to be compulsory and automatic; how were the differences between the member-states as to power and size to be expressed in terms of votes and representation; and who was to control the entire system as it became operative? These considerations provided the undertones for lively discussions as to the practical issues, namely where to start the process of integration and how, and what was to be the procedure of enforcing the Communities' decisions within the six member-states. The delegates were well aware of the necessary limitations – but would they throttle the newly born child? On the other hand too much freedom would be liable to cause resentment for fear of imperilling national sovereignties, again with fatal results. The offspring had to receive just the right amount of support and nourishment to survive and prosper without embarrassing its progenitors. An obstetrical problem of the first magnitude indeed!

Employing extreme caution, the planners had drafted the Treaties in such a manner as to provide the Communities with Policy Directives rather than with detailed Rules. Only a limited number of specific agreements and detailed lists, which were considered essential to get the economic co-operation between the Six off the ground, were set out in protocols and annexes attached to the main Treaty. The fundamental directives were phrased in such a way that they could by consent be regarded as sacrosanct as the American Constitution, without embarrassing any of the participating Governments by contentious references to detail. These declarations of intent were accompanied by a basic time-table, with ample escape-clauses in case of difficulties. On the other hand the functions of the new Institutions, the proportionate representation of the six states on Committees and other sub-organizations, voting procedure and the system of implementing any agreed policy were laid down with precision and in some detail.

By the end of 1957 all the legislative Assemblies of the Six had ratified the E.E.C. Treaty as well as the Euratom Treaty, with comfortable majorities in every instance. The embarrassment over E.D.C. in 1954 had been successfully avoided. The Treaties were ceremoniously deposited in the archives of Rome, and the great experiment was about to begin.

(2) THE PRINCIPLES

The step up from common control over coal and steel to the integration of six national economic systems, including their nuclear energy programmes, was very great indeed. The lives of 180 million people would be affected in many respects, probably irrevocably. Failure might well bring down the entire edifice, including E.C.S.C. The grand concept of the E.E.C. Treaty is best appreciated when one reads the impressive list of its eleven important objectives: the elimination of customs duties and quantitative restrictions on imports and exports and on similar measures; a common customs tariff and a common commercial policy; the free movement of persons, services and capital; a common agricultural policy; a common transport policy; the avoidance of distortion of competition (e.g. abolition of restrictive practices); the co-ordination of economic policies and the maintenance of an equilibrium of balances of payment; 'approximation' of relevant municipal laws; the establishment of a Social Fund; the establishment of an Investment Bank; and the Association of certain overseas countries and territories.

The tools supplied for the accomplishment of these tasks were four independent Institutions: an Assembly of delegates, a Ministerial Council and a Commission for each Community, and a Court of Justice. The Court and the Assembly were to be common to both Communities as well as to E.C.S.C., but the Ministerial Councils and the Commissions were individual organizations within each Community. As far as the Councils were concerned, this actually meant little more, for the time being, than that the respective specialist Ministers would deal with Coal, Steel and Nuclear Energy, whereas the Foreign Ministers or any other useful departmental Minister or Secretary of State would sit on the E.E.C. Council. The two Commissions, and the High Authority, were truly distinct bodies, set up to represent the new Europe *vis-à-vis* the six national Governments, whose views were to be expressed by the three Ministerial Councils. The Councils and Commissions were to have the assistance of a large Economic and Social Consultative Committee on which all interested parties were to be represented by delegates.

The 'Common Market' was to be established in twelve years, by three stages of four years each, subject to modification in the event of trouble. If the machinery were to come to a halt – a realistic possibility in view of the complicated system of initiating, accepting and implementing major policy matters – there was to be an Arbitration Board to make binding decisions in respect of future procedure and to ensure the eventual implementation of the agreed common policies. In the event its services were never required.

Following the recital of objectives, the second Part of the E.E.C. Treaty, commonly referred to as the 'Treaty of Rome', sets out, in four 'titles', the procedure to be adopted as regards the implementation of the free movement of goods, the agreed common agricultural policy, the free movement of persons, services and capital, and the common transport policy. We shall see in due course that it was not considered wise to follow this sequence when it came to carrying out these directives. The third Part states the Community Policy concerning the integrated economic life of the Six: rules for commercial practices (competition, companies, dumping, state-subsidies, fiscal regulations, and the desirable harmonization of certain municipal laws), general economic and social policy and the establishment of a European Investment Bank (E.I.B.). Part Four deals with the proposed Association of overseas countries and territories, while the fifth Part defines the establishment of the four Institutions and of the Economic and Social Committee, including the financial provisions relating to these bodies. The final Part provides the new Community with a 'legal personality', i.e. with a separate identity in law, and lays down some specific legal and administrative rules. Article 237 of this part contains the provision for admission of other European states as full members: by the unanimous approval of the member-states' representatives on the Council, after the latter have obtained the opinion of the Commission. (See below, pp. 44 *et seq.*)

The Treaty was concluded for an unlimited period (Art. 240), and no provision was made for the resignation or expulsion of a member-state. Presumably the first contingency was regarded as highly improbable but also beyond effective sanction if a particular Government so decided, whereas the second was inconceivable in practice. The basic principle of the new Europe was and remains the obligation to make certain concessions in case of dissent. Ultimate compromise on matters of importance within the Community is of paramount importance.

Although the limits of the economic activities of a modern state are pretty wide and very elastic, these objectives cover almost every aspect. It was the intention to 'harmonize' and 'integrate' the entire economic systems of the Six in accordance with the principles and methods tested in connexion with E.C.S.C. The conception was unashamedly federal: none of the member-states would be able to impose positive measures upon any of the others, while all major and basic decisions would have to be agreed with unanimity, at least for the time being. The purpose of these measures and precautions was to ensure gradual progress by common consent and without causing 'national' reaction. For some years to come the rights of member-states to resist any undesirable interference with their sovereign authority on matters of principle would be safeguarded. Later there would be gradual transition to majority decisions, in respect of practically all proposals or implementations.

The Community and its Institutions were established as independent organizations, free from direct national interference. They were to be protected from political as well as from financial pressure. This was not achieved, however. The Community is not expected to become financially independent before about 1975. Even the Ministerial Council was conceived not merely as a conference of Cabinet representatives from six countries, but as an integral part of the Community administration charged with tempering the Commission's desires for further integration and common policies, by attention to the consensus of the political climate in the member-states at any given time. The new Parliament, which was the enlarged E.C.S.C. Assembly in a new dress, was given only limited powers. Within its limitations, however, it enjoyed a considerable measure of freedom from control particularly as regards subjects for discussion or investigation.

Right through the web spun of customs unions and common policies there runs a common thread: harmonization and integration within the Community, and a common tariff wall facing the outside world.

(3) THE ANNEXES TO THE E.E.C. TREATY

Only about one half of the E.E.C. Treaty volume is taken up by what might be called the Treaty proper, set out in 248 articles. There are numerous specific Regulations and references to named commodities to allow for the implementation of at least one of the common policies without delay. It was rightly feared that some of these matters, if discussed again at lower levels, would hold up work for quite a while and might even re-open topics on which agreement had already been reached. Some of these provisions are of particular interest to British readers, as they are indicative of the type of 'special' arrangement which is possible within the general context of the Treaty, quite apart from concessions as regards transition periods.

There are four long lists of detailed tariff headings relating to specified articles in respect of which reductions are laid down; a list of agricultural products agreed to be made subject to the new common policy; a description of the 'invisible' transactions in respect of which no new restrictions would henceforth be allowed; and a list of the overseas countries and territories to which special Association rights would be accorded as per the fourth part of the Treaty.

Then there are nine protocols of widely differing character. An Investment Bank is set up for the Community, some German territories, where the Basic Law of the Federal Republic does not apply, are specially considered; financial concessions were made to protect the French franc from certain dangers and disadvantages due to financial stipulations in the Treaty itself, a precaution which eventually proved ineffective because it was inadequate, but which is of historical interest in view of French criticism of the weakness of the pound more than a decade later; the difficulties arising out of the peculiarly backward economic conditions in Southern Italy are taken care of next; then there are provisions to assist the agricultural industry of Luxembourg; the position of certain imports from associated overseas territories is clarified; there are measures to ensure harmony between E.C.S.C. and E.E.C. as regards imports of some products from Algeria; the maintenance for six years of duties and charges relating to mineral oils and their derivatives is specially permitted; and the terms of the Treaty are applied to Netherlands New Guinea.

These protocols are followed by a Convention consisting of three Parts: an implementing agreement in respect of the Association of a number of overseas countries and territories with E.E.C., mostly concerned with former colonial possessions of some of the member-states. A Development Fund is established to make it possible for financial aid to be given to these countries on behalf of the Community acting as an entity.

This is one of the major 'outward-looking' features of the Treaty: the Fund is centrally administered by the Commission, and the Council annually determines each country's financial contribution. Aid is given to assist these 'emergent' or 'under-developed' areas to improve their social institutions as well as for investment purposes of 'general' interest. In this instance 'qualified' majority decisions (i.e. voting by two-thirds majority) are already permitted. The member-states are given 100 votes, as follows: Germany and France 33 each, Italy, Belgium and the Netherlands, 11 votes each, and Luxembourg 1 vote. (This is unusual, as normally Italy is accorded the same number of votes as France and Germany.) It will be readily seen that the two major voting blocs cannot ensure the necessary majority without at least the Luxembourg vote. The annual amounts to be contributed to the Fund by the member-states are specified in detail.

The other two Parts of this Convention relate to banana imports into Germany and coffee imports into Italy and the Benelux countries, rather minor matters compared with Part 1.

The Treaty contains further a list of the Community's privileges and immunities, according special status in law to the new 'Civil Service' on whom would fall the duty of operating and administering the entire complicated machinery. Also set out is the Statute of the new Court of Justice, with definitions of the positions of its judges and other functionaries and a number of procedural rules of a general nature.

The Treaty then continues with another Convention, whereby the Parliament, the Court and the Economic and Social Committee are formally established. Provisions are made for the financing of these bodies. There follow declarations on the part of the principal signatories in which they signify their willingness to conclude agreements with other countries (another outward-looking feature), to assist the city of Berlin in view of its peculiar position and to enter into Association agreements with the independent countries of the franc area and with certain other countries.

The Final Declaration sets out an intimation by the French Government to propose to their national Assembly legislative measures whereby applications for patents relating to certain defence matters, including atomic research, shall be released for publication after a certain quarantine period.

Thus ends this blend of general directives and detailed provisions, wherein directives of most fundamental importance are frequently succeeded by rather minor provisions relating to specific commodities or matters of rather ephemeral importance.

The Treaty constitutes a fine piece of draftsmanship in many respects. The E.C.S.C. blue-print has been adroitly adapted to the much wider conception of supra-national economic integration. The result of the Messina deliberations emerges in the shape of a Twelve Year Plan for a Western European Economic Federation. The term 'economic policy' has been applied in its widest sense: many cultural and political objectives are touched upon and formally declared subject to the harmonization work of the Commission, provided there is the essential consensus among the six governments.

The independence of the Institutions, the careful 'weighting' of the votes accorded to the member-states and the deliberate apportionment of power between the initiating and driving forces of the Commission on the one hand and the Council of Ministers (of necessity required to look over their shoulders and pay due regard to the mood of the nations concerned) on the other – these are realistic provisions designed to take the Treaty right out of the realm of Utopia and into the harsh reality of modern politics. Almost incidentally a new class of Europeans was created, for it was evident that there would have to come into existence a small army of supra-national Civil Servants who, with their families, would form the nucleus of a growing European bureaucracy, frequently referred to as 'Eurocrats'.

It was now 1958, and it seemed quite probable that the strange infant might not merely survive but even turn out to be somewhat precocious. Its six progenitors were already beginning to worry about signs of juvenile delinquency . . .

CHAPTER IV

The European Coal and Steel Community

We have referred to the setting up of this specialized Community as a kind of pilot scheme. Although it has now been largely merged with the two later Communities, the present position of this organization must be briefly described.

HEADQUARTERS AT LUXEMBOURG

The administrative Headquarters are at Luxembourg, from where control is exercised over the huge coal fields in Lorraine, Luxembourg, the Ruhr, Northern Italy and in other parts of Europe, the extensive iron and steel industries of the Six and certain auxiliary plants. The Coal/Steel Community, originally operated by the High Authority, was designed and functioned as a kind of miniature federation.

We have already mentioned that the Treaty by which it was created and which was signed on 18th April 1951, was in some respects more 'supra-national' in character than the later Treaties of Rome. In 1951, the shadow of the Second World War still hung over Europe and there was the ever-present menace from Stalin's Russia. Pressure from the outside makes for co-operation between nations. When this pressure had eased some years later, the Treaties of Rome were drafted on more functional and general lines, exhibiting rather fewer characteristics of a supranational nature.

The liaison between the governments of the six member-states of E.C.S.C. and the High Authority was originally maintained by the Council of Ministers, in this instance composed of the departmental Ministers concerned with the coal and steel industries of their respective countries. The High Authority had to *consult* with the Council as regards its decisions, but it was not necessarily obliged to follow the Ministers' advice.

Since 20th July 1967, the E.C.S.C. in essence forms part of the European Community. Its primary duties are the supervision of the 'common market' in the products under its control (all connected with the coal and steel industries, and including many by-products), research and investment, fair competition and (a vital obligation as regards the mining industry) redundancy and re-training. One of the principal results of the establishment of the single Community has been to enable the Commission to formulate a co-ordinated energy policy embracing coal and its products, gas, natural gas, oil, electricity and nuclear energy.

E.C.S.C. remains vitally concerned with controlling the prices charged by the industries under its supervision, with maintaining the stability of freight rates and with working conditions. Restrictive practices are kept in check by general directive or by specific legal action, production is aided by a steady flow of technical information and know-how across the frontiers of the Six and the Community has been able to re-settle, re-train and re-house a fair proportion of the labour forces (particularly in the coal-mining industry), who lost their jobs in the course of transition from coal to other fuels in industry or for other reasons.

In accordance with the provisions of the basic Treaty, E.C.S.C. is and always has been financially self-supporting. It raises the necessary funds by imposing levies on the coal and steel industries of the member-states. In a way it has become the victim of its specialization: it controls one of the principal sources of energy (coal) and one of the principal basic industries (the production of iron and steel). This was a useful combination when the predominant objectives were the prevention of war and the testing of this type of supra-national organization in Europe. Today, the threat of war may be less real in view of the equilibrium of nuclear armaments and the more conciliatory attitude of a rather more prosperous Soviet Union. The test whether E.C.S.C. as an organization would be workable, and whether it could be effectively operated by six nations acting

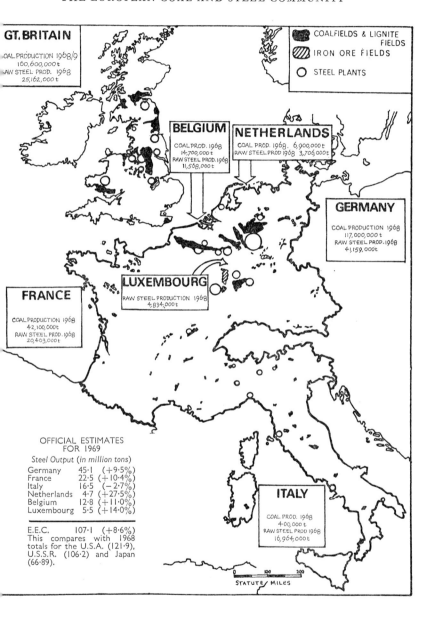

GT. BRITAIN

COAL PRODUCTION 1968/9
160,600,000 t
RAW STEEL PROD. 1968
25,162,000 t

COALFIELDS & LIGNITE FIELDS

IRON ORE FIELDS

○ STEEL PLANTS

BELGIUM

COAL PROD. 1968
14,700,000 t
RAW STEEL PROD. 1968
11,568,000 t

NETHERLANDS

COAL PROD. 1968. 6,900,000 t
RAW STEEL PROD 1968 3,706,000 t

GERMANY

COAL PRODUCTION 1968
117,000,000 t
RAW STEEL PROD. 1968
41,159,000 t

LUXEMBOURG

RAW STEEL PRODUCTION 1968
4,834,000 t

FRANCE

COAL PRODUCTION 1968
42,100,000 t
RAW STEEL PROD. 1968
20,403,000 t

OFFICIAL ESTIMATES
FOR 1969

Steel Output (in million tons)

Germany	45·1	(+9·5%)
France	22·5	(+10·4%)
Italy	16·5	(−2·7%)
Netherlands	4·7	(+27·5%)
Belgium	12·8	(+11·0%)
Luxembourg	5·5	(+14·0%)

E.E.C. 107·1 (+8·6%)
This compares with 1968
totals for the U.S.A. (121·9),
U.S.S.R. (106·2) and Japan
(66·89).

ITALY

COAL PROD. 1968
400,000 t
RAW STEEL PROD 1968
16,964,000 t

0   100   200
STATUTE MILES

together had been successful. In due course sensible administration required the combined administration of *all* sources of energy through the medium of a single European Community with its own special 'power' departments, linked to the 'coal' sector of E.C.S.C. and the energy production side of Euratom. In this way, all basic sources of energy, including the new wealth of natural gas, are now conveniently co-ordinated.

The production of iron and steel is now administered jointly with other basic industries, and the remaining sectors of E.C.S.C. and Euratom may soon be combined to form the comprehensive Scientific and Technological Research and Development Department of the European Community, in accordance with the common energy policy proposed by the Commission.

It is probable that the Merger Treaty, which became effective on 20th July 1967, will one day be followed by a Consolidation Treaty to replace the three existing Treaties. This possibility is viewed by many with a good deal of apprehension. The European scene of 1970 is very different from that of the Fifties. There are grounds for thinking, so it is said in the 'European Capitals', that such a Treaty would in all probability be a good deal less supra-national than the old Treaties – that much would be lost through the merger. The people who hold such opinions pin their hopes on the reasonable assumption that it will take some time to draft such a treaty, and that when it is ready there will have been some resurgence of European thought and feeling, and, quite probably, the Community itself will have been enlarged by the admission of new members.

CHAPTER V

The European Atomic Energy Community (Euratom)

E.C.S.C. was the 'pilot' Community. E.E.C. was set up to achieve the principal 'first-line' objectives of European unification – namely a common economic policy within and a common economic front towards the outside world.

The third Community, Euratom, has been treated in a rather off-hand manner by most commentators dealing with the new Europe.

It began its life as a very specialized common market of its own. It was created by a second Treaty signed at Rome, on the same occasion as E.E.C. Its main purpose was to carry out joint research and development work in the field of atomic energy and for its peaceful exploitation. This 'Euratom Treaty', signed in March 1957, came into force on 1st January, 1958. At that time most politicians as well as many scientists confidently expected a more rapid development of this new source of power, and they were justly concerned with securing for Europe adequate access to the essential raw materials, proper research facilities and an orderly transfer from the established sources of power to atomic energy without excessive redundancies, bottle-necks and similar difficulties. This 'transfer' proved to be much slower than anticipated, partly due to cost factors, and partly due to the discovery of 'natural' gas in Europe and under the sea, in large quantities.

They agreed on a number of specific objectives: Euratom was to ensure the procurement, use and supervision of nuclear materials within the Community. It was given what in those days was considered an adequate research budget. Much of the available money was to be spent on setting up nuclear research and development centres, so that today there are four of those: at Ispra (Italy), Geel (Belgium), Karlsruhe (Germany) and Petten (Netherlands), of which the first-named is much the largest. These centres were set up in accordance with the Community's first 'Five-Year Plan', during 1958–1962. The operational budget at that time amounted to only about £75 million. Out of this relatively small fund, the salaries of about 2,000 members of the research staff had to be paid, as well as the construction of the centres and the entire research programme.

On 19th June 1962, the Ministerial Council approved a proposal by the Euratom Commission in respect of its second 'Five-Year Plan', 1963–1967. The first budget total was almost doubled, to about £150 million. In pursuit of its endeavours to provide Europe with its own reactors, the ORGEL programme at Ispra (near the Lago Maggiore in Italy) which has been almost completed, and other reactor programmes were initiated subsequently including work on a 'pulsed' reactor (SORA). Much of this work was done in conjunction with countries outside the Community, particularly the United States, with which there are not only exchange arrangements concerning know-how but also comprehensive research and production arrangements. The 1969 budget was based on estimated expenditure of about £130 million for a single year. The research and training budget for 1970 amounts to about £136 million.

The number of staff employed is now rising towards 3,000. Further recruitment and training are vital tasks for those in charge of the scientific departments, as the Community is broadening its research work in several directions. It is hoped one day soon to enter the field of reactor sales and thereby to recoup a fair proportion of the increasing expenditure.

Euratom had its own Commission of five members (Luxembourg had no representative), who were nominated by the Governments of the member-states for four years' tenure of office. There were a Community Secretariat, a Research Department as well as several Committees concerned with the atomic industry's external relations, security, information, health, personnel and finance. An independent agency had been set up to negotiate and control the procurement of the expensive essential raw materials, and there were several ancillary sub-committees. Liaison was established and maintained with the United States, Canada and Great Britain. Some of the auxiliary services shared between Euratom and E.E.C. have already been mentioned.

The Treaty establishing a single Council and Commission for the European Community led to the merger of the administrative responsibilities of Euratom with those of the other two Communities. The principal result for Euratom is its growing role as the central organization for the energy production and distribution of the Six. It would be Europe's largest 'Ministry of Fuel and Power'. In the process of this development it may absorb some of the duties of E.C.S.C. as well as of some of the departments of E.E.C. concerned with research and production of energy. In January, 1969, the Council of Ministers decided that by 1st January, 1971, the Community was to have a permanent oil reserve for 2 months, under central control.

An incipient common energy policy has been outlined by the Commission, including equal access to supplies, price supervision and harmonization of fuel and power prices.

The space research and production programme is also about to be centralized within the Euratom organization, but such commercial activities as the sale of reactors and the exploitation of know-how will in future probably be handled by the economic departments of the Community.

When one compares these activities with the scientific achievements in this field in the United States, the more recent acceleration of nuclear work for civil uses in the U.S.S.R. and the developments in Britain, the accomplishments of Euratom are not very spectacular. However, it is beginning to catch up. It must be stressed that Europe started far behind the three countries mentioned, that Euratom had little scientific and only limited financial assistance in the initial stages, and that collaboration between France and her five partners has not been very easy. The French, having developed their own atomic research programme, in due course produced their own 'atomic' bomb. Work for peaceful utilization was carried out simultaneously: as so often, the civil research work was aided in many ways by the development of military programmes. It was largely due to these French enterprises and the desire of the French government to keep France in the military 'atomic race' that the joint research work among the Six did not accelerate earlier, but the incidental know-how acquired by the French research workers concerned with the military exploitation of their work, together with the rapid progress now being made in Germany, may yet bring about a more sustained rate of progress towards achieving practical results such as the production of Communication satellites and small reactors for industrial use.

There is already quite considerable impetus behind some of the projects, both scientific and financial. Atomic energy has been accorded massive priority as far as power is concerned; the research programme is wide and fairly imaginative, and new industrial reactors are being introduced on a broad scale. A nuclear merchant vessel, the 'Otto Hahn', has been completed in Germany for experimental uses, with financial contributions by Euratom. This vessel has successfully completed her trials and her reactor has become critical. At present the Community is concerned with developing its own reactors. It is important as early as possible to reach the stage when the Community will be able to construct these costly items of equipment in its own factories. The two principal member-states, France and Germany, do not at present pool their technological information; indeed France pursues a vigorous 'national' programme of her own. What is more, there is a good deal of 'reserved' research work: by mutual agreement each member-state need merely certify a research centre or production unit as of a military nature, and all information and research work connected therewith will be at once classified as 'secret' and withheld from distribution to the Community.

Most of the functions of Euratom will probably be absorbed by the 'Energy Sector' of the European Commission. Future expenditure is bound to increase.

In March 1968, the Commission recommended to the Council a programme of joint enterprises in the fields of nuclear industry, with direct Community participation in the joint enterprises capital. The total civil nuclear budget of the Community for 1968/72 is estimated as $5,000 million. The fusion of the Communities and – possibly – the joining of new member-states is likely to provide the opportunity for a massive upward re-assessment of the Euratom plans. In February, 1969, the Commission stated that E.C.S.C. and Euratom must pool their resources to implement a European energy policy. They forecast that by 1980, about 60 per cent of the Community's energy requirements might have to be obtained from 'outside', and such dangerous 'dependence' had to be avoided.

The rapidly developing training and ancillary departments of Euratom must be briefly mentioned here. Young scientists are being trained in increasing numbers, much work is being carried out to render their handling of highly dangerous substances less perilous. There is a major biological research programme devoted to these tasks.

In view of the frequent arguments about international control of nuclear research and testing, it is of interest that Euratom has successfully employed teams of inspectors to check stocks and supervise tests for some time past.

The principal research centres themselves are gradually developing into true centres of European scientific study. At Ispra, the ORGEL reactor project has been a technological success. At Petten, north of Amsterdam, another reactor development programme is under way. At Geel, in Belgium, a nuclear study centre is being built up for work in nuclear metrology, while at Karlsruhe, In S.W. Germany, research into the uses of new substances is being carried out.

Incidentally, in or near these centres new European schools for the sons and daughters of the Euratom workers and other Community employees have been set up, and we shall return to these interesting projects in due course.

This is probably the most convenient place to mention Europe's belated space exploration and research efforts. The two principal projects are E.L.D.O. (the space launcher programme) and E.S.R.O. (the space research programme). Neither of these projects, however, is being handled by Euratom at the present time. Following the merger of the Commissions, such work is likely to be allocated to Euratom's eventual successor, the Energy and Research Department of the European Community.

Space research is a field where the U.S. has achieved a tremendous lead over all others with Russia alone providing viable competition. There are still some opportunities for a concerted European effort to catch up with the leaders. However, the system of development at present employed does not seem to be very effective to achieve the common objective: the E.L.D.O. scheme, organized in co-operation with non-member states, was originally developed to use the Australian Woomera site for the experimental launching of a European satellite. High costs, and comparatively unsatisfactory results have led to defections, including the United Kingdom. There were too many cooks engaged in the preparation of this costly dish. Whereas the United States have twice successfully landed men on the moon, the European prototype rocket is still earth bound and beset on all sides by the political rivalries and financial difficulties of the various countries involved. On 6th December 1967, S.E.T.I.S. (Société Européenne pour l'Etude et l'Intégration des Systèmes spatiaux) was formed (including two British participating companies), to develop the fourth stage of the E.L.D.O. rocket. By the end of 1968 several rather unsuccessful tests had been carried out, and in February, 1969 M. Lefèvre, the chairman of the E.L.D.O. Council, expressed 'deep regret at the reduction of the British contribution by $16 million to $24 million.' Britain is now no longer 'interested' in these experiments.

On the other hand, the sister project, E.S.R.O., Europe's space research organization, is far from defunct. It may not yet be too late for a number of schemes to be developed for realistic (not merely prestige) reasons. The planners seem to have learned their lesson: the established Community procedure of retaining complete central control over any multi-national project is apparently essential to ensure steady progress. Although in this field, too, France has gone ahead alone, there are sound reasons for hoping that her efforts will yet benefit the Community as a whole. There is much useful know-how to be acquired by the civil research teams from the experience gathered as the result of military experimentation. It has been

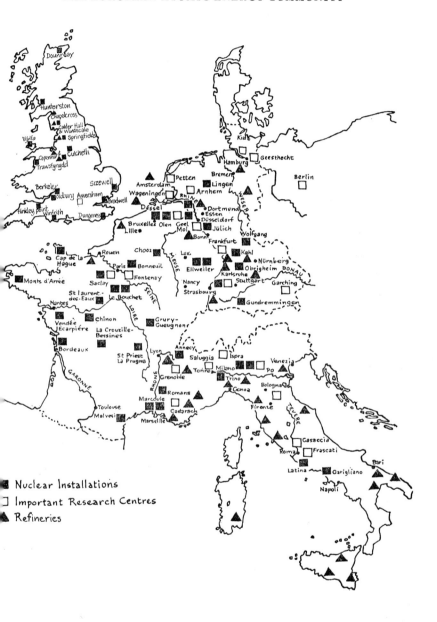

Nuclear Installations
Important Research Centres
Refineries

indicated that Britain may at least maintain her contributions to this field.

European research into the civil uses of atomic energy has come a long way in 13 years. Countries which might never have been able to obtain fissile materials at all, even for peaceful uses, have been enabled to enter the field of nuclear research. The distribution of raw materials has been controlled – there has been no recorded instance of misuse. The Community is one of the world's most industrialized areas and its potential energy requirements are very great indeed. There will soon be a real need for all the nuclear power they can produce, for the energy requirements of the Community are likely to rise steeply in the near future. Some power stations have already been built. Several more are scheduled, and scientific help on a considerable scale is being provided by the U.S. under a bilateral Agreement signed in 1958, which remains in force.

Euratom has also signed treaties for mutual aid with Britain, Canada, Brazil and the Argentine Republic. The Community now stands fourth amongst the 'nuclear' regions of the world. This is not by any means only a matter of prestige or economic preference: the provision of nuclear energy has vital security advantages for the members of the Community, for whom the steady supply of oil is likely to remain precarious. Pipe lines are vulnerable and so are most oil wells, but underground power stations at home can do much to guarantee essential supplies of energy and power. A 'joint enterprise' scheme for the utilization and conveyance of oil and natural gas was recommended by the Commission in 1969.

Euratom will undoubtedly cease to exist as a separate entity, but the vital need of power supplies for Europe, under safe European control, will remain one of the essential tasks of the Community.

CHAPTER VI

The Institutions of the European Community

When the administrative success of E.C.S.C. had satisfied the Spaak Committee as to the workability of the 'Institution' system, the latter was duly adopted for E.E.C. and Euratom. Both these Communities were set up, each with its own Commission to carry out the executive and administrative work, and with a Ministerial Council representing the governments of the six member-states. The European Parliament and the Court were formed as separate and independent Institutions to be shared by all three Communities. An important feature adopted from the E.C.S.C. scheme was the Consultative Committee, a very large forum for maintaining constant contact between the many interested parties in the six countries at all levels.

On 8th April 1965, a Treaty was signed by the six governments to merge the three Councils and Commissions into two single Community bodies, a European Council and a European Commission. Although this Treaty was in due course ratified by all the member-states, its implementation was held up for some time, until 20th July 1967, partly because some of the member-states felt that this important decision could conveniently be used as a bargaining counter in dealing with the French Government's claim to appoint a Frenchman as the next President of the Community, and partly because of the ever-present apprehension among the administrators, that any change in the then prevailing political climate, was likely to have 'anti-integration' results.

As it was, in 1967 the term of office of the first President of the Commission, Prof. Hallstein, was coming to an end. The selection of his successor presented many problems and feelings were running rather high for some time, until M. Jean Rey, of Belgium, a member of the Commission since 1958, was appointed. He took office on 6th July, 1967.

We must now consider the new unified European Community, as constituted by virtue of the implementation of the Merger Treaty. It consists of a Commission (or Executive), a Council (of Ministers), a Parliament and a Court, the four Institutions of the Community of Europe.

A. THE COMMISSION

(1) ITS WORK

The Commission is the senior executive organ of the Community. Under the three Treaties the Commissions were charged with the drafting and implementing of 'decrees' or laws in accordance with these Treaties or with Council decisions. This activity constituted the general legislative power of the three Commissions, and the unified Commission is now charged with this important duty.

Apart from such abstract law-making, the Commission also makes individual 'Decisions', either in pursuance of a directive in one of the Treaties or in accordance with one of the Regulations made thereunder. Such Decisions do not necessarily affect a national government or one of its departments, but may be 'aimed' at a company or even an individual. They range over a wide field. Thus among the many hundreds of such Decisions made every year (the number is increasing), there may be such divers matters as an order to comply with a tariff quota, the determination that a certain measure constitutes a concealed subsidy and must be discontinued, or a formal permission granting temporary exemption from compliance with a specific Regulation.

In conjunction with this aspect of its duties, which brings the Commission into contact with many sectors of the public (although it deals far more frequently with departments than with individuals), its officials are obliged to supervise as well as scrutinize many types of commercial activities.

The following are examples of activities which may require a Decision by the Commission: it may have been reported to the Commission that in a certain trade, in a certain area, restrictive practices of a prohibited nature are actually in force. Or that the full force of a Community law is being evaded by some firm re-exporting certain goods. The Commission will carefully investigate such a report. If there seems to be a reasonable foundation for it, the competent Commission department will get in touch with the alleged transgressor and require him to take the proper action prescribed by the legal provision applicable. If this fails, the matter may have to be taken by the Commission before the European Court, but such a step would be exceptional.

Well over one thousand such Decisions have been made by the E.E.C. Commission year by year in the past and many more by the other two Executives. Uncertainties as to the meaning or intention of certain provisions made in connexion with the implementation of the Common Agricultural Policy have caused a minor flood of matters requiring clarification, but this will probably subside again soon as each major issue is interpreted and explained. The Commission is nowadays able to go further than merely to order something to be done or to be avoided: through their administrative staff they can actually keep the resulting activities under observation and watch the effect of their rulings in practice.

This part of the Commission's activities – individual Decisions – constitutes a sizeable portion of the day-to-day work of this Institution. This is essentially Civil Service work – the beginnings of a European Civil Service system.

In effect the Commission plays the part of a master mediator. Senior civil servants, meeting in almost continuous session, are not likely to be baulked by any but the most insuperable differences. (The same applies to the Council of Ministers, in ordinary circumstances. The basis of 'unification' is accord by mutual concessions.)

However, the most important and far-reaching aspect of the Commission's activities concerns the initiation of Community policies. This process is of vital significance throughout the whole Community system and affects the rate of its development and indeed its very existence. It is this formula, tried and found adequate as regards E.C.S.C., which now ensures that the Community develops in accordance with the Treaties, in harmony with the wishes and capabilities of the member-states and under the positive supervision of the European authorities themselves – not an easy task by any standard.

Of course, the Treaties themselves contain a number of 'enactments' which require nothing more than enabling provisions, as they are compulsorily and automatically applicable in all the member-states by virtue of their inclusion in the Treaties. Typical examples are the abolition of customs and the reduction of quotas. But most Treaty provisions are of a much more general nature. It is usually left to the Institutions (in practice, the Commission in conjunction with the Council) to pass the measures required to implement the policies and directives outlined in the Treaties. We have seen what a wide field is covered by them. But it is not necessary to request the national governments or their parliaments to give their assent as to detail: what is laid down in the Treaties constitutes basic 'European Law' and when specific legislation is subsequently passed in connexion therewith by the Commission and the Council, this automatically becomes applicable in every member-state, as and when decreed.

This process of policy initiation is obviously most important. In this way supra-national measures are agreed and automatically added to the six national legal systems. The E.C.S.C. High Authority and the Euratom Commission were limited in their respective scopes and their powers were of necessity specified in detail and limited by the Treaties, whereas we shall not know the full extent of the unified Commission's powers until all the common policies prescribed in the Treaties are in operation.

The underlying principle of this policy-initiation process is that as regards major matters, decisions by the Commission require approval by the Council. The procedure is as follows: The Commission decides, usually after lengthy and detailed preliminary discussions with many Committees, experts and representatives of interested parties, that the time is opportune to implement one of the Common Policies set out or indicated in the Treaty of Rome. Let us assume that policy is the 'Common Transport Policy' as per the E.E.C. Treaty, Articles 74–84. After some initial 'market research', let us suppose the Commission feels justified to go ahead. A detailed submission is drafted and discussed with the Council. It will by that time be known whether there are any strong objections to going ahead as far as any of the six governments is concerned. When the policy has been 'initiated' by submission to the Council, the subsequent process of implementation is governed by strict rules. (It is worth bearing in mind that without the Commission's action the Council could not have done anything at all about the Transport Policy – it had to be stirred into action).

There follows a discussion usually referred to as a 'dialogue', between the Foreign Secretaries of the Six, in this instance assisted by their Ministers of Transport and other senior ministerial officials for the Council, on the one side, and the Commission on the other. The latter body is itself highly departmentalized, and there now ensues a good deal of specialized Committee work. It is worth noting at this stage that the European Parliament is gradually 'coming in' to participate in these preliminary discussions, thus converting the dialogue into a 'trialogue'. The Commission recommended in 1969 that this process should be accelerated.

Eventually the Commission's proposal may be formally submitted to the Council. It will still be the Commission's draft and their 'Bill', as it were. They would not have gone as far as this unless the chances of obtaining eventual approval had been considered reasonably good. This means the climate in the six member-states must be more or less right as regards the adoption of the policy concerned.

In due course the Council will make up its six-fold mind. It is provided by the Treaties that crucial decisions of this kind must be unanimous, at any rate for the time being. As from the beginning of 1966, the commencement of the Third Stage of the Common Market, the requirement of unanimity should have been replaced by 'weighted' decisions, i.e., a two-thirds majority. The French Government held up this step, but eventually agreed to a tacit and gradual transition process on the understanding that no vital policy matters would be passed against the specific opposition of any national government.

The Council can throw out the Commission's submission and that would be the end for the time being. If the Council is not unanimous in its decision yet the Treaty concerning the issue under discussion requires only a majority decision, they can either accept the proposed draft as it stands by the prescribed majority, without being able to amend it, or reject it outright. On the other hand the Commission can at this stage, if they feel this would save the situation, amend the submitted draft as re-submitted to them and amend it. The amended draft is then returned to the Council, who at that stage then must accept it or reject it as it stands.

The basis of this system is negotiation, and the principal object of such negotiations is to enable the Commission to implement the Treaty policies according to its principles but without upsetting the national governments of the member-states. On the other hand the Council has no power to alter such important drafts itself. What this procedure really achieves is that the Commission provides the ingredients for the dish while the Council decides whether it is digestible as far as the member-states are concerned. The meal is cooked by the Commission, but only after the Council has expressed a definite desire for its inclusion on the menu.

There is another major task to be performed by the Commission, namely, to ensure compliance with the Treaty provisions themselves. Here the Commission will act on information laid against a member-state, and in appropriate cases will require the latter to justify its action or practice. If the member-state does not act as requested, the Commission prepares an Opinion (a considered statement) which may require the state concerned to abide by the law within a certain time. If even this request fails, the Commission may take the matter to the European Court. In recent times about 7–10 such disputes have occurred every year. Although the implementation of additional common policies may temporarily swell the number of cases where there are such differences of views, this increase is likely to abate in due course, as soon as the major issues have been decided and the difficulties ironed out.

These processes and procedures followed a similar line of development in each of the three Communities – the High

Authority and the two Commissions working roughly along the same lines. Of course there was this difference that due to the specialist nature of the industries under their care, the work of the High Authority of E.C.S.C. and of the Euratom Commission tended to be rather more limited in scope than that of the E.E.C. Commission. Nevertheless, there have been a number of important cases where the High Authority had to take action against member-states of the Community. The Community of today has inherited those duties, and the 'Eurocrats' in Brussels are never slow to act irrespective of the fact that states make difficult opponents.

(2) ITS COMPOSITION AND COMMITTEES

The Commission of the European Community consists of fourteen members, each of whom is in charge of a Directorate-General. The immediate control of these 'Departments' (comparable to inchoate Ministries), is in the hands of Directors-General. In addition, there is a Spokesman Department, which handles such matters as official pronouncements and formal communications, and three 'services', concerned respectively with Statistics, Legal Matters, and Information (P.R.O.).

The members of the Commission are pledged to work in complete independence of their respective national governments, and of any national or sectarian interests. They reach decisions by majority vote and accept joint responsibility for their actions, in the same manner as a national cabinet.

The collaboration and interplay between the Council and the Commission provides the motivating and operating force behind the Community. It is from these forces that it is hoped a Political Community will eventually develop, by empirical and gradual growth.

This Commission relies a great deal on the large Economic and Social Committee of 101 members (24 each from the three major member-states, 12 from the smaller states, and 5 from Luxembourg). It has numerous sub-committees. This Committee has assisted both E.E.C. and Euratom from the beginning and has proved to be of great value as an internal link within the Community. It is a vital link with the public sectors, as many divergent interests are represented. Moreover the Committee is often consulted by the Council on matters of practical detail in connexion with Directives or other legal enactments, and is thus doubly valuable to the Community.

There are numerous specialized Committees and sub-organizations, some of which are in frequent session. Much of the Community's work is in fact done in Committee. The total number of Committee sitting days is quite impressive.

The Directorates-General are essentially European 'Government Departments'. They include many of the divisions normally found in a national government, such as Social Services, Agriculture, etc. The Commission delegates to these departments a great deal of responsibility for work of lesser importance or not of a contentious nature. This is usually done by 'proxy-assent', *i.e.* the assent of the Commission members to a non-contentious proposal is obtained in advance and the members need not then be called together for discussion. If there is a dispute, it is dealt with in the course of one of the weekly meetings of the Commission. The steady flow of rulings and decisions seems to indicate that this system is fully utilized.

(3) THE MERGER

The Commission has 14 members, not more than 3 from any member-state. They are full-time officials, not permitted to engage in any other occupation and subject to removal by the Court, on application to that Institution by the Council or by the Commission itself. Its members are appointed by 'common consent' between the governments of the member-states. The Commission is fully independent, financially or politically, as far as the national governments are concerned.

The members are always appointed for 4 years and are then eligible for re-appointment. There are a President and three Vice-Presidents. The Parliament continues to have the power to force the Commission to resign en bloc by passing a vote of No Confidence, one of the few 'real' powers of the Parliament, but not one which has ever been used.

There is a good deal of speculation in the 'European capitals' concerning a possible sequel to the implementation of the Merger Plan, namely the substitution of the three basic treaties by a single Consolidation Treaty. The question is being asked whether such a Treaty is likely to be rather less supra-national than the older treaties. Would it even preserve the *status quo* in Europe? Many people feel that the answers to these questions will depend on the prevailing mood at the time in the various countries; and it is considered that it may be wise to postpone the drafting of such a Treaty until ex-President de Gaulle's influence no longer affects progress in Brussels.

Another incidental result of the merger may be the removal of E.C.S.C. from Luxembourg which would be strenuously resisted by the Grand Duchy, whose revenue from the presence of the Community within its borders is of very real importance to its well-being. The Luxembourgers wish, at the very least, to be allowed to become hosts to some other European organizations. A related issue is that concerning the eventual choice of a European administrative capital. The choice nearly fell on Brussels some years ago, but the Belgians then unsuccessfully opted for Liège which did not otherwise command much support. The choice now seems to lie between Brussels and Luxembourg.

The unified Commission is a very large organization, with some 8,000 civil servants and an annual budget of many hundred million pounds sterling. More than forty Committees work in the huge concrete headquarters in the Avenue de la Joyeuse Entrée in Brussels, whose many offices are being filled to capacity with European administrators. This is the nerve centre from where the economic affairs of some 180 million people are being conducted (not counting additional millions in the associated countries). Here are the offices where much of Western Europe's agricultural policy will be decided, not in the Agricultural Ministries of the Six. There is no single nation in the world nor any other group of nations, with an economic potential as great as that of these six neighbouring states, and the power concentrated in Brussels may well exceed that of Washington and Moscow in the days to come.

B. THE MINISTERIAL COUNCIL

The formula was: one Council of Ministers for each Community. The intention was: to provide a permanent high-level link between the essential 'Community' authority, namely the Commission, and the governments of the Six. Yet it was not to be an antithesis, Community *vs.* national governments, but a synthesis, the Community co-operating with a special body representative of the national governments and embodying their full authority.

The Special Council of E.C.S.C. and the Council of Euratom were of necessity composed of the competent departmental Ministers and their senior assistants. The E.E.C. Council spanned a wider field. Each national delegation was headed by the Foreign Minister, assisted by one or more other Ministers, usually chosen from those in charge of one of the following departments: Finance, Economics, Industry, Agriculture, Transport, Social Services, Labour, Communications, Research and European Affairs, or their principal Secretaries of State.

The scope far exceeded that implied by the word 'economic'. But so did the range of activities covered by E.E.C.

(1) THE COUNCIL'S WORK

By Article 1 of the Merger Treaty of 1967, the new Council takes the place of the three original Councils.

The Ministers do not themselves attend at every Council meeting, but are frequently represented by their Senior Assistants. We have already made reference to the Council's role in connexion with the implementation of major community policies. In the first instance a proposal is submitted to the Council by the Commission. If a unanimous decision is required the position is quite straightforward. But if a 'weighted' majority vote is sufficient (in accordance with the Treaties or in conformity with the gradual introduction of the majority vote), then the following system comes into play: Under Article 148 of the E.E.C. Treaty, and by similar provisions in the other two Treaties, the Councils made their decisions by a majority vote unless 'otherwise provided' in the Treaty. If the majority required was 'qualified', the member-states had 'weighted' votes, as follows: Germany, France and Italy: 4 votes each, Belgium and the Netherlands: 2 votes each and Luxembourg: 1 vote. Twelve votes (a two-thirds majority of the total of 17 votes) were required when the Treaties stipulate a proposal to the Council by the Commission. Twelve votes were also required in all other cases (*i.e.* a simple majority did not suffice), but there was a further condition that to constitute a positive vote by the Council these twelve votes must come from at least four members. As there were six members, the joint votes of the three major powers were insufficient for a positive vote, for their 12 votes would only have been contributed by three members. But the joint votes of any combination of five members always sufficed to outvote even one of the major powers endowed with 4 votes.

If a member abstains – and this can be an important 'let-out' – those present are not thereby precluded from adopting a measure 'with unanimity', so that it is possible to register a token protest without holding up the Council's work.

As from the beginning of 1966 the Council was to have gone over to such weighted majority decisions in most instances, but as we have seen this development was held up for political reasons. However, in due course most Council decisions will probably be made by a two-thirds majority (12 votes), possibly in some instances with an additional condition as to the actual number of members required to vote in favour of the decision under consideration.

The Ministerial Council maintains several permanent links with the Commission; for the purpose of working out and implementing, new common policies. These links in practice are provided by departmental Committees, on which both institutions are represented, and which are in almost constant session.

The working procedure adopted by the Ministerial Council is broadly as follows: if the subject-matter before it is a proposal concerning policy submitted by the Commission, the matter is referred for study to an *ad hoc* Committee made up of Senior Officials assisted by experts, or to one of the Permanent Committees.

All these Committees are supervised by the Committee of Permanent Representatives, which is an important body consisting of senior officials. As the Commission is represented at all the ensuing committee meetings, this procedure is essentially a continuation of the 'dialogue' referred to earlier.

Actual decisions can only be made by the Ministers who are their respective countries' plenipotentiary delegates, but in minor matters agreement is often reached at an earlier stage between Council and Commission and the final decision is then a mere formality.

In the case of decisions on matters of greater importance, however, there are naturally lengthy discussions between the Ministers and the Commission. It is in connexion with such matters that the Council, by a unanimous adverse vote, can reject any proposal made by the Commission, but where in cases of a split between the Ministers, the Commission's proposal either stands as it is or must be referred back to the Commission for reconsideration.

Another task delegated to the Council, which is of considerable practical importance for many of the Senior Officials of the Community, concerns the salaries, allowances and pensions of the President and members of the Commission and of the senior personnel of the Court which are fixed by the Council, by qualified majority vote.

There are other matters of policy in respect of which the Council has decisive influence. It can hold up the consideration of common policies at an early stage and generally dictate the tempo of the Community's development. These are activities essentially based on the Ministers' powers *qua* their national ministerial authority and not so much by virtue of their membership of the Council of Ministers.

(2) COMPOSITION OF THE COUNCIL AND ITS COMMITTEES

The E.E.C. Council consisted of six Ministers, each with voting powers according to a special weighting system whereas the E.C.S.C. and Euratom had Councils of six and five Ministers respectively, each assisted by specialist Committees.

The single Council, established in 1967 by Article 1 of the Merger Treaty, has inherited the 'powers and competences' of the three parent Councils. The Presidency is held in rotation for a period of six months by a representative of each of the six member-states, and its work schedule is prepared by a Committee consisting of the six Permanent Representatives (Art. 4).

There are a number of permanent committees formed on departmental lines, as well as *ad hoc* committees set up as and when required. They are linked to the Committee of Permanent Representatives, which consists of six Ambassadors located at Brussels with their staffs. These Representatives act on behalf of their respective Ministers on many occasions, a matter of necessity as after all the Ministers have to fulfil their duties at home as well.

The Council is also represented at sittings of the Economic and Social Committee, whereby contact is maintained with the leaders of opinion of the various domestic interests in the six member-states.

(3) THE MERGER

The Treaty under which the Commissions and Councils were merged has been previously considered. Its effect on the three Councils of Ministers was less significant than on the Commissions. The Councils had already been merged in all but name, so that the consequences of the implementation of the merger treaty were mostly in the administrative field, and even in that respect very little remained to be done.

The Committee of Permanent Representatives fulfils an essential role as a body of ministerial deputies 'in residence' at Brussels. It maintains a permanent connexion with the Commission on behalf of the Ministers.

It is probable that in the not so distant future the procedure of reaching decisions by majority votes will be accepted as the normal practice – so that the veto will disappear in respect of all but the most vital issues. The single Council has retained the crucial power to make essential decisions, it still seems to consider it its duty to temper the desire for further and expedited integration with a measure of caution dictated by national sentiments and political contingencies, while at the same time carrying out its obligation to implement the objectives and directives of the Treaties – or perhaps, one day, of a single Treaty. It is probable that the new Council, to a much greater extent than the three separate Councils, will be able to consolidate its position as a true Community organ, not merely as a delegation of Ministers. The wider the scope, the greater the task. And as the Community grows, the standing of the Council as one of its integrated and essential organs may be enhanced – at least that is the planners' intention. The 'enlargement' of the Community might lead to a larger Council, but too many members might weaken its efficiency. It is possible that a Community of 10 members would have a Council of only 14 members, as at present.

C. THE EUROPEAN PARLIAMENT

(I) DEVELOPMENT

The European Parliament is, as we have seen, a development on a broader basis of the old E.C.S.C. Assembly. That 'Common Assembly', set up in September 1951, to keep a measure of public control over the two principal community industries, consisted of 78 parliamentary delegates from the member-states. It had practically no executive powers, although it could 'discuss' the Community's Annual Report (which is still submitted to the Parliament), and it was empowered to bring about the resignation of the entire High Authority by passing a 'No Confidence' vote with a two-thirds majority.

It was a safety-valve, but there was little need to use it. Gradually its administrators enlarged their sphere of influence as Parliamentarians are wont to do. The right to convene extraordinary sessions was fully utilized, and the terms of reference were exploited to their very limits. A rudimentary procedural system developed and as the Community succeeded in staying alive, so did its Assembly.

Nothing was done to curb the development of this embryonic Parliament. In 1953 its rules of procedure were amended to allow for the representation of political parties. Three parties, the Christian Democrats, the Socialists and the Liberals were officially given financial aid (through the Assembly's budget), and in the Spring of 1954 all the party leaders consolidated their positions in public by making formal Statements in the Assembly declaring their parties' views concerning the Community's policy. As from that time on the Assembly, within its occupational limitations as an organ of a specialized Community, was able to assume a much more pronounced supra-national character than for instance the Consultative Assembly of the Council of Europe.

By 1957 the Assembly was obviously a going concern. It was therefore decided, after prolonged discussion, to build it up into a 'European Parliamentary Assembly' for the three Communities, by way of a protocol to the E.E.C. Treaty of Rome.

The new Assembly met for the first time on 19th March 1958, at the 'House of Europe' in Strasbourg, the venue of the Council of Europe. In March 1962, it was officially re-named the 'European Parliament'.

(2) COMPOSITION

The Parliament consists of 142 members, who are all delegates from their countries' respective national parliaments. There are 36 members from each of the three major member-states, 14 each from the two smaller ones, and 6 from Luxembourg.

The delegates sit in a semi-circle, according to their respective party allegiances. A party to be formally recognized must consist of at least 14 members. At present there are 4 parties in the House: the Christian Democrats, the Socialists, the Liberals and the E.D.U. (European Democratic Union) which consists entirely of French 'Gaullists'.

At the time of writing there are 53 Christian Democrats, more than half of whom are German or Italians, 36 Socialists, all members of the various Social Democratic parties, 25 Liberals, mostly members of rather small national splinter parties with liberal leanings, and 18 members of E.D.U. (European Democratic Union), a break-away from the Liberals on the part of the French Gaullist supporters, who by this action seriously reduced the strength of the Liberals in the House. There are also 9 'Independents', 7 of whom are Italian Communists. The Italian delegation is now proportionately representative of the national Parliament. The total number does not reach 142, as not all the parties are represented at full strength.

Each country is entitled to select its delegates according to its own wishes. At the present time this is being done in the following manner:

	Upper House	Lower House	Total
France	12	24	36
Germany	—	36 selected by proportionate representation	36
Italy	18	18	36
	By absolute majority vote		
Belgium	7	7	14
	By proportionate voting		
Netherlands	4	10	14
	By proportionate voting		
Luxembourg	—	6 nominated by a Committee	6
Total number of delegates			142

All the systems of selection employed incidentally have the effect of excluding small minority parties from representation, which is regarded as an essential precaution during the early stages of European Parliamentary experimentation.

The domestic arrangements are of interest. The members sit at long curved tables arranged in six sectors, facing the President on his daïs. Rather more people have to be accommodated than the 142 members, for the sessions are also attended as of right by representatives from the Council and the Commission, and there are a number of Parliamentary officials. (In practice the Commission is fully represented, but the Council usually sends only a few observers.)

Viewed from the President's chair, the Council's eleven delegates sit in front, to the extreme left. Next, proceeding from left to right, we have the political parties in the following order:

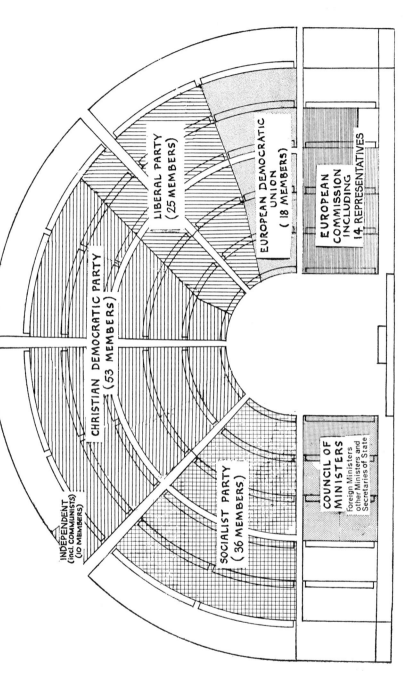

INDEPENDENT
(incl. COMMUNISTS)
(10 MEMBERS)

CHRISTIAN DEMOCRATIC PARTY
(53 MEMBERS)

LIBERAL PARTY
(25 MEMBERS)

EUROPEAN DEMOCRATIC
UNION
(18 MEMBERS)

SOCIALIST PARTY
(36 MEMBERS)

EUROPEAN
COMMISSION
INCLUDING
14 REPRESENTATIVES

COUNCIL OF
MINISTERS
Foreign Ministers
other Ministers and
Secretaries of State

THE EUROPEAN PARLIAMENT IN SESSION

Communists (not officially a 'party'), Socialists, Christian Democrats, and Liberals, the E.D.U. members sitting next to the last. In each case the front bench is occupied by the party leader and his principal aides, while the remainder of the delegates sit in alphabetical order within their respective party groupings. The fourteen representatives of the Commission sit on the President's right, in front of the members. (See diagram, page 59.)

(3) PROCEDURE

The President and his eight Vice-Presidents are elected by secret ballot. They are ex-officio members of the Parliamentary Standing Committee. There have been no difficulties in the past as to the allocation of these positions according to the nationalities, but the political parties are not unnaturally always keen to exploit the 'fair distribution' principle to their own maximum advantage.

Voting is usually along party lines but there are no whips and party discipline is not unshakable. In the occasional clash between national and party allegiances the former is likely to prevail (each member is also a member of his national assembly) and parties may then be split. The Socialists are the most homogeneous group as they all belong to fundamentally similar national parties. They maintain rather strict party discipline which is, however, not always observed by all members. The largest party, the Christian Democrats, who are mostly Catholics, are also well organized and the tendency here is to tighten party cohesion. Both these parties are in favour of greater integration, but the Socialists also want 'democratization', a term which is sometimes defined as 'modern European Socialism'.

The Liberals are a less rigidly organized party. They represent more than a dozen medium and small parties. They are on the whole very enthusiastic Europeans.

The E.D.U. group constitutes the opposite of the type of party it was originally hoped to develop. Its members are all French, and all are opposed to further integration and centralization at the present time. In fact, they and the Italian Communists may be regarded as a kind of 'European Opposition'.

In some respects the E.D.U. is obviously French rather than European, and their battle cry of 'Europe des Patries' is not the slogan of the followers of MM. Monnet, Spaak and Hallstein.

Voting in the House is carried out as follows: – If a vote is called for, the President demands a show of hands. If there is no obvious majority, the 'Ayes' rise and the 'Noes' remain seated. If there is still no conclusive result, or if at least 10 members demand it, a roll-call is then taken. (This is only permitted if at least 71 members – half the full number – are present.) However, even if there is no quorum, voting by show of hands or by rising and remaining seated is permissible unless at least 10 members object, so that non-controversial decisions can be taken without a quorum of members being present.

The plenary sessions are open to the public, but not those of the Committees. Any of the four Community languages may be used by speakers, and there is a 'simultaneous translation' service by which every address is rendered in the other three languages.

(4) THE WORK OF THE PARLIAMENT

There are about 6 to 8 full sessions per year (either ordinary or extraordinary), which means that the House sits for about 30–40 days in all. The two ordinary sessions are held in May and October, and on the additional occasions the House meets in extraordinary session. Although the number of plenary session days is rather small (the delegates must also attend sessions at home!), the total number of Committee working days is high. One or more of these Committees is in session at almost any day throughout the year.

According to the Treaties, the Commission is responsible to the Parliament and to nobody else. What does the Parliament do to carry out its part of this arrangement? Perhaps the best way to describe it is that it may stir the Commission into action if it wholly fails to take certain steps under the Treaty, or may gently set it 'on course' if it appears to be unduly swayed by one or other of the national governments. Then again, the Parliament is consulted prior to the submission to the Council of any major proposal or draft by the Commission. In the last resort, the Parliament could 'sack' the entire Commission, a procedure which has never yet been put to the test.

The real spade work is done in Committee. There are ten large Committees of 29 members each, concerned with the following subjects: Political Affairs, External Trade, Agriculture, Social Affairs, Internal Market matters, Economic and Financial Affairs, Co-operation with developing countries, Transport, Energy, and Research and Cultural Affairs.

These departmental divisions are more or less co-extensive with the Commission's Directorates. As regards nationalities, each of these Committees is composed in accordance with a proportionate system, under which there are 7 delegates each from the large states, 3 each from the smaller ones and 2 from Luxembourg.

There are also three smaller Committees of 17 members each, concerned with Health Protection, Budget and Administration, and Legal Affairs. Here the 'national ratio' is 4 : 2 : 1. Within each national group of Committee members the prevailing relative strengths of the political parties are taken into consideration as far as possible when members are appointed.

Members of the Parliament can make their presence felt in several respects: they can ask questions in the House, they can put written questions to the members of the Commissions and they can participate in debates. There is a system of questioning the authorities based on 'Question Time' in the British House of Commons.

The eventual publication of these verbal interchanges ensures that carefully considered replies are given, and if a matter is raised adroitly and persistently, useful results can often be achieved. Furthermore, the attendance of responsible Commission members (by request) even at Committee meetings not only helps to clarify the more difficult issues, but may also lead to second thoughts on the part of the Commission.

It is a piquant possibility that a Minister, having avoided grilling in his national Parliament, may yet be taken to task in the European Parliament, by the very same member, and on the very same issue.

We have already mentioned the fact that the Parliament is edging in on to the Council/Commission dialogues, and also its fundamental right under the Treaties to supervise the Commission's budget.

(5) ELECTORAL REFORM?

In May 1960, the House adopted a draft convention in accordance with the terms of the Treaty of 1957 to the effect that 'the Assembly shall draw up proposals for elections by direct universal suffrage . . .'. The agreed procedure envisages two stages: during the first stage the Parliament would be enlarged to have 426 members, two-thirds of whom would be elected by direct suffrage to sit for 5 years, while the remainder would still be national delegates. All nationally recognized parties would be permitted to nominate candidates. During the second stage the remaining delegates would be gradually replaced by additional elected members.

Such a large Assembly would have to be given additional powers, otherwise there is little point in going to the trouble of bringing it into being. Each state would probably be allowed to have its members elected according to its own wishes and convenience. It is not thought likely that this Convention will be implemented for some little while, but the general re-allocation and re-arrangement which would become necessary if new member-states were to join, might possibly be considered as providing a reasonable opportunity to introduce at least the first stage of the Draft Convention.

In December 1969 the Commission proposed that from 1974 the Parliament should have final control over the Community's budget, which by that time would be met out of the Community's levies and tariffs. It was recommended that even if the Council was against the budget proposals, the Parliament should be able to carry the day by a two-thirds majority. The self-financing Community would thus in practice be able to submit its budget direct to the Parliament, for ultimate approval by the latter.

D. THE EUROPEAN COURT

(1) COMPOSITION AND PROCEDURE

The fourth of the independent Institutions is formally known as the Court of Justice of the European Communities.

This Court is located in a modern office building in the rue de la Côte d'Eich, at Luxembourg. It is in many ways a unique tribunal. There are seven judges, who are assisted by two advocates-general, all of them appointed by inter-governmental arrangement from jurists practising or admitted in the member-states and of high competence and eminent standing. The judges elect one of their number to be the President of the Court for two years, and also elect a President for each Chamber (there are two) for a period of one year. There is a Court Registrar charged with the usual administrative duties, and two advocates-general share the duties of presenting the issues to the Court, impartially and so as to provide the essential assistance to enable the Court to arrive at a fair decision. Many of the disputes involve complicated issues of fact and law.

The Court, which developed from the small tribunal originally provided for E.C.S.C., is permanently in session. Although it may divide into two chambers, this only happens when it deals with administrative matters, such as proceedings brought against officials of the Community, or by such officials against Community Institutions. The Court almost always sits in plenary session. The official languages are German, French, Italian and Dutch, and commonly the plaintiff decides which language is to be used throughout the proceedings. However, if the defendant is a member-state or, say, a company registered in a member-state, the language of that state will be used.

The procedure is laid down in various official documents. Appeals against actions by the High Authority had to be brought within one month of the date when such act was published or notified; the time limit in respect of appeals against E.E.C. or Euratom was two months, which limit is now generally applicable. Certain non-contractual claims against the Community become statute-barred (*i.e.* cannot be brought at all) after five years.

The member-states and the Institutions have to be represented before the Court by an 'agent', who may be assisted by counsel or by an advocate. All other parties must also be legally represented, the right of audience being restricted to advocates who are members of the bar of their respective countries.

An action is commenced by a petition to the court, setting

out the claim (analogy in English Law: Statement of Claim). This is filed with the Court and a judge-rapporteur then has the case assigned to him, so that he can make the necessary legal and administrative arrangements and supervise the conduct of the case. The defendant then files his defence, and there may be further pleadings. When the pleadings are closed, the judge-rapporteur decides whether a case has been made out for investigation. If so, this may be carried out by the Court itself, and the latter may for this purpose ask the parties to attend, call for documents and hear witnesses as to facts as well as experts. In due course, the Court usually orders a full report to be made of this investigation.

Either at the conclusion of such an investigation, or without one having been held, the President of the Court will fix a date for the hearing. On that occasion the pleadings will be read, counsels' arguments heard and the advocate-general will make his submissions on law and facts. The Court will in due course announce its decision. It speaks 'with a single voice', *i.e.* there are no dissenting judgments. All proceedings except the judges' deliberations prior to their decision are open to the public. The Judgment is signed by the President and the members of the Court and also by the Registrar. There is no right of Appeal except that a re-hearing may be requested in the event of a mis-trial.

There are some ancillary functions which the Court may discharge: it may be asked to interpret its own judgments at the request of a Community Institution; it may have to reopen a dispute in order to take into account evidence which was not previously available, and this is possible even after judgment, until 10 years have elapsed: and it may be asked by domestic (national) courts to give preliminary rulings by way of inter-pretation.

The Court's judgments can be enforced just like those of ordinary national courts of law. Costs are usually paid by the losing party, but no court fees are payable.

(2) WORK AND JURISDICTION

One of the duties of the Court is to test and review the decisions and decrees of the Council and the Commission with regard to their legality under the terms of Community Law as set out in the Treaties or in Regulations made thereunder. It also has power, (when required to do so, for instance, by the Parliament) to stir the Council or the Commission into activity if either of those bodies is not taking due action as prescribed in a Treaty or under a Regulation.

Under certain special conditions a private individual may ask the Court to force the Council or another Institution to take a certain action, if it has failed to do so in violation of its Treaty obligations.

The Council and the Commission may bring disputes before this tribunal, and so may companies as well as individuals. In the case of the two last-mentioned, however, there is a restrictive condition: they may only have recourse to the Court if a decision is actually 'addressed to them' or is 'of direct and specific concern to them'. This provision prevents many companies and individuals from making use of the Court as far as disputes under the E.E.C. or Euratom Treaties are concerned; the older E.C.S.C. Treaty is rather more generous: as long as a decision 'concerns' the company or individual or is considered by them 'a misuse of power affecting them', they may have recourse to the Court.

The Court also acts as mediator between Community Officials and may give opinions at the request of a member-state or an Institution. The number of such opinions given exceeds 1,200.

All the Court's decisions and findings are in due course published in the four official languages as well as occasionally in other languages, such as English, if the matter is of general importance.

The Court has automatic and compulsory jurisdiction within its sphere of activities, which is unusual for an international tribunal. The member-states as well as the Institutions and any other organization or person within its competence are bound by the Court's decisions. In 1969, fines were imposed on several British and Swiss companies for alleged violation of the Community laws against restrictive trade practices. These decisions were made without those companies having submitted to the Court's jurisdiction. It has yet to be decided specifically whether the Court has jurisdiction over companies registered outside the Community but operating within it.

(3) THE COURT AND THE NATIONAL TRIBUNALS

In theory every national court should refer to the European Court any problem of interpretation concerning 'European Law' as contained in the Treaties, the Regulations etc., if its meaning does not appear to it to be certain or clear. This is an optional procedure and inferior national tribunals *may* use it. If, however, the particular court which is baffled by a certain Treaty provision or regulation happens to be the supreme court of a member-state, it *must* refer the matter to the European Court.

It is an unquestionable principle that as regards subject-matters within its jurisdiction, the Court's decision constitutes the law of the Community, and is as such applicable in all the member-states. On such points of interpretation of provisions in the Treaties or the Regulations, and as regards any other matter concerning what may be broadly termed 'Community Law', the domestic courts are therefore bound by the European Court's decisions. In a number of cases national courts have upheld the provisions of 'Community Law' against those of municipal law.

(4) GENERAL COMMENTS

The European Court is in many respects one of the most 'complete' Institutions of the Community. It is wholly independent of the six governments and also of the other three Institutions and has adequate powers to conduct its hearings and enforce its decisions. Its decisions take precedence, if there are divergent opinions or contrary judicial views, over the decisions of any national court concerning matters of 'Community Law'. No major modifications are at present proposed as regards its composition or jurisdiction except that presumably the implementation of further common policies and/or the admission of additional member-states as full members may make the appointment of further judicial personnel desirable.

E. THE PRINCIPAL SUB-ORGANIZATIONS

(i) THE ECONOMIC AND SOCIAL COMMITTEE (E.E.C. and Euratom)

This committee was set up by the E.E.C. Treaty (Articles 193–195) and the Euratom Treaty (Articles 165–167), as a consultative forum available to both communities (E.C.S.C. had its own consultative committee). It has 101 members, of whom 24 hail from each of the three major states, 12 from each of the two medium states and 5 from Luxembourg. These members are nominated by the Councils of Ministers on governmental recommendation for periods of four years. The committee has its own small Secretariat, and is under the administrative control of an 'Office', consisting of its President, two Vice-presidents and twelve of its members.

This committee is a typical 'Community Organ'. It operates by way of informal discussion and debate. Its principal functions are to bring together the civic leaders in every one of the member-states and from all social and economic walks of life. It provides the essential contact between the Communities on the one side and all manner of organizations and private individuals on the other. It is through this committee that industry and commerce can conveniently bring their views and opinions to the notice of the Community leaders.

The committee is composed of industrialists, farmers, representatives of various transport undertakings, trade unionists, tradesmen and craftsmen, members of the professions and other representatives of the working and producing public. In the absence of directly elected Parliamentary representatives, this is the principal point of contact between the Community officials and the people in the six member-states.

In practice it operates through the medium of a number of specialist sub-committees, set up to deal with specific problems as and when they arise in the course of the implementation of the Treaty directions. The active sub-committees at the present time are concerned with agriculture, the further implementation of the common economic, transport and social policies, the services, overseas territories, with health problems arising out of nuclear research work as well as with economic problems connected with the 'nuclear' industries.

The committee is located in Brussels. The Ministerial Council and the Commission *must* refer to it in respect of many matters before they can deliver a formal Decision. Apart from this requirement under the Treaty that it must be consulted in advance, the committee is at all times available for voluntary consultation by any of the Institutions.

Its meetings are held in private. The present members will hold office until 4th May 1970, when they will be eligible for re-appointment. The method of appointment is of interest. Every member-state submits a list containing twice as many names of suitable candidates as will be allocated to it. This list is then considered by the Commission and in due course trimmed to the correct proportions in respect of each state by the Council. The latter must reach its decision by unanimous vote.

Among the present trade-unionist members are two Italians who represent Communist-controlled unions. Several French Communists, who also had been nominated for membership, were not included in their country's final list. This point is worth noting as it indicates a typical aspect of Community procedure: where nominations to any Community organization are left to a member-state, the latter is perfectly free to select its representatives according to the particular procedures preferred by its government for the time being, provided (presumably) that this procedure does not violate any principle of Community Law. There is a definite limit beyond which the Community will not at present interfere with the sovereign rights of the member-states.

(2) THE EUROPEAN INVESTMENT BANK

The bank is located at Brussels. One of its principal 'general objectives' is to ensure the maintenance of a workable financial equilibrium between the member-states. It was much concerned in May, 1969, with the 'back-flow' arrangements, after speculators had unduly depressed the French franc (as well as the U.S. dollar and the Pound Sterling), to the embarrassing advantage of the German Federal Bank. The Bank also promotes development projects within the Community area, without deriving any profit from such operations. It is a semi-independent organization within the Community orbit. The Bank has available capital partly subscribed and partly guaranteed, of more than $1,000 million. Loans in excess of $750 million have been authorized.

It is controlled by a Council consisting of the six Ministers of Finance, which is responsible for the acquisition of the necessary funds and their use by the bank. This Council nominates an administrative governing body and a directorate, and ratifies the annual budget. The administrators – there are twenty-four – deal with such matters as the granting of credits, fixing interest terms and general financial policy. The directorate, which has seven departmental committees, is responsible for the routine work. Loans have been made to France, for gas and potash mining enterprises, to Italy, for motorways and electricity undertakings, to Belgium, for road works, to Turkey, to build railways and factories, as well as many others, including loans to territories such as the Ivory Coast, for a fruit canning factory. In May 1969, assistance was given to the Dutch salt industry. The Bank is also participating in the financing of the Bosphorus bridge. For funding purposes, the E.I.B. recently raised about £6¼ million in Belgium, and £10 million in Italy, by means of bond issues.

(3) THE EUROPEAN SOCIAL FUND

This fund has the specific purpose of financing important schemes such as the re-training and re-employment within the Community of workers who have lost their jobs as the result of the running down of certain industries, changes of policy etc. A board of administrators supervises not only the allocation of funds but also the manner in which any grants made out of the Fund are used.

The 'migrant' workers in the Community have special social and welfare problems. They have been placed under the special supervision and care of a Consultative Committee solely charged with looking after their well-being.

In the summer of 1969, the Commission proposed a radical

increase of the Fund's budget, to enable it to finance wide re-training schemes, and to give it powers to allocate assistance as and where and how it wished. By 1968, over $80 million had been spent to assist over one million people.

The contributions are made by the member states in the following proportions: France and Germany, 32 per cent each, Italy 20 per cent, Belgium 8·8 per cent, Netherlands 7 per cent and Luxembourg 0·2 per cent.

(4) THE TRANSPORT COMMITTEE

This is a large committee of experts who have for some time been working on problems concerning the eventual implementation of a common transport policy. Although their brief is limited under the E.E.C. Treaty to the consideration of matters connected with land and inland waterways transport only, even within this limited field they have not yet reached the stage where they could begin – with some hope of eventual success – to formulate the draft of a proposal for a common transport policy. On 1st January 1968, a joint advisory committee on social matters in inland waterways transport was set up.

The Common Transport Policy, which developed from the work of this Committee, has so far resulted in the issue of 'Community haulage licences' (about 1,200), a maximum/minimum tariff for international road haulage, a law regulating transport cartels, some common safety rules and a number of 'Community-wide' common procedures. This is of course only a beginning, but the effects of unified transport regulations are of such obvious advantage to all that smooth progress is anticipated.

(5) THE 'ASSOCIATION' ARRANGEMENTS

We shall in due course refer to the Arrangements of Association between the Community and several European and non-European countries. The supervision and realization of these agreements is entrusted to a number of Association Councils (each concerned with a single Associate country or group of Associates), whose work is co-ordinated under the control of a special Directorate-General of the Community. The three

THE FOUR 'INSTITUTIONS' OF
'THE SINGLE EUROPEAN COMMUNITY

COMMISSION
14 MEMBERS

DIRECTORATES-GENERAL

COMMITTEES
Economic and Social
Monetary
Technical
etc.

FUNDS
European Social
Overseas Development
Agricultural
(EAGGF)

ORGANIZATIONS
European Investment Bank
Nuclear Supply Agency
Research Centres

Other
Committees
Funds and
Organizations

SERVICES IN COMMON
Statistical — Legal — Information

COMMISSION

PARLIAMENT

COUNCIL OF MINISTERS

COURT

LOCATIONS: Brussels and Luxembourg.

Association Councils so far set up are all located in Brussels, where Community representatives can conveniently maintain constant contact with the delegates (Ambassadors and special representatives) from the associated countries.

At this stage it may be helpful to set out the basic organization of the Community in simple diagrammatical form. Following the implementation of the Merger Treaty in 1967, the European Community has been organized as shown diagrammatically on the preceding page.

CHAPTER VII

The Six at Work

(1) WHAT HAS BEEN ACHIEVED?

It is not easy to make a fair assessment of the achievements of a going concern, at any given stage. And the European Community is very much a going concern, although its progress has neither been smooth nor regular. From 9th May, 1950, to the present, the path to unity has been marked by success and failure, rising hopes and sudden disappointments. Yet in several respects the Treaties have been translated into reality and whatever the future may bring, Europe will never be the same again.

It is neither difficult to criticize the mistakes and miscalculations of the past nor to indulge in starry-eyed anticipation of the thrills of unity to come. It is rather more hazardous and complicated to make an unbiased assessment. Some of the principal objectives of the Market are laudable by any standard: avoidance of another European war, better living standards and social security, improved trading conditions and a more competitive rate of technological progress. What has the new Community system done to realize these objectives? In the final analysis, like any other human organization it is likely to prove as useful – or as ineffective – as the people concerned with it permit it to be.

What have the Six achieved since those early days of the Declaration by Robert Schuman in the Salon de l'Horloge, nearly twenty years ago?

The Coal and Steel industries have been effectively integrated. It was a programme involving what is called sectoral economic integration, *i.e.* integration limited to one or more industries or occupations, and to certain ancillary processes and operations connected therewith. The E.C.S.C. Treaty is a rather more detailed code than the E.E.C. Treaty of Rome – due to its being concerned with a programme for two specialized industries whose problems were clearly defined, and for which it was possible to plan ahead with a degree of certainty.

A common industrial policy has been evolved over the years, in accordance with General Objectives regularly issued by the High Authority. Investment and research, restrictive practices and re-employment, new developments and effective financial autonomy – these were some of the matters which had to be dealt with by an experimental organization placed in control over two heterogeneous industries.

The coal industry continued to contract throughout the period under consideration, while steel production, having more than doubled during the first 10 years, was beginning to run into a period of comparative stagnation and partial recession.

The 'Institutional' effectiveness of the new Community was well and truly tested. The Parliament was empowered to participate in compiling the High Authority's budgets and, to a limited extent (by way of endorsing appointments), to help with selecting the members of that body. Its debates contributed a good deal towards the harmonious evolution of the common policies.

The Court had numerous opportunities to rule on a great variety of disputes concerning the application of the E.C.S.C. Treaty. A body of legal precedents began to emerge, and with it a growing degree of certainty as to what was implied by the Treaty and the complex system of Regulations made thereunder and how the process of integration was to be continued.

The co-operation between the Special Council of Ministers and the High Authority was effective and useful according to most of those concerned.

The success of this European pilot scheme and its adaptation in connexion with E.E.C. and Euratom have been mentioned earlier. The fact that the severe set-back in connexion with the failure to organize a Defence Community was fully overcome was proof of the resilience as well as of the sound structure of the 'Four Institutions' system.

The Community is by now well established in the life of Europe. It is frequently said that it has passed the point of no return. Prognostications of this kind are dangerous – many political and economic organizations have disappeared without trace although at one time it seemed as if they were destined to endure for centuries.

Yet the Community gives the impression that it has come to stay for a long time. It has had the valuable advantage of 'natural growth', something which previous unions and affiliations between nations have conspicuously lacked, including even the United Nations.

The common policy to establish freedom from internal tariffs within the Community area and a common External Tariff towards the outside world, has been fully in force as from 1st July 1968. At that stage the Community became for most practical purposes a single economic unit or 'home market' for the Six. The implementation of the First Policy (Title 1) of Part Two of the E.E.C. Treaty of Rome: the Free Movement of Goods, has been completed.

The E.E.C. Treaty is in essence an economic charter to smooth the way for eventual political unification. The free flow of goods within the area and a homogeneous customs 'wall' towards non-member states is regarded by the European authorities as an essential corner-stone for the edifice to be constructed.

In the meantime, Euratom, too, made a good deal of progress prior to its integration within the Single Community. The nuclear common market has ensured the supply of the essential raw materials to the Six. Several large research centres have been set up, power stations have been built and joint research programmes launched in collaboration with other countries, in particular with the United States. Now efforts are being made to build more suitable reactors in Europe, instead of having to rely on the purchase of these expensive items of equipment in other countries.

Together, the three Communities succeeded in bringing into

existence a common labour market; new and expanding industries have had the effect of drawing migrant workers from one member-state to another, and from outside into the Community. This migration has produced new problems of welfare and social adjustment, which in turn have required the application of thought and finance to bring about acceptable solutions.

The Bank and the Funds have been busy. On a number of occasions member-states have urgently required temporary assistance to prevent an excessive drift of Community assets in one direction. The various Funds had to be replenished rather more quickly than anticipated, particularly as large sums were needed for re-training, re-housing and re-organization, mostly in connexion with the contracting mining industry.

The first European Development Fund (E.D.F.) which was distributed during the years 1958–1963, placed a total of $581\frac{1}{4}$ million by way of grants, etc., and $423\frac{1}{2}$ million were allocated as advances out of the 2nd E.D.F. This latter fund amounts to $1,000 million, much of which was advanced to the 18 African States and Madagascar (the Yaoundé partners). Of the grand total all but a very small fraction (about $17.4 million) is non-repayable, the rest being subject to low interest rates over 40 years.

The first E.D.F. was mostly earmarked for economic and social investments, while the second was used principally for agricultural and industrial production to make the African states concerned more competitive on the international markets. So far, about 600 different projects have been financed in this way. Another $70 million have recently been provided for the use of the Associate partners and for countries 'specially linked' to the Community.

Considerable progress has been made as regards the proposed common policy to ensure the free movement of persons, services and capital. The documentary burden on what one might call the 'travelling public' has been drastically eased, although some formalities remain. The free movement of workers has been facilitated to such an extent that it can probably not be pushed further for some time. By a new Regulation, not yet in force, it is intended to follow up the lifting of the

Customs barriers by a corresponding simplification of 'free' travel within the Community. There now exists a system of ensuring that 'foreign' workers from within the Community area are permitted to apply for all vacancies arising within any member-state. Indeed, by virtue of recent Regulations it is no longer necessary for vacancies to be offered to local nationals prior to making them available to migrant workers from anywhere within the Community, although in special emergency situations member-states may temporarily restrict employment to their own nationals, for limited periods and as regards specified employment only. This restriction must be lifted again as soon as the emergency situation has ceased to exist. A good deal has been done to improve living conditions: in many localities small 'colonies' of migrant workers have been set up. The inherent perils in such a scheme – such as for instance temporary animosity between Turkish and Greek workers within the Community – have been successfully contained.

These 'common policies' and their concomitant effects have contributed to the development of the Community. The improved and 'harmonized' economic and social conditions within the Community as a whole have stimulated trade in the steel industry and minimized the recession in the mining industry. Similar beneficial effects were also felt in those branches of heavy industry which are concerned with the supply of nuclear material and the building of new power stations, to mention just two instances.

The first Directive under Article 58 of the E.E.C. Treaty was approved in March 1968. It co-ordinates the legal guarantees required of companies seeking to establish themselves in more than one member-state. These guarantees affect not only the shareholders but also third parties.

The third common policy to be implemented was that concerned with Agriculture. There had been grim forebodings. Agriculture is mankind's oldest industry, and food being of such vital importance to us all, many people are likely to be extremely sensitive and suspicious if they feel that the production and cost of their basic foodstuffs are being 'tampered with' in any way.

European farmers and other food producers have for long

been privileged and protected in many ways. They may not always have paid good wages to their men, they may not themselves have enjoyed many of the comforts available to town dwellers, but they did manage over the centuries to create a way of living as it suited them. And on the whole they did not fail their respective countries. Yet, as theirs is one of the key industries to keep the people going in time of war, the agricultural communities of Europe have long enjoyed conditions of considerable national seclusion and independence. A *common* Agricultural Policy? Perish the thought! The farmers seemed prepared to fight such a proposition every inch of the way – they would block the roads, destroy their produce. . . .

They didn't, in the end. After many fierce protests and demonstrations, after the battles had been continued at the conference tables through the night, while the clocks remained stopped to keep within the formal time limit, the delegates from the Six eventually accepted a compromise solution. The Commission submitted its much amended proposals setting out the policy to be implemented to the Council of Ministers in December 1963. These proposals recognized the need for a basic 'support' price for farmers within the Community, for provision of aid to the producers and for stabilization of the prices of the essential products. Thus the first hurdle was safely taken.

By the summer of 1965, the policy had been generally agreed, and further proposals were then put forward by the Commission to complete the programme.

The principal objectives are to ensure the free sale and purchase of agricultural products in the Community area; the financing by the Community of the cost of 'market support' for agricultural produce as well as subsidies for exports to countries outside the Community; and the total integration of the agricultural trade policies of the Six *vis-à-vis* outside countries.

The Commission was able to remove the trade barriers as regards farm products within the Community area on 1st July 1968.

Instead of tariffs and import restrictions, a levy system has been introduced, whereby the industry itself is helping to neutralize the differences between price levels in the various member-states for an interim period.

When this transition stage is over, specific individual price levels will be fixed for every agricultural product or groups of products. It is in this connexion that the French Government insists on financial compensation, the price for its relaxation of General de Gaulle's anti-unification attitude.

The operation of the centralized finance system for European agriculture, together with the eventual integration of the national agricultural policies, will mark the completion of the programme set out in Title II of the E.E.C. Treaty, Part Two. By the end of 1967 more than half the Community's farm produce had been organized in a single market. All levies on grain, pork, eggs and poultry within the Community had been abolished, and levies on importing from outside countries were the same for all member-states. Sugar was among the products in respect of which final 'price integration' came into force on 1st July 1968.

A good deal still remains to be done: there will have to be uniformly valid 'Euro-licences' for import and export into and from the Community, relevant taxation and legislation is due to be 'harmonized', and national aids to agriculture, which are still at variance in the member-states, ought to be levelled out so as to avoid 'distortion of competition', which is contrary to the Treaty of Rome.

A peculiar position has developed in connexion with French agriculture. France is the only genuinely autarchic country in Europe and for that reason the French Government expected French grain exports to other Community members to rise sharply, thereby offsetting some concessions made by France in other spheres.

However, the percentage of French exports of wheat to the other five member-states actually fell in 1966, and Italy bought more maize from the U.S. than ever before, although French maize was available. It is a fact of modern economic life, that 'strings attached' to loans can overcome and upset any agricultural plans.

Progress has been made towards a more uniform tax system, by introducing a tax based on the French 'value-added' principle. However, Italy and Belgium were authorized by the Council, in December 1969, to postpone the introduction of T.V.A. until

1st January 1972. The other four members have now introduced the system, on a uniform basis. Furthermore, the Commission proposed to the Council of Ministers in the autumn of 1967 a system of tax reform including provisions for 'European Companies', *i.e.* companies which would be able to operate freely from anywhere in the Community without fiscal or legal obstacles. A start was made to 'harmonize' from 1st July 1968 all taxes affecting capital movements, mergers and investment. All tax disadvantages due to national legislation within the Community are scheduled for abolition, and it is further suggested to provide uniform 'investment stimulation' throughout the member-states, by introducing identical fiscal incentives. The Commission also proposed a number of common tax arrangements in connexion with company mergers across the national frontiers of the Six. By February 1970, the Council had not agreed to these proposals.

Not very much so far has been done to integrate the member-states' transport policies, one of the principal common policies to await full implementation. The E.E.C. Treaty of Rome only refers to rail, road and inland waterways (Article 84). Yet even within these limits the transport industry is strangely averse to standardization. There has been widespread fear that such a process would eventually lead to the elimination of many of the existing operators – a fear which to some extent may prove to have been well-founded.

Some of the individual measures to facilitate road haulage have been mentioned earlier. There has been some co-operation between the railway operators in the Community, who are in every instance the member-states themselves, and only limited concerning operations by carriers on road and waterways. However, a Directive has been issued setting out the essential requirements of a common transport policy. The Commission has laid down two outlines in principle so that rules can be drawn up.

(a) to enable people to set up as carriers of goods by road in national and international transport, irrespective of which member-states they belong to, and

(b) to control the capacity of national goods transport by road.

The proposed rules are intended to provide uniform legislation as to carriage by road by nationals of the member-states anywhere within the Community, while at the same time avoiding undue restrictions against other nationals. The control of the available capacity is intended to facilitate the introduction of a uniform licensing system, on a geographical (not necessarily national) basis, with strict 'market supervision' to avoid duplication of services, transport starvation in unpopular areas, uneconomic services and other anomalies and misuses.

In December 1967 the Council at long last reached agreement as to the method of implementing a common transport policy; agreement as to 'normalization' of railway accounts and on public transport generally was reached by the end of 1968.

Under the 'Leber Plan' it was intended to harmonize, by July 1968, the more important national transport regulations, and to help the railways by restricting road transport in accordance with agreed principles. The originator of this plan was the German Minister of Transport, and this 'aid to railways by law', a very controversial issue, was intended to be tried out in Germany by way of a test scheme, but the Commission has proposed drastic limitations and amendments. Far-reaching proposals have been tabled by the Commission for an integrated trunk route system throughout the Community. A beginning has been made to improve the arrangements relating to the navigation on the Rhine.

It is possible that some progress may soon be made through the medium of the European Conference of Transport Ministers. As far as air transport is concerned, the Treaty leaves matters in the hands of the Council 'for future reference'. Five countries of the Six operate highly competitive national air line systems, in addition to a number of independent operators. There is no effective 'Euro'- system, although two of the principal national operators have concluded a bilateral agreement. All the Six are, of course, members of I.M.C.O. and I.C.A.O., respectively the world organizations for shipping and air transport. The first stage of the Transport Policy was completed in March, 1969, when six of the seven basic Regulations had been adopted by the Council, and only one, concerning dual taxation, remained inoperative.

As mentioned earlier, an incipient common energy policy of

four basic points was submitted to the Council of Ministers in February, 1969.

In conclusion we must refer to the work done to eliminate some of the more common practices in restraint of trade. Price fixing, restrictions on production, market-sharing arrangements, interference with free tenders, dumping, state subsidies and discriminatory tax restrictions or inducements have all been made subject to control by the European authorities or illegal by virtue of special regulations. It is in connexion with the enforcement of these prohibitions that the European Court has lately been kept very busy.

We shall in due course turn our attention to 'incidental' achievements of the Community, such as the European schools, the harmonization of legal provisions, cultural developments, the creation of the 'Community spirit' and other plans for integration, material as well as spiritual. (See pp. 106 *et seq.*)

The ultimate objectives of the Treaties have at all times been the pacification and political unification of Europe. The Six are but a part of Europe, and the effects of a common economic policy are not directly felt by the ordinary citizens. Nevertheless, the Community seems to have extended its activities a long way beyond the Treaties, and the process of integration has had many remarkable side effects.

(2) IS THE COMMUNITY 'OUTWARD-LOOKING'

One of the more serious allegations which can be made against any organization which co-ordinates protective measures by its members against outsiders – and which has frequently been made against the European Community – is that it is 'inward-looking' and protectionist.

The Community's Common External Tariff is, of course, essentially a protective measure. It will undoubtedly have diversionary effects on some trades, by redirecting goods from being exported to one of the Community countries to customers elsewhere. (For instance, cheap Danish eggs some time ago flooded the British market because they could not 'get over' the Community tariff wall.) But in fairness it must be said that the Common Market countries have made all kinds of efforts to come to terms with other countries, and there is now a fairly sophisticated system of 'external relations' which must be considered.

(a) ASSOCIATIONS WITH OTHER COUNTRIES

In the first instance, there are the 'Association Arrangements', with non-European countries and territories under Article 131 of the E.E.C. Treaty and 'with any country, group of countries or international organization' under Article 238 of that Treaty. The overseas countries and territories with which such special arrangements were concluded in the first instance are listed in Annex IV of the Treaty itself. They are all of them former colonial possessions of one or other of the member-states, or of the United Kingdom.

The Associations so far formed are with two European countries, namely Greece and Turkey, and Treaties have also been concluded with a group of seventeen African states, with Madagascar, Nigeria and of late with Tanzania, Zambia and Uganda, all of them former British colonies. The arrangement with Nigeria was at long last ratified on 19th January 1968 on behalf of the six member-states. Such arrangements require the unanimous approval of the Council, and the Parliament must be consulted. The Treaty itself, which formally provides for Association with non-European countries, but not with European states, may be 'extended' in order to make associate membership agreements possible.

Association with the Community is a contractual arrangement, embodying reciprocal terms. The Associate member acquires no administrative or other control within the Community, but merely commercial rights and, possibly, some duties. The Associates may be compared to holders of non-voting and not fully paid-up shares in a limited company.

The first Associate member was Greece (November 1961). Under the supervision of a special Council composed of Community representatives and Greek government officials, projects are now under way to modernize and improve the economic structure of that country, with particular emphasis on her agriculture. The chief purpose is to assist the Associate eventually to 'catch up' with the Community, by the elimination of old-fashioned practices, by the reorganization of backward industries, and by the introduction of modern (preferably Community-type) measures. The Greek economy is weak in many respects. It is nevertheless anticipated that by 1983, at most 22 years from the conclusion of the Agreement, Greece will be able to take her place as a full member of the Community. In the meantime she will receive assistance by being permitted to make use of the Community's tariff reductions in many ways like a full member, without having to lay open her own economy to the flood of Community goods which would otherwise result from the making of reciprocal arrangements. The volume of Greek trade has increased since the signing of this agreement, most of the increase being due to more active dealing with the Community over a wide range of commodities. This tendency has been sustained for some years and still continues.

In July 1963, the Community signed an Agreement at Yaoundé in the Cameroon Republic, with a group of eighteen African states. This Agreement came to an end on May 31, 1969 but was duly prolonged for five more years. It is essentially an extension of the benefits of the E.E.C. Treaty to these newly independent countries, with many special conditions and provisions to allow for the specific situations in what are economically erratic states. The Agreement provides for liberal financial aid, technical assistance (as regards roads, health, education etc.), and for a permanent system of administrative co-operation between the Community and the Associate Group. An Association Council has been set up which is assisted by a special Committee charged with the implementation of the various provisions in detail, by a 'Parliamentary Conference' (an assembly of delegates), and a special Court of Arbitration. This organization constitutes something like a miniature Community of its own, whose portals are open to further applicants. At its full meeting in December 1967, when 54 members of the Parliament and 54 parliamentary delegates from the African states (3 per state), attended, the main problem ahead was agreed to be the relative lack of profitability of the African

In 1966 Nigeria signed a separate Association Agreement with the Community. Kenya, Uganda, Tanzania, Morocco and Tunisia have made similar association arrangements. This is clear indication of the extension of the Community's influence as an entity beyond the frontiers of the former French Colonial Empire into the areas of British influence.

states' exports, and ways and means to remedy this, other than by loans or donations, which would only temporarily improve the position. A number of economic remedies of a more permanent nature were proposed by M. Armengaud of France (the official rapporteur) and accepted by the Conference. Kenya, Tanzania and Uganda have concluded a very similar Association agreement, which was signed in July 1968, in Brussels, and this Agreement, the 'Arusha Agreement', was approved by the Parliament on 1 October 1968.

The two national groups which are partners under the Yaoundé Agreement have declared that neither will take any action to hinder the eventual political unification of either Europe or Africa. In May 1968, the Yaoundé Committee of 36 representatives (18 parliamentary deputies from the Community, and 18 from the African states), decided to renew the Yaoundé Agreement.

On 1st December 1964, Turkey became an Associate member of the Community, thereby extending the link with the Six further to the East. A list of Turkish commodities was drawn up and these goods now enter the Common Market at preferential rates. Recently this list was extended to cover additional ranges of articles. Substantial loans have been extended to Turkey by the Investment Bank to effect economic improvements, particularly in the Eastern provinces. It is now expected that Turkey will soon be able to carry increased economic burdens, and to enter upon a transition stage prior to becoming a full member of the Community.

The recent special Association agreement with Nigeria, provides for mutual trade preferences, without financial aid from the Community. This is known as the 'Lagos' Agreement.

Association Agreements with Tunisia and Morocco were signed in March, 1969. These Agreements are effective for 5 years, when they will be reviewed. They have the effect of making both these countries full Associates of the Community. Malta has begun negotiations for similar purposes.

(b) PACTS AND AGREEMENTS

The Community in its corporate capacity is able to conclude

trading pacts with other countries on behalf of all its members. This is an unusual international practice which sets it apart from other economic groupings of nations. In 1963 E.E.C. signed an agreement with Iran, another with Israel in 1964 (which was replaced by a 'preferential' 5-year agreement in February 1970), and a 3-year pact with Lebanon in 1965. Negotiations for a special trade pact with the entire Community have been begun with Yugoslavia. Community officials speak with pride of these instances when the Economic Community has acted as a single entity *vis-à-vis* third parties. In February 1970, the Community was engaged in 'trade talks' with at least nine countries: Argentina, Austria, Japan, Lebanon, Malta, Spain, U.A.R. and Yugoslavia.

(c) SPECIFIC PROJECTS

A number of projects have been launched by way of co-operation between several members of the Community on one side and an individual country on the other. The European Space Research Organization (E.S.R.O.) and the Launcher Development Organization (E.L.D.O.) are cases of such co-operation between member-states of the Community and one or more non-member states. There are a number of agreements between Euratom and other countries. The nuclear merchant vessel 'Otto Hahn' was built under the terms of a special arrangement between a Community (Euratom) and a member-state (Germany). The 'Dragon' agreement, for the joint operation of a gas-cooled reactor in Dorset (by the Community and six other countries), has been fruitful, and now runs until 1973.

Apart from such formal arrangements between individual sovereign states and one or more members of the Community, there are innumerable consortium arrangements linking companies within and without the Community borders to each other.

(d) DIPLOMATIC LINKS

The Communities have established many diplomatic links with the outside world. In some instances they have set up embassies

ASSOCIATIONS WITH E.E.C.

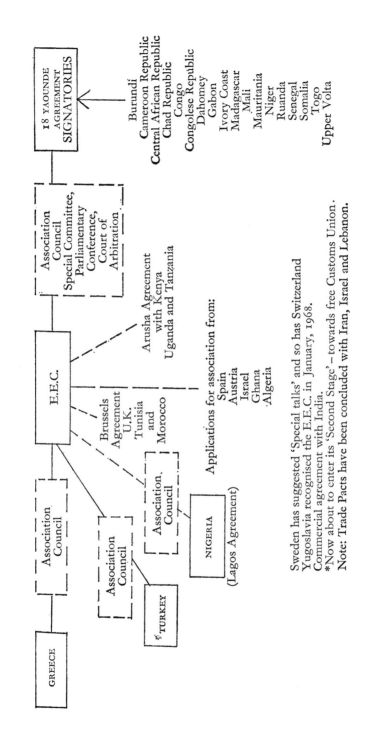

18 YAOUNDE AGREEMENT SIGNATORIES

Burundi
Cameroon Republic
Central African Republic
Chad Republic
Congo
Congolese Republic
Dahomey
Gabon
Ivory Coast
Madagascar
Mali
Mauritania
Niger
Ruanda
Senegal
Somalia
Togo
Upper Volta

Association Council Special Committee, Parliamentary Conference, Court of Arbitration.

E.E.C.

Arusha Agreement with Kenya Uganda and Tanzania

Brussels Agreement U.K. Tunisia and Morocco

Applications for association from:
Spain
Austria
Israel
Ghana
Algeria

Association Council

NIGERIA (Lagos Agreement)

Association Council

Association Council

TURKEY

GREECE

Sweden has suggested 'Special talks' and so has Switzerland Yugoslavia recognised the E.E.C. in January, 1968. Commercial agreement with India.
*Now about to enter its 'Second Stage' – towards free Customs Union.
Note: Trade Pacts have been concluded with Iran, Israel and Lebanon.

abroad (e.g., the E.C.S.C. Embassy in London). Most major states apart from Russia and the Republic of China and their respective allies and satellites have Permanent Representatives (Ambassadors) accredited to the Community Headquarters in Brussels. Yugoslavia is expected to do so soon, following her official recognition of the Community. These Ambassadors to the Community are invaluable intermediaries particularly when preparatory work is to be done. The 'Iron Curtain' countries do not officially recognize the Community as such, but there are definite signs that it may not be long before one or other of them will make commercial arrangements with the Six in their corporate 'Community' capacity.

(e) OTHER POINTS OF CONTACT

There are world-wide financial contacts through the Investment Bank. There is a formal Parliamentary link with the Council of Europe, particularly through the annual joint session of the two Parliaments, with active participation by the Commission. And there are links with G.A.T.T., with other members of the 'Kennedy Round', and through many other connexions in the world of finance.

(3) FACTS AND FIGURES

Statistics are anathema to many. Yet what better proof is there of a promise fulfilled or a target missed than the quantitative details relating to the subject-matter? And the true place of the Community in the world of today emerges best by way of comparisons in respect of a reasonably wide selection of topics.

In order conveniently to achieve this objective of fair comparison and to paint a reasonably accurate picture, while at the same time paying due heed to the sensitivity of those who are appalled by tables and percentages, most of the relevant statistics have been grouped together within the confines of this sub-chapter.

References to the 'Community' are only to the Six unless otherwise stated. The metric and decimal systems are employed throughout. Figures relate to 1968 unless otherwise indicated.

Abbreviations used: m. (million), sqkm. (square kilometre), E.F.T.A. (European Free Trade Association).

The Community area is 1,167 m. sqkm. (with European associates, 2,070 m. sqkm.). This is very much less than the area of the U.S., 9,363 m. sqkm., or of the U.S.S.R., 22,402 m. sqkm., and about the same as that of the E.F.T.A. countries, 1,277 m. sqkm.

The population of the Community is 186 m., with its European associates, 228 m. The population of the U.S. is 201 m., of the U.S.S.R., 238 m., and of the E.F.T.A. countries 99 m.

It is apparent from these figures that the Community is comparable with the U.S. and the U.S.S.R. in being a compact population area, but that it has a very much greater population density than either of these nation-states.

The Community's potential labour force numbers about 74 m., which is nearly twice that of E.F.T.A. and about the same as that of the U.S. There are no recent figures to hand concerning the U.S.S.R., but the labour force of that country in 1964 was 104 m.

The total number of unemployed in the Community at the end of 1968 was 1·2 m. (Germany about ·2 m., France ·2 m. and Italy ·6 m.), whereas in the U.S. the number was about 2·6 m. In the U.K. there were at that time about ·6 m. wholly unemployed.

One way of comparing the 'efficiency of employment' in several countries is to tabulate the respective rates of increase of their gross national products (G.N.P.). From such a comparison some conclusions can be drawn as to the relative productivities in the various countries. If we take 1963 as the 'basic index' year (being 5 years after the E.E.C. began to operate), we see that by 1968 the Community's index had risen from the basis of 100 in 1963 to 117·3, whereas the U.S. and E.F.T.A. had respectively achieved indices of 127 and 116. (There is no reliable comparison index figure for the U.S.S.R.)

Let us now look a little more closely at some of the component indices, which together produce these G.N.P. figures.

The annual growth rates over two 5-year periods provide some interesting comparisons:

	1956/61	1961/66
Community	5·3%	4·9%
E.F.T.A.	3·5%	3·6%
U.S.	2·2%	5·6%

AGRICULTURE

In 1967, the Community had 71 m. hectares of agricultural land under cultivation, compared with 31 m. hectares in E.F.T.A., about 441 m. hectares in the U.S. and 601 m. hectares in the U.S.S.R.

In spite of its far smaller area, the Community managed to produce 60 m. tons of cereals, compared with 170 m. tons produced by the U.S. and 117 m. tons by the U.S.S.R. It marketed about twice as much meat as E.F.T.A., about the same amount as the U.S.S.R. but only half of the U.S. production. The emphasis in the Community is on the production of beef and pork, the output of lamb and mutton being rather less important.

As regards dairy products (an important sector of Britain's imports from the Commonwealth and E.F.T.A.), the Community in 1967 produced about two and a half times as much milk as E.F.T.A., more than the U.S. and about as much as the U.S.S.R. The Community also produced more than three times as much butter as E.F.T.A., more than either the U.S. or the U.S.S.R., and nearly twice as many eggs as E.F.T.A., more than the U.S.S.R. but a good deal less than the U.S. with its huge mechanized battery farms.

ENERGY

(1968 figures (*see Table on facing page*) in equivalents of a million tons of coal.)

The Community figures for 1968 show a decrease of about 6 per cent as against 1967.

	Coal	Lignite	Crude petrol-eum products	Natural gas	Primary elec-tricity	Total
Community	198	29	21	25	40	313
E.F.T.A.	178	3	4	3	68	256
U.S.	491	·8	586	586	82	1,746
U.S.S.R.	444	78	379	240	37	1,178
Japan	51	—	1	1	33	87

PRODUCTION GENERALLY

(Basic index 100, for 1958, except where otherwise indicated.)

Industrial production has increased in all the principal comparison areas. The rise in the Community has been from 100 to 164, in E.F.T.A. to about 157, in the U.S. to 167, in the U.S.S.R. to 200, and in Japan to 291 (1967 figures).

The Community produced nearly 50 per cent more iron ore than E.F.T.A., about three-quarters of the total U.S. output, but less than half of the U.S.S.R. production. The Community's output of pig iron and steel was not much less than that of the U.S.S.R., and not much less than that of the U.S. It was three times as high as the total E.F.T.A. production.

The Community is the largest producer of cement in the world, just ahead of the U.S.S.R.

In 1968 the Common Market countries produced very nearly 7 m. passenger cars and more than half a million commercial vehicles. The comparative totals in the rival producer areas were, respectively:

E.F.T.A.: 2·1 m., ¾ m.; U.S.: 8·3 m., 2·1 m.; U.S.S.R.: about 350,000 and 650,000; Japan: 3·5 m., 1·9 m.

In the same year the Community's yards launched over 2·6 m. tons of merchant shipping, compared with 3·0 m. tons by E.F.T.A., ·4 m. tons by the U.S. and 8·5 m. tons by Japan.

TRADING FIGURES

In 1968, the Community imported about $61,836 m. of goods

and exported $64,191 m., a positive trade balance of nearly $2·4 m.

Comparison figures (exports f.o.b., imports c.i.f.):
E.F.T.A. $37,590 m., $31,030 m., negative balance: $6,560 m.
U.S.: $33,088 m., $34,227 m., positive balance: $1,139 m.
U.S.S.R.: $9,410 m., $10,634 m., positive balance: $1,224 m.
Japan: $12,989 m., $12,973 m., negative balance: $·016 m.

These figures demonstrate the economic strength of the Community, which handles more than a quarter of the world's imports as well as of its exports. Its total turnover is greater than that of any other nation or grouping of nations. During 1967 the negative balance of the Community began to change for the better with the result that a positive trade balance with the rest of the world was at last established.

The individual import and export totals in respect of every member-state have risen year by year for some time – an indication of progress, albeit only Germany regularly had a consistently positive trade balance within the Community of late, while Belgium/Luxembourg have recently managed to achieve an export surplus. This process continued throughout 1969.

An analysis of the origins and destinations of the Community's imports and exports respectively is illuminating. Imports by member-states from within E.E.C. have been rising faster than those from E.F.T.A. or from any other large trading area. On the other hand, Community exports within E.E.C. have not expanded any more rapidly than sales by the Community as a whole to the U.S. Sales to E.F.T.A. have not developed so rapidly of late. It is interesting to observe, however, that the Community's trade with E.F.T.A., the U.S.A. and the U.S.S.R. is rising at the expense of dealings with the rest of the world. It would seem that the economic effect of a trading area is two-fold: increased trade within the area, and increased trade with other 'giant' trading areas, to the detriment of commercial dealings with 'independent' or 'isolated' states. In 1968 about 8 per cent of the Community's imports came from the Associated Territories Overseas, to which about 6 per cent of the Community's total exports were sold.

In 1967, the Community's exports to the East European

Countries were over $2,140 m., and imports from those countries, $1,980 m. The corresponding figures for E.F.T.A. were $1,382 m. and $1,684 m.

SOCIAL SERVICES ETC.

Comparisons of social services, standards of living and similar conceptions should be approached with caution. There are many vague contingencies, due to national habits, educational standards, population density, climatic conditions, etc., which could make nonsense of the most careful analysis. The examples here provided are therefore only intended as a rough guide.

From 1960 to 1966 the value of the social security benefits received by people in the Community rose by about 80 per cent, a more rapid rise than could be noted elsewhere.

In 1966, there were in the Community 149 doctors per 100,000 inhabitants, compared with 120 in E.F.T.A., 153 in the U.S., 210 in the U.S.S.R., and 111 in Japan.

The people in the Community kept body and soul together by an intake of an average 2,860 calories per person per day, which compared with about 3,100 in E.F.T.A. and the U.S. In 1966, they tried to improve their living accommodation by building about $1\frac{1}{2}$ m. new 'units' (houses, flats or apartments), while in E.F.T.A. they added 600,000, in the U.S., $1\frac{1}{2}$ m. and in the U.S.S.R., $2\frac{1}{4}$ m. At the end of that year the people in the Community were duly accommodated in such a way that there was between .6 to 1 person per room, in E.F.T.A., .7 to 1.1 (.7 in Britain), in the U.S., .7, and in the U.S.S.R., where there is still considerable overcrowding, 1.5.

In the Community there were 163 private cars for every 1,000 inhabitants, a slightly higher ratio than in E.F.T.A. (Britain and Sweden have a high 'car-frequency' rate), where the figure was 158, but not nearly as many as in the U.S., 397, or one car per fewer than three persons. In the U.S.S.R., there were but 4 cars for 1,000 persons. Out of 1,000 people in the Community, 170 owned a television set, compared with 209 in E.F.T.A., 408 in the U.S., and 68 in the U.S.S.R.

During the period under review the total wealth of every member of the Community increased very considerably. The indices of ordinary shares also rose until recently, the average increase in the Community stock exchanges being 72 per cent, while the member-states' reserves of gold and convertible currencies rose from a total of $11,900 m. in 1958 to $21,107 m. in 1967. The indices have lately resumed their respective rises, and the reserves have continued to increase. The holdings of member-states at the end of 1967 were as follows: Germany, $6,738 m.; France, $5,848 m.; Italy, $4,148 m.; Netherlands, $2,104 m.; and Belgium/Luxembourg, $2,220 m. By comparison the U.K. held $2,733 m. and the U.S. $14,277 m.

Even a cautious analysis of this statistical cocktail demonstrates that the compact Community possesses a very wide range of raw materials (remarkable in view of its comparatively small area), and is capable of producing many sophisticated substitute materials where it lacks adequate natural resources. It is the world's most active export/import area, and its inhabitants on the whole enjoy a very high standard of living. The economic potential of the Community is immense, but it is stressed by those who hold executive positions within its principal organizations that this potential can only be fully utilized under the aegis of political unification.

(4) THE NEW EUROPEANS

It is probable that one day there will be a heated argument as to who actually first conceived the new Community in its present shape. Several men might lay a claim to this distinction but it is still much too soon to accord any definite preference to this personage or to that. Yet among those who will undoubtedly rank with the leading contenders we can safely name Winston Churchill, Guy Mollet, Paul-Henri Spaak, Jean Monnet, Robert Schuman, Konrad Adenauer, Alcide de Gasperi, Joseph Luns, Joseph Bech and General Charles de Gaulle.

In 1950 the conception of 'One Europe' was neither novel nor original. On the other hand the empirical procedure adopted by the planners of the new Community had never been tried before, and the time chosen by them – only five years after the end of the Second World War – made many observers shake their heads.

What has been achieved so far is of course largely due to the inspiration given by those early leaders and their devotion to an ideal. Yet they could never have succeeded without the able assistance of a number of distinguished personages from the six member-states, who were willing to lend a hand when it came to navigating the untried vessel 'Community' across the uncharted seas of European co-operation.

The reader may wish to know a little about the people who at present occupy some of the most responsible positions in the Community. Space does not permit the mention of those who held those appointments in the past, and it may well be that some of those mentioned will have been replaced by the time this book appears in print. With these reservations in mind, the writer believes that the European Community will appear rather more real to the reader if he has a little personal information about some of the men who run it.

(The following abbreviations have been used: B:Belgium, F:France, G:Germany, I:Italy, L:Luxembourg and NL: Netherlands.)

THE COUNCIL OF MINISTERS

On the 1st July, 1967, the single Council came into being and its first Chairman was Willy Brandt (G).

In accordance with normal Common Market procedure, the national delegations are headed by the Ministers of Foreign Affairs of the six member-states, namely J. M. A. H. Luns (NL), Maurice Schumann (F), Pierre Harmel (B), Walter Scheel (G), Aldo Moro (I) and Gaston Thorn (L).

The Secretary-General of the E.E.C. Council is Christian Calmes (L, 54), a barrister, who after a period of imprisonment in Germany during World War II worked for many years in the Luxembourg Ministry of Foreign Affairs. His office is at 2, rue Ravenstein, Brussels.

The six Permanent Representatives of the member-states are: D. P. Spierenburg (NL), J.-M. Boegner (F), J. van der Meulen (B), Hans-Georg Sachs (G), Bombassei di Vettor (I) and A. Borschette (L).

THE COMMISSION:

The President of the Commission is Jean Rey (B, 66, Secretarial, Legal Service) who started his career as a lawyer in Liège. He was a Liberal member of the Belgian Parliament in 1939, and after release from a prisoner of war camp where he spent the years from 1940–1943, became Minister of Reconstruction in 1949, and thereafter Minister of Economic Affairs. From 1958 he served as a member of the E.E.C. Commission with special responsibility for external relations.

There are four Vice-Presidents. Sicco L. Mansholt (NL, 60, Agriculture) has always been concerned with agricultural matters. He is a graduate of the School of Tropical Agriculture in Deventer, and was a farmer for a number of years. He entered the Dutch Parliament as a member of the Socialist Party, and was Minister of Agriculture from 1945-1948 and again from 1951–1956. He became one of the Vice-Presidents of the E.E.C. Commission in 1958 with special responsibility for agriculture, and was himself the originator of the Community's common agricultural policy.

Lionello Levi-Sandri (I, 58, Social Affairs, Personnel, Administration) has worked as a civil servant for many years, in a number of Italian Ministries. He is an expert on matters concerned with labour and social questions. After war service in North Africa he commanded a Resistance Brigade in Northern Italy. In 1948 he became a Counsellor of State and in 1961 was appointed a member of the E.E.C. Commission, in charge of social affairs, and a Vice-President in 1964.

The third Vice-President is Fritz Hellwig (G, 56, General research, nuclear research), who was a professor at several German universities. He was a prisoner of war from 1943–1947 and entered industry on his release. In 1956 he became a member of the German Parliament, sitting as a Christian Democrat, and as such was a delegate to the European Parliament from 1959. He was a member of the E.C.S.C. High Authority from 1959 until its dissolution in 1967.

Raymond Barre (F, 44, Economic and financial affairs, Statistical office) is the youngest Vice-President. He studied law and eventually became an official of the Ministry of Industry.

He was a member of a large number of government organizations, chiefly concerned with planning, manpower costs, and technological research.

There are nine other members of the Commission.

The Belgian member is Albert Coppé (57), formerly a professor of Economics at the University of Louvain. He was a Christian Social Deputy and later held office as Minister of Works, Economic Affairs and Reconstruction. M. Coppé was the Vice-President of the E.C.S.C. High Authority.

Guido Colonna di Paliano (I, 60, Industrial affairs) is a professional diplomat. He was Deputy Secretary-General of NATO from 1962–1964, when he became a member of the E.E.C. Commission until its dissolution.

Hans von der Groeben (G, 61, Internal markets, Commercial and fiscal matters, regional policy) is a civil servant. After service in the German army he became an official in a provincial Ministry of Finance. In 1955 he headed the German delegation to the E.E.C. section at Brussels, and in 1958 was appointed a member of the E.E.C. Commission.

Henri Rochereau (F, 60, Development Aid) is a lawyer, and was for many years an Independent Republican senator. In 1959 he was Minister of Agriculture in M. Debré's government, and in 1962 joined the E.E.C. Commission.

Emanuel Sassen (NL, 57, Competition) is another lawyer. He was a deputy (Catholic People's Party) from 1946–48 when he became Minister of Overseas Territories. He represented his country in the old E.C.S.C. Common Assembly and was appointed a member of the Euratom Commission in 1958.

Victor Bodson (L, 66, Transport) was at various times a Socialist deputy. In 1961 he was elected to his country's Council of State, after periods of appointment as a Minister in 1940–44 (in exile, London), and again in 1944–47 and 1951–59.

Jean-François Deniau (F, 40, External trade) is the 'baby' of the Commission. He participated in the formation of the E.E.C. and served in several Ministries. He was in charge of the E.E.C. Commission's delegation during the negotiations in 1961–63 with the British government concerning the British application for membership. In 1967 he was French Ambassador to Mauritania.

Wilhelm Haferkamp (G, 45, Energy) is an economist and trade unionist. He served for several years on the Executive Committee of the German Trade Union Council and was a member of the E.C.S.C. Consultative Committee from 1958–1966 and again in 1967. He was a Socialist Landtag deputy.

Edoardo Martino (I, 58, External Relations) became a Christian Democrat deputy in 1948 and thereafter held office as Under-Secretary in several Italian Ministries.

The Executive Secretary of the Commission is Emile Noel. The President of the important Economic and Social Committee is Louis Major (B) and its Secretary-General, Jacques Genton. This Committee has 101 members and held more than 75 full meetings.

For the purpose of internal co-ordination between the Commission and the Directorates-General, responsibilities have been divided as follows:

Group 1: General Economy (Chairman: Barre, Deputy: Hellwig).

„ 2: Industry (Chairman: Groeben, Deputy: Colonna).

„ 3: Agriculture (Chairman: Mansholt, Deputy: Deniau).

„ 4: External Relations and development aid (Chairmen: Martino and Rochereau).

„ 5: Social Affairs (Chairman: Sandri, Deputies: Coppé and Haferkamp).

„ 6: Membership applications and association requests (Chairman: Hellwig, Deputy: Sassen).

„ 7: Administration (Chairman: Rey, Deputies: Sandri and Bodson).

Thus the distribution of portfolios in this first 'European Cabinet' is in line with the system of numerical weighting within the Community. The three major countries are each represented by two chairmen and (except for France), by two Deputies, while Belgium and the Netherlands both have one appointment in each category, and there is one Luxembourg member.

THE EUROPEAN COURT

The European Court has seven judges. The President is Robert Lecourt (F, 60), formerly French Minister of Justice. A lawyer before the War, he became a Resistance leader and in 1945 a Deputy to the National Assembly, representing the M.R.P. He held ministerial office in 1948/49 and again in 1957, was appointed to the Tribunal in 1962 and elected President on 9th October 1967.

The President of the first Chamber of the Court is now Joseph Mertens de Wilmars (B, 56), a specialist in administrative and European law. From 1952–1962 he was a member of the Belgian Chamber of Representatives. The other members of this Chamber are Prof. Ricardo Monaco (I, 59), who held numerous legal appointments connected with international law at various Italian Universities until 1956, when he was elected to preside over the State Council, and Andres Mathias Donner (NL, 50), a former Chamber President. He was active in the Dutch resistance movement during the Second World War, and became Professor of Public and Administrative Law at Amsterdam University in 1945. M. Donner also served on several Commissions and is a member of the Academy of Science.

The other Chamber is presided over by Albert Trabuchi (I, 61), another academician and a lecturer in law at various Italian Universities. In 1945 he became Director of the Institute of Civil Law at Padua, and he is also a member of many institutions devoted to the study of international law. The two members of this Chamber are Dr Walter Strauss (G, 68) and Pierre Pescatore (L, 49). Dr Strauss was retired in 1935 for political reasons and after the War held various provincial ministerial appointments in Germany and from 1949–1963, when he was appointed to the Court, he was Secretary of State in the Federal Ministry of Justice. Judge Pescatore was employed in the diplomatic service from 1946 until he became a lecturer in law at Liège University in 1951, where his chair was that of European Community Law.

The two Advocates-General are MM. Roemer and Gand, and the Clerk to the Court is M. van Houtte.

The Court sits at Luxembourg, where there are two Court Rooms, the Registry and various administrative offices.

THE EUROPEAN PARLIAMENT

The President is Alain Poher (F, 59). M. Poher is a civil engineer. After the War, in 1945, he became Chef de Cabinet to Robert Schuman, and, in 1953, President of the Senior Council of Trade. In 1957 he was made Secretary of State for the armed forces (marine). He is a Senator representing the Popular Republican Party, and on 28th April, 1969, became the temporary successor to General de Gaulle as President of France.

There are seven Vice-Presidents, Edoardo Battaglia and Enrico Carboni (I), Hans Furler and Ludwig Metzger (G), Cornelis Berkhouwer (NL), Joseph Wohlfart (L) and Fernand Dehousse (F).

The Secretary-General, whose office is at 19, rue Beaumont, Luxembourg, is H. R. Nord (NL).

Meticulous care has been taken to distribute executive positions fairly among the member-states. This system of fair allocation has been applied even to some of the less important functions. It is noteworthy that the Information and Spokesman groups are staffed in such a way as to preserve neutrality, and it is here that one occasionally meets nationals of non-member states, who incidentally, are frequently at least as 'European' in outlook as their 'Community' colleagues.

The need to ensure the fair apportionment of executive positions, the proper allocation between members of parties, the weighting of votes according to various considerations, including national affluence, size of population and power, and scrupulous observation of the quadrilingual rule (an expensive system) make for a complex and sophisticated organization. One cannot by consent eradicate the schisms of centuries by any easy method. It appeared to the writer that many of the new European 'Civil-Servants' are well on the road towards developing into 'European nationals'. Counting their families, some 60,000 people are now employed within the Communities. As time passes, these men and women will themselves become one of the human factors of the new Europe for which they are working.

No biographical survey of the Community, however brief,

would be complete without more detailed biographical details of at least four of the vital personalities concerned with the creation and the early life of the Community, namely MM. Schuman, Monnet, Spaak and Hallstein.

ROBERT SCHUMAN was born in Luxembourg in 1886 and became a lawyer. He was French Under-Secretary of State for Refugees in 1940 and in due course, after the war, became Foreign Minister as well as Prime Minister of France. It was his Declaration of 9th May 1950, while he was Foreign Minister, which gave the impetus to the eventual building of the European Community. He was Minister of Justice until 1956, and throughout a member of the M.R.P. in the French Chamber. He then became President of the European Parliament and held this position until March 1960. Robert Schuman died on 4th September 1963.

JEAN MONNET, the 'Father of Europe', was born in 1888 and after working in his family business (Finance) became Deputy Secretary-General of the League of Nations in 1919, at the age of 31. He later returned to the world of finance, but at the outbreak of the Second World War became Chairman of the Anglo-French Co-ordinating Committee. After the fall of France, Winston Churchill appointed Monnet as a member of the British Purchasing Mission in Washington. He then joined the Free French Forces in Algiers and in 1950 was the principal author of the Schuman Plan. In 1952 he was appointed President of E.C.S.C. but later resigned to head the Action Committee for the United States of Europe. He was awarded the Prix Charlemagne in 1953.

PAUL-HENRI SPAAK was born in 1899 and became a lawyer. In due course he held a great variety of Ministerial appointments, including the Ministry of Foreign Affairs in 1935–1938, when he became Prime Minister of Belgium for the first time. During the Second World War he was the Foreign Minister of the Belgian Government in exile, but became Prime Minister again in 1947. M. Spaak has presided over almost every important international association, e.g., the U.N. Assembly in 1946, O.E.E.C. 1948–1950, the Council of European Recovery, 1948, the Consultative Assembly of the Council of Europe, 1949–1951, and the International Council of the European

Movement, 1950–1955. He was Secretary-General of N.A.T.O. during 1957–1961, and in 1961 took office again as Deputy Prime Minister until his recent retirement. M. Spaak was accorded a very large number of honours and distinctions, including the award of the Prix Charlemagne in 1957.

WALTER HALLSTEIN was the first President of the E.E.C. Commission, from 1960–1967. He had held appointments as Professor of Law at various German Universities. In 1950 he headed the German Schuman Plan delegation and in the following year became Secretary of State in the Ministry of Foreign Affairs at Bonn. He was first elected as President of the E.E.C. Commission in 1960 and re-elected in 1962 and 1964 to this, the most senior of the Community's appointments. Dr Hallstein holds numerous honorary doctorates and other honorary degrees and distinctions from academic and other bodies all over the world, including the Prix Charlemagne (1961).

CHAPTER VIII

The Way Ahead

(1) A COSTLY ENTERPRISE

Today the European Community is without doubt the most influential and powerful supra-national organization in the World. Not since the formative years of the United States of America has there been a movement of such magnitude to combine the efforts and policies of independent national entities.

The costs are great. The Six have had to allocate very large sums to the European budgets. Each state makes a contribution in accordance with a fixed scale: the three major powers pay 28 per cent each, the two medium states 7.9 per cent each, and Luxembourg 0.2 per cent. Although the Commission may relieve a country of this liability under certain circumstances, such a contingency has not so far occurred. There have been threats of 'withholding' these financial allocations, but in fact the member-states have kept to their respective obligations. Every year the ever-increasing estimates are duly laid before the Councils and after due acceptance by these bodies, before the Parliament which has the right to make amendments. If there are none, the budget is taken as agreed. If amendments are made, the budget is referred back to the Council, who may wish to reconsider it together with the Commission, prior to the final decision by the former. All accounts are subject to an independent audit.

At present this costly organization is entirely funded by the member-states as a huge 'extra' in addition to their respective national budgets but this procedure is due for review, possibly in connexion and simultaneously with the drafting of a Consolidation Treaty. The receipts from the Common External Tariff charges, from the agricultural import levies and other 'Community' income may then be utilized, together with other common assets, to make the complex and costly European administrative system more or less self-supporting. The Commission has recommended that 'self-financing' should begin in 1974. The Community would then begin to become independent of the financial stranglehold of 6 – or in any event 3 – national Exchequers. This is an essential pre-requisite of political independence and unification.

Apart from these essential financial considerations, all the member-states have had to expose their respective exchequers to certain major economic risks ever since the Community began to function. Failure at an early stage might have been shrugged off, but after some years the interlinking of the national economies and financial systems had developed to such an extent that severe economic difficulties besetting one of the three major states were certain to affect most seriously all the other countries within the Community. Political instability in Italy, the excessive purchasing power of the D-Mark prior to up-valuation, and the recurring French monetary crises during the closing stages of the de Gaulle era were cases in point. Somehow, the Community survived all these turbulent periods.

As the Community is not yet really self-supporting, the edifice might yet collapse, with serious effects on the Six. Was it wise to invest so much in Europe, to expose the respective national economies to such serious risks in support of policies over which each member-state can only exercise partial control?

(2) WIDENING HORIZONS

One of the reasons usually advanced by those who speak with conviction in favour of the Common Market as it is today, is that there is much more to it than obtaining economic advantages and securing peace in Europe. One is referred to the manifold side-effects and incidental developments caused by the creation of the Communities. For instance, the new Community Law had definite incidental effects on the laws of every member-state, and there was a kind of chain-reaction which led to considerable assimilation of new commercial legislation in the Six. Moreover, there has been a certain amount of deliberate 'harmonization'. This process is specifically encouraged by the E.E.C. Treaty of Rome. Thus, to give an example, the legislators and the courts in the member-states have endeavoured to adjust their respective mercantile laws, to bring about a measure of conformity and to avoid inconvenient discrepancies wherever possible.

Beneficial effects were also due to the rising tide of increased trade within the Community, which in turn brought about increased contacts between the people of the Community member-states. Whether in connexion with commercial pursuits or through taking holidays 'abroad' but within the Community, the people in the six member-states have certainly got to know each other a lot better. The free movement of migrant workers has led to additional human contacts. (Which incidentally caused a certain amount of misunderstanding and trouble.) But beyond any doubt the mass movement of workers has enabled large numbers of men and women to earn their living in other parts of the Community, who would otherwise never have gone so far afield except in time of war as invaders, but not as welcome visitors and peaceful workmates.

General satisfaction with this increasing rate of social contact and the beneficial effects of the various legislative harmonization measures have helped to generate a wide demand for administrative and industrial standardization. This was very much in accordance with expectations. While the removal of tariff restrictions was agreed to be useful, not many people would derive direct benefit therefrom and more concrete proof of integration was required. In due course widespread demand arose for 'Euro'-projects of many kinds. There were many items clearly in need of harmonization, e.g., patents, trade marks, bills of lading and other commercial documents, safety requirements, minimum standards, consumer protection, and it was evident that there were hundreds of other matters where unification, harmonization or standardization, call it what you will, could make life easier and cheaper. During the past decade, on the occasion of many international conventions, these matters have been discussed at great length. As a result there has been some progress, although not very much. Change is costly, and it is often not easy to persuade an individual, let alone a state, to make a change in order to fall in with someone else's usage. It is possible that there may be early and important progress towards the mutual recognition of legal rulings by the courts of the member-states. The Commission has submitted a draft convention to this effect, which would supplant the cumbersome and incomplete system of bilateral arrangements now in existence.

Much more noticeable is the rapid rise in the volume of inter-Community cultural exchanges. This is a most congenial basis for international co-operation, but even so cultural and social relationships have improved a good deal faster than most people expected. Whether we scan the sports pages and observe the large number of teams and individuals travelling across the national borders, or the amusement guides, where there is ample evidence of cultural interplay at all levels, or glance into the bookshops to see the quantities of translated books and many volumes even in their original 'Community' languages – the impression is certainly one of a cosmopolitan approach to life far beyond what was customary before the Second World War.

In this connexion it is rewarding to take a brief look at the European Schools. They bear witness to a most successful albeit comparatively humble experiment. Years ago some officials of the Coal and Steel Community in Luxembourg felt that their children might benefit from being educated in a supra-national school, with special regard to the international origin and transient domicile of their parents. A small private school was set up, and so successful was it that (with the aid of six Ministers of Education, which must surely make this the most powerfully supported school in the world), this venture developed into a system of six European Schools with several thousand children. They are respectively located at the Community centres in Luxembourg, Brussels, Varese, Mol/Geel, Karlsruhe and Bergen. The director of each school may be of any one of five member-state nationalities, but not of that of the country where his school is located. One half of the pupils have to be children of Community officials, but the others may be the sons and daughters (the schools are co-educational) of any resident in the particular town. The spirit in one of these schools visited was most refreshing. It is obvious that the linguistic training will prove invaluable. The 'European Baccalauréat', which the pupils can obtain at the end of their course, is internationally recognized. In 1969, 178 were awarded. For 1970 it is planned to commence 6-year courses for an international baccalaureate, for students in non-member countries, including Britain. The Commission has recently recommended the establishment of a 'European University'.

There is a College of Europe, already, in Bruges. This is not a Community venture, but one of its principal supervising officials is a senior officer of the Commission. At this College postgraduate courses are held in European subjects, which may be of great assistance to aspirants for Community employment.

It is now an established fact that a wide economic union, like the European Community, is bound to produce results far beyond and perhaps rather outside the planned co-ordination and integration of selected national economic policies. Few people could have foreseen this with any degree of certainty 20 years ago, as no such attempt at supra-national integration had ever been made. Yet it is apparent from the speeches and writings of people like Monnet and Schuman that in their view a proliferation of the effects of economic union was not only regarded as probable but was regarded as one of the important advantages of the 'empirical method' employed in the reconstruction and co-ordination of Western Europe. The 'spin-offs' due to European integration may well prove at least as valuable as the results of planned unification.

(3) THE 'COMMUNITY-SPIRIT'

Twenty-five years after a war which involved almost all its peoples, the Continent of Europe is still split into two distinct sectors, East and West. There is as yet no reliable indication that any country to the East of the Iron Curtain will do much more than 'recognize' the Community and trade with it as a single entity. In March 1968, Yugoslavia formally recognized the Community and appointed a special Ambassador to Brussels. Poland, too, has recently shown increased interest in trade and cultural relations with the Community, with which it has held bilateral discussions for the past two years. Rumania and Czechoslovakia may yet seek closer contact with the Community before long. As for the European states to the West of the Curtain, they are themselves still divided into two groups according to their economic and political allegiances. Firstly, there are the countries of the Community, their European Associates and those members of E.F.T.A. which have made it clear that they would enter the Community as full members or join it as Associates if an appropriate arrangement could be made. The other group consists of those members of E.F.T.A. who may not at present be able or prepared to come to terms with the Community, and of Spain, which remained uncommitted until 1967. On 21st September 1967, negotiations began between the E.E.C. and the Spanish government, with a view to reaching a bi-partite Agreement, in two stages. Stage one is intended to last 6 years, and the second stage would follow if and when possible. The Community would lower its tariffs over 4 years by 60 per cent, while Spain would effect a 40 per cent reduction over 6 years. These talks were still continuing in 1970.

This division of Europe is not regarded as more than a temporary state of affairs by senior Common Market Executives. Many expect that before long practically the whole of Western Europe will be prepared and even eager to make some kind of arrangement with the Community, at any rate for trading purposes or even more intimately, while with the Eastern states it may be possible to agree on much closer commercial ties, possibly on a Community-Eastern Europe Trading Pact basis. The U.S.S.R. is believed to be no longer wholly averse to such a project.

At any rate, in spite of occasional tension, such as between Turkey and Greece over the Cyprus issues, there is today little danger of serious conflict between the nations of Western Europe. These countries were the customary battlegrounds of the past, and there is justification for the view that the virtual elimination of the risk of armed conflict in that area by itself constitutes a major step towards world peace. Western Europe now enjoys a reasonable prospect of stability and prosperity, it is argued, and instead of expelling millions of fugitives to foreign lands, the nations of Europe have themselves become a beckoning asylum for many.

Yet underneath the surface many old quarrels still persist. In Belgium, in the Tyrol and around the West German Republic's Eastern frontiers, the establishment of the Community has not wiped the old slates completely clean. However, the creation of a common commercial border following the completion of the C.E.T. wall in 1968, had a salutary 'shock' effect on many European countries. The prospect of having to trade 'over' this wall was by no means encouraging. As the Six and any other members which may join it in the future, become economically and politically more and more integrated, their own national cohesion and unity may begin to slacken. And when this happens, the 'genuine' national groups, such as for example, the Bretons, the Celts, the Walloons and the Flamands may come to the fore again, not so much as nations but as ethnic entities. The Belgian election results of April 1968 support this view: both Nationalist groups doubled their representation. Without incentives to serious rivalry, and powerless to conduct wars, these comparatively small 'natural' units may be able to live together more amicably. All Europe might gain from such a development. It is a fascinating prospect for peoples like the Scots and the Welsh if the United Kingdom were to enter the Community. The recent electoral successes by Scottish and Welsh Nationalists are in some quarters regarded as possible symptoms of such devolution in Great Britain.

At any rate, a measure of 'Community spirit' has already been engendered by the development of the Common Market. The loosening of the restrictions previously imposed on travel and trade between the nations, increased prosperity and a lessening of mutual suspicions have contributed to a feeling of interdependence, an incipient belief in Europe, among substantial numbers of people. National and religious prejudices die hard, but they are weakening. If they can be replaced by justifiable pride in the achievements of, say, the ethnic groups, this could be all to the good.

It is easy to exaggerate these tendencies. Harmonization and integration measures, even economic unification on all fronts, can achieve only limited objectives. Most people are not affected directly by trading arrangements and international administrative measures. The 'little' common markets, the Europeanization in sport, the arts and learning generally, wider travel, more liberal educational measures – all these things are likely to be effective in the long run only as long as there are no strong contrary developments. At the present time there exists in the Community countries a conciliatory spirit which might grow enormously as the years go by. The comparatively slow growth of a 'European' feeling, more or less unaided and without propaganda, may well in the end have more valuable and lasting effects than the deliberate creation of a Utopian superstate in too much haste.

(4) PLANS AND PROJECTS

Community officials are fond of saying that their organization cannot afford to rest on its laurels. Its objectives at present are the full implementation of the common Agricultural Policy, harmonization of fiscal provisions, progress in connexion with an effective common transport policy, an improved social policy, greater emphasis on regional development, the creation in the near future of a single European Community as an administrative entity, a Community Treaty of Consolidation and a radical change in the manner of financing the Community.

When in February 1967, the Finance Ministers of the Six at long last agreed on the introduction of a uniform 'value added' tax system in the Community (as from 1970) they were taking a vital step forwards as regards fiscal harmonization. The system to be adopted differs radically from the comparable British taxes – purchase tax and corporation tax. 'Value added' tax (T.V.A.), which is imposed every time goods change hands after something has been done to increase their value in respect of the value thus added (*i.e.*, on present value less previous value), allows for a simplified system of Government (or Community) rebates. It would also permit a variation of the existing 'turnover' tax now levied in the Community countries.

Superimposed upon these planned developments is the possibility of adding several new European Associates, and in due course, at least four additional full members including the United Kingdom. Beyond these plans there hovers the ultimate objective, the Grand Design, namely political unification. Here opinions differ greatly as to what may have to be done and what ought to be done. There are many human as well as administrative contingencies to be taken into account.

Another 'outline' Treaty setting up a European Political Community? Or the gradual proliferation, by design, of the political side-effects of E.E.C.? It might be possible, it is argued, to arrange for the presence of Commission representatives at national cabinet meetings and in national assemblies, in a consultative capacity. A Minister for European Affairs in each member-state might be appointed by the Commission, with national government and Council consent, to attend relevant meetings of the national government concerned.

The implementation of a common policy as regards the member-states' financial operations would help to further such plans. As the Economic Community grows so its demands on the member-states' monetary contributions will increase. Ever larger slices of the national budgets will have to be allocated to the Community funds. Not unnaturally many people have come to the conclusion that as soon as possible there should be a stabilization of the rates of exchange within the Community, together with the establishment of a considerable degree of central control over the national Banks of Issue, common planning of short-term loans and kindred arrangements by the member-states and eventually a common currency. Such propositions are being widely canvassed in financial circles in the Community. Developments along those lines would in turn facilitate the projects proposed in respect of greater harmonization of social policies. If there is common control over large proportions of the national funds of the Six, sooner or later it may be found easier to finance the European social schemes through a central authority rather than in accordance with provincial or national schemes ultimately financed, directly or indirectly, by means of funds borrowed on the international money markets.

The plans for the development of the European Parliament have already been mentioned. Direct elections and enhanced powers are considered to be likely items on the agenda before another decade has gone by.

There is a marked and widespread desire to enable the Community to speak with a single voice on every reasonably opportune occasion. Such a development would probably lead to other groups of nations making similar permanent or *ad hoc* supra-national arrangements – one such possibility has already been mentioned in connexion with the feasibility of an economic agreement between the Community and a number of Eastern European states acting in common. The Yaoundé Agreement is a useful example of how such pacts may be made. Successful arrangements of this kind are bound to trigger off sympathetic reactions elsewhere and the small flames of international co-operation which may thus be lit are not likely to be snuffed out very easily. In furtherance of these projects, the Commission in April, 1969, put forward a 3-year plan to remove all remaining trade barriers, enlarge the Community and strengthen its ties with other countries, and to make the 'merged' Community financially self-supporting, on the lines described earlier.

(5) DIFFICULTIES AND OBSTACLES

The traditional objections to supra-national agreements in Europe are political and emotive. They stem from the days when even simple customs agreements between two or more powers were regarded as threats to the existing balance between the nations. From the German Zollverein in 1834 to modern times there have been numerous plans and schemes to facilitate economic relations in Europe. Some of these were little more than cloaks for military alliances, but others were economically quite practicable. Europe, however, does not usually take kindly to proposals of customs unions and *prima facie* suspects the thoughts behind all schemes for voluntary integration between nations. Thus the only political amalgamations which were (temporarily) successful have invariably been those which were imposed by force upon a number of defeated states. It was the realization of the implications of this tendency, the consideration of what could (and did) happen if and when the prevalence of inter-European rivalries enabled a single state to subjugate most of the Continent, which led to the creation of E.C.S.C. after the Second World War.

Outspoken opposition to the new European Community has by no means been subdued by the comparatively successful operations of the Common Market. Apart from purely economic arguments as to detail, there are in Europe today at least three major factions of 'anti-marketeers'. In the first instance there are the Revanchists mainly (but not exclusively) in Germany and Italy, for whom the reversal of the outcome of World War II is the principal objective. The division of Germany and the loss of some previously Italian territories are opportune reminders of the recent past, and it is not difficult to fan the flames of irredentism, even in an era of comparative prosperity.

The second group are the Communist parties of Europe. Since the U.S.S.R. does not recognize the Community as a separate entity, the Communists in the Community area are formally opposed to the Common Market as a capitalist scheme to perpetuate the exploitation of the working classes and a potential threat to the Eastern European democracies. There are several large Communist parties in the Community, particularly in Italy and France. However, now that the growing controversy between the Soviet Union and China has reminded the Russian leaders of the fact that they are more closely bound to Europe than to Asia, it seems that opposition from this quarter may give way to a measure of co-operation. In March, 1969, seven Italian Communists took their seats in the Parliament as members of the Italian delegation, and their demands for 'real European policy' did nothing to unsettle the Parliament. In France a recent Opinion Poll indicated that a majority of Communists now favoured the existence of a European Community.

The third group is amorphous. It extends from the more out-spoken 'Gaullistes' to super-chauvinists in every country.

The reasons underlying such 'nationalist' hostility to the 'Market' are many and varied. Unhealthy internationalism, spineless commercialism, selling this or that country 'down the river', unnatural alliances – these are some of the anti-Market slogans at present in vogue. The influx of foreign workers, the undermining of the trade-unions' authority, the alleged undercutting of wages, the weakening of national unity through foreign interference and the undoubted erosion of sovereignty are among the results of European economic integration which are most severely criticized.

It was due to considerations of this nature that the Fouchet Plan had to be shelved. That plan had been the Community's first detailed attempt to set out a number of essential measures for European political integration. In its original form it is as good as dead.

It will take more than majorities in favour of the 'Market' expressed by public opinion polls and the spread of prosperity to silence opposition to the Community idea from these quarters. The national differences between the sovereign states of Europe are very deep. It is always dangerous to interfere with the real or illusory independence of a proud people, and sovereignty is inflammable stuff.

Even inside the Community the further integration of the Six meets with constant opposition on these grounds. The former President of France was determined to ensure the leadership of his own country within the Community; as far as political unification in Europe is concerned, some kind of superficial alliance of a traditional type between the Six represented his most progressive plan. There is all the difference in the world between a Pact and Integration, between an 'Europe des Patries' and de Gaulle's 'Patrie Europe'. It is not so very important how integration is achieved, whether by some form of federation, or confederation, or condominium. But if the states of Europe are unwilling or unable to proceed further on the road towards integration than the present stage of economic union, then (according to most of the leaders of the Community) the entire edifice may once again be in danger of utter collapse. But, reply the supporters of de Gaulle, do you really wish to have foreigners run your nation's affairs, depend on aliens for the security of your country and the well-being of your family, reduce your national parliament to the status of a County Council and be dependent on distant bankers for the viability of your country's economy? Put like that, the prospects sound alarming to many.

It is with this type of 'opposition by conviction' principally in mind, that some leading circles in the Community are content to go easy for a little while as far as the introduction of further 'common policies' is concerned. Not many like to see the Ministerial veto used for the purpose of calling a halt to progress, nor does anybody want to bring about another period of abstention by a member-state (like the refusal by the French delegation to attend any meetings of the Commission for six months to emphasize their attitude concerning the introduction of the majority vote envisaged by the E.E.C. Treaty). With so many smouldering fires still hot below the outwardly calm surface of Western Europe and with one of the principal member-states so recently under the complete influence and control of a patriotic leader clearly opposed to taking any steps towards political integration for many years, most people agree that it would be unwise to re-negotiate any existing agreements or to embark upon new ventures. 'What we have we must keep', will be the motto for some time to come. It was therefore with the utmost caution that first the Commission, and (at their suggestion) the six Prime Ministers met to re-open the gates of the Conference Chamber. 'Enlargement' of the Community may well mean re-negotiation of at least some parts of the Treaties.

CHAPTER IX

The European Free Trade Association (E.F.T.A.)

(1) THE REASONS WHY

From the very start the conception of the new European Community had been something much more far-reaching and permanent than the creation of just another Customs Union. After the limited pilot scheme, there followed the extension of the newly developed formula to the entire field of the national economy and of the peaceful uses of nuclear energy. We have seen in what general terms the Treaty directives and resolutions are set out. This very generality made it possible to go gently beyond the limited field of trade and economics, and to apply the processes of harmonization and integration to other spheres of human activity.

The ultimate objective had always been political unification. Clearly, the broader and deeper the basis of preliminary integration, the more solid the foundations on which it would be possible eventually to construct the edifice of a politically united Europe.

Every signatory to the Treaties of Paris and Rome bound his country 'for good' (with certain specified exceptions and exclusions) to abide by the provisions and stipulations of these three Pacts. The Treaties were concluded for an unlimited period. The admission of other states as full members is subject to the unanimous approval on the part of the Council, following the Commission's recommendation to that effect. It is an exclusive Club.

In 1957, when the Rome Treaties had been signed, the widening of the process of European integration became more apparent. The total population of Europe was nearly 450 million. Only about 40 per cent had been united for economic purposes under the new Community's aegis. About 120 million Europeans, in seven countries, were cut off from the rest by the Iron Curtain which divided the Continent into Western and Eastern sectors. Rather more than 175 (now 184) million lived in the six countries which made up the new Community. This left about 150 million people in uncommitted states. Of these, Britain was by far the most important trading nation, but several of the other economically neutral states also played major roles in world commerce.

The United Kingdom, alone among the major powers of Europe, had emerged uninvaded and undefeated from both World Wars. She had been the only bastion of Free Europe until with the massive help of the American Armies and the resurgence of the Soviet forces, the occupation of Europe was gradually brought to an end. In 1945, the world was prepared for the problems of Peace by the edicts of the Big Three – the U.S.A., the U.S.S.R., and the United Kingdom.

By Spring 1948, of the men who had three years earlier brought the War to a successful conclusion, only Stalin remained in power. Roosevelt had died and his former Vice-President, Truman, had succeeded him. Churchill had been ousted at the polls by the leader of the Labour Party, Clement Attlee. In May 1948, as President of the Congress of Europe convened at the Hague, Winston Churchill declared to the world at large that European economic and political union was essential and that some of the several nations' sovereign rights would have to be merged to that end. Churchill was at that time undoubtedly Europe's greatest living statesman, and even out of office his words were accepted as the considered expression of Europe's desires. Churchill was Europe's voice, by right and acclamation. The position which the United Kingdom might occupy in relation to this project of a Europe unified economically and politically was never specified. The fine phrases were greeted with enthusiasm and relief – details were neither asked for nor provided.

In Britain, the Labour Government was fully occupied with problems of social reform and industrial reorganization. The Hague Declaration, emanating from a Continent so recently liberated after a massive collapse, was not considered relevant to the United Kingdom's own specific and more pressing problems. In October 1951, Winston Churchill was returned to office. By then, Britain had already refused to join E.C.S.C. as a founder member, although she had consented to have observers present in Luxembourg to watch proceedings from a distance.

The extension of the Community system after 1957 provoked the European neutrals to a reconsideration of the position. The erection of a uniform customs wall around almost half the trading potential of the Continent measured by population – and even more by actual trade – could not be shrugged off lightly. Still, Britain felt no more inclined to sign the Rome Treaties than the Paris Treaty of 1951. The time was not considered opportune for such a step and suddenly it was too late to join as a founder member and too early to apply for admission as an additional candidate.

The British Government thereupon formulated a compromise proposal, a European Free Trade Area to embrace all the sixteen nations which during the immediate post-war period had been recipients of American 'Marshall Aid'. This Area would therefore have embraced the Six as well as most of the uncommitted nations of Western Europe. A special committee of the Organization for European Economic Co-operation (O.E.E.C.) was set up under the chairmanship of Britain's Paymaster-General, Reginald Maudling, and discussions ensued – ranging over many possible variants of association and (possibly somewhat prematurely) over many details concerning the reduction of tariffs by stages – which lasted for over a year without achieving any definite results. An essential difference soon became apparent, between the British approach to the problem in hand on the one side, and that of some of the new 'Europeans' on the other. The British delegation desired a wide but loosely defined system of customs and tariff relaxations by mutual agreement and consent. Most of the others in O.E.E.C. preferred a tight and rigid programme of scheduled tariff abolition, in accordance with a fixed time table. The British approval was purely economical and tentative, whereas of the majority of the negotiators most were in favour of permanent economical union with a view to ultimate political unification, while a few remained undecided between the two schemes.

The Maudling plan envisaged no integration for defence nor political unification of any kind. In November 1958, these preliminary discussions ended in deadlock, no common platform having been found. By then the Six had been busy with the implementation of the Rome Treaties for nearly a year and were about to make a start with lowering the customs barriers within the Community walls. At that stage Britain once more approached the nine nations which had been concerned together with her in the recent abortive talks with the Six. After prolonged discussions another conference, this time without the Community members, was convened at Stockholm, and on 20th November 1959, a Convention was signed by which the European Free Trade Association was established. It was in due course ratified by its seven signatories: Britain, Austria, Denmark, Norway, Portugal, Sweden and Switzerland. These countries, the Seven, were situated all round the Community and due to their peripheral positions in Europe had few common frontiers. Nevertheless, in spite of the disadvantage due to its members' geographical position, E.F.T.A. soon valiantly challenged the Community's system of co-ordinated reduction of tariffs and customs. E.E.C. put on the pressure: trade within the Community rose by 5 per cent in a single year. E.F.T.A. could not quite match that, but even so managed a respectable rise of trade volume between its member-states of $2\frac{1}{2}$ per cent over the same period.

The two groups have remained economic rivals ever since. The volume of trade between their respective member-states is increasing simultaneously. But there are no bridges. And it is really only in the fields of lowered tariffs, duties and customs that there is rivalry, because beyond that sphere E.F.T.A. does not compete. As we shall see, the two are not really comparable at all, except as regards that single aspect. It is a bit like comparing a motor car with a hoop – each has a wheel but the hoop has nothing else.

(2) WHAT E.F.T.A. IS AND DOES

The Stockholm Convention was ratified in May 1960. In one major aspect it resembles the Treaties of Rome: it is couched in general terms and consists largely of principles and objectives for the respective governments respectively to abide by and to achieve. And again rather like the E.E.C. Treaty of Rome, the initial tariff reductions and the quotas due for immediate abolition are spelled out in detail in the Convention itself.

The principal objectives of the Free Trade Association were specified as follows:

Economic expansion, full employment, increased productivity, financial stability and higher living standards, trade between the member-states under conditions of fair competition, avoidance of significant disparities between member-states as to conditions of supply of raw materials, harmonious growth of world trade, and progressive removal of trade barriers.

The list reads like an excerpt from a letter by any Minister of Trade or Commerce to Santa Claus; or like a catalogue of objectives which a prospective Minister of Economic Affairs promises to achieve at election time. Two essential differences are at once apparent which distinguish this 'programme' from that contained in the E.E.C. Treaty: there is no mention at all of any non-economic objective, nor of any proposition to achieve a common policy as between the member-states themselves even in the limited sphere of economic progress. No political or social integration, no common defence plan, no common policies, not even a Common External Tariff. There could be no doubt whatsoever: the E.F.T.A. signatories were content to aim at progressive elimination of tariffs and customs as between themselves, while maintaining their individual quota systems and duties *vis-à-vis* all third parties, including the Six. This arrangement was in many respects the same as the Maudling Plan which had been proposed as an alternative to the development of E.E.C. and which had at that time been rejected by the Six as too limited and too vague. The E.F.T.A. Convention, it was stressed, would not affect national independence nor the principles of sovereignty. The member-states would facilitate trade without sacrificing their rights to determine their own economic policies.

This was all very well for seven states as heterogeneous as the members of E.F.T.A. Separated geographically by the central core of the Community, economically even more incompatible than the Six, common policies would have been very difficult to implement, even if the respective governments had wished to go so far.

By 1961 many people had begun to wonder whether in the circumstances it had been worth while to set up E.F.T.A. at all, as it would hardly be useful as a foundation for a bridge to span the gulf between the Six and the Seven. The comment on behalf of E.F.T.A. was simply that it was not meant to be part of a bridge at all, but a multi-national economic arrangement to offset any adverse effects on the trading efforts by the Seven due to the policies pursued by the Community. In any event, the purely economic and somewhat temporary nature of the E.F.T.A. arrangement made the Association a creature utterly different from the Community.

Almost ten years have passed since the birth of E.F.T.A. in May 1960. What has the Association achieved during that time? By and large it has attained its limited primary objectives, namely the abolition of many tariffs between the member-states. The qualification is necessary because although the inter-Association tariffs on all listed goods have by now been eliminated, not all goods passing between the Seven are 'listed' for this purpose, as we shall see.

(3) THE ORGANIZATION OF E.F.T.A.

The administrative apparatus of the Association is far less sophisticated than that of the Community. It is, however, perfectly adequate for the limited sphere of trading operations between the Seven in accordance with the terms of the Convention and their well-established procedural system.

The principal organ of this international (not supra-national) organization is its Council, which has its headquarters at Geneva. In that city, at 32 Chemin des Colombettes, there is a Secretariat of moderate size, with four departments: Trade policy, General and Legal, Economic, and Press and Information. There are the usual administrative and finance services to assist the Secretariat in connexion with specialized work in those directions.

The Council itself operates as a double-tier organization, in this way: There are at Geneva seven permanent delegations, representing the member-states, whose respective leaders hold ambassadorial rank. They convene weekly to deal with routine matters arising out of the ordinary trading transactions between the Seven. The upper tier consists of those Ministers of the member-states' Governments who at any given time hold the relevant departmental appointment of 'Minister of Trade' or 'Commerce', and these seven Ministers meet from time to time either at Geneva or in one of the E.F.T.A. capitals to discuss and agree future policy and other matters of general importance.

A new Chairman of the Council is elected every six months, the appointment passing from state to state by rotation. There are six departmental Standing Committees which deal with the various aspects of the Association's work: Customs, Trade Experts (who are specifically charged to take care of the more complicated and detailed rules and regulations), Consultative, Economic Development, Agricultural Review and Budget. The Consultative Committee is rather similar to its sister organizations within the Community. It consists of small delegations of three to five members each from every member-state, representing the leading industrial, commercial and professional interests, including employers and trade unions.

On this Council every member-state has a single vote. The Council itself deals with all contentious matters, including alleged infringements of the E.F.T.A. rules and regulations, complaints and failures to co-operate. Decisions may be given by a simple majority vote, but formal 'Recommendations' in respect of important matters are normally required to be passed unanimously.

Territorially the E.F.T.A. Convention applies to all the European possessions of the member-states, with some minor exceptions, and also to Liechtenstein as the result of the Principality's customs union with Switzerland.

In 1961, Finland became an associate member of E.F.T.A. and is now represented on a special eight-nations Council. Iceland has recently been accepted as an additional associate member. Unlike the Community Treaties which are perpetual and contain no provisions for either the resignation nor the expulsion of a member-state, the E.F.T.A. Convention permits a member to withdraw after giving twelve month's notice. Altogether it constitutes a much more conventional type of international agreement.

(4) E.F.T.A. TODAY

The Association has managed to speed up its limited programme of tariff abolition, and the last 'internal' tariffs on listed goods were abolished at the end of 1966. There has been progressive elimination of the members' protective duties on industrial products 'eligible for area tariff agreement' – *i.e.*, goods of E.F.T.A. origin and consigned from one member-state to another. As a counter-measure to the Community's wide-ranging tariff reductions, the term 'industrial products' in the above context has been very generously interpreted to embrace almost every kind of article except certain listed agricultural and marine products.

Still, the E.F.T.A. list of commodities to which the recent total abolition of tariffs applies, is limited. This limitation arises by virtue of the term 'of E.F.T.A. origin'. In many instances the imported raw materials or the components of such listed goods will have had the benefit of 'drawback' or other duty relief. The delicate problem therefore arose as to the temporary treatment of such goods, from the point of view of imposing duties, until permanent measures could be introduced more or less painlessly. Accordingly, intermediate arrangements were made in respect of such goods. From 1970 onwards the duty-free importation of such articles can be refused if they are made of imported goods or components and can be classified as having benefited by 'drawback' or other financial privileges to the disadvantage of similar goods or articles made within the E.F.T.A. territories and without the benefit of such fiscal advantages.

Obviously the Community's recent harmonization and

integration efforts have aroused great interest in the commercial circles of the E.F.T.A. states. No comparable E.F.T.A. schemes are, however, under contemplation at the present time. The volume of trade between the Seven doubled from 1959 to 1964 and until the middle of 1965 this upward swing continued at a regular rate. It has now slowed down and shows signs of an opposite tendency.

With the completion of the external tariff wall around the entire European Community the seven E.F.T.A. members were driven to trade at an increasing rate with each other, whenever it was a reasonably economical proposition to do so.

Although the original terms of reference for the Trade Association were limited within rather narrow confines, it was interesting to read in one of the Organization's Annual Reports that schemes are to be introduced soon to facilitate the employment of E.F.T.A. nationals in member-states other than their own, to take more effective measures against restrictive practices and even to make provisional tariff arrangements as regards the export of agricultural products. It seemed as if the belief that E.F.T.A. was not quite at the end of the road, was causing its leaders to broaden its basis beyond the terms of the Stockholm Convention, at any rate for the benefit of those members which had not lodged an application in Brussels. But now, with three of its members on the verge of joining the E.E.C., with Austria and Sweden willing to make 'special arrangements' with the Community, it would seem that the Trading Area's usefulness is coming to an end.

Although E.F.T.A. has managed to operate successfully a system of tariff abolition which would help its member-states to take the great step across the gulf into the Community with less risk than might otherwise have been the case, the actual efficacy of these measures with regard to Community membership has yet to be tested. In this connexion the activities of the Association's Economic Development Committee which of late have increased considerably, are of interest. This body gives advice in respect of the development of 'backward' areas in the E.F.T.A. countries.

In 1967, when three member-states of E.F.T.A. applied for admission into the Community, the homogeneity of the applicant state's economy played a major part in the Commission's deliberations and subsequent 'Preliminary Opinion' concerning the anticipated results of such membership, *vis-à-vis* the Community as well as the applicant state, and in 1969, the Commission's 'Revised Opinion' again made reference to the 'E.F.T.A. effects'. It is evident that the free trade arrangements among the Seven did much to condition the present applicants for the stresses and strains of the Economic Community.

The E.F.T.A. leaders in their formal addresses sometimes use expressions such as 'if the Association still exists at that time'. Its temporary nature has never been denied but it is by no means clear how such an end will come about.

(5) E.F.T.A. AND THE COMMUNITY

The E.F.T.A. countries, together with their Finnish associate, have a total population of about 100 million, which compares with about 220 million in the Community with its two European associates. In spite of this 2:1 population ratio in favour of the Community, and notwithstanding the latter's geographical advantages, it is obvious that the absorption into the Community of some of the larger Association members would make a tremendous difference to the standing of the Community thus enlarged *vis-à-vis* the U.S.A. and any other rival. On the other hand, not every country may be suitable for membership of the Community. This view was emphatically repeated in 1969.

In 1967, the Commission stated formally, 'As regards Europe, the Community has always believed that membership was the solution most in conformity with the Treaties for those democratic countries which have attained a sufficient degree of economic development'. Insufficient national economic homogeneity might be considered a major obstacle.

The E.F.T.A. countries are capable of considerable economic expansion: the Association's total G.N.P. rose at about the same rate as that of E.E.C. during recent years, a faster rate of expansion that that of even the American economy during the same period. Of course, when it came to the actual G.N.P. figures (not merely the rates of expansion), that of the U.S.A. was still more than 40 per cent greater.

A merger or a bridge joining the two European groupings has been included on many international agendas in recent years. However, all the discussions and schemes achieved nothing at all. While there are tenuous 'links' through the common membership of such organizations as the Conference of Fishing Countries and the European Patent Convention, the Austrian government's application to become a kind of special associate of E.E.C. was for years the only tangible sign of a rapprochement. This particular move will most probably lead to nothing more than a special bilateral Community-Austria Agreement, as under the terms of the post-war Treaties with Austria, the latter country is prevented from concluding any kind of union with Germany. However, negotiations in this connexion are still proceeding, albeit at a leisurely pace.

In the words of Professor Hallstein, 'the success of the Common Market led to the foundation of E.F.T.A.'. The volume of trade between the two groupings has increased greatly. These commercial ties plus the respective geographical locations of the states concerned, gradually eroded the widespread aversion to genuine integration. In the autumn of 1967, apart from Austria, which was obliged to follow an individual line, Norway, Denmark and Ireland joined the United Kingdom as applicants for membership, and Sweden also made an approach. Portugal and Spain appeared to be desirous of attaining associate status. Switzerland alone did not take any positive steps.

The other alternative – a strengthening of the present E.F.T.A. arrangements – is probably not a practicable proposition in the long term. There have been signs of some 'institutionalization' in the E.F.T.A. system, as well as suggestions to harmonize some of the member-states' fiscal laws. But these indications of preparation for future development must not be overrated. The Association's span of life is likely to be lengthened or shortened in an inverse ratio to the success and prosperity of E.E.C. Already the four Scandinavian members have concluded a separate customs union, Nordek, the first stage of which is to be completed by the end of 1970, and the second two years later.

The organization of E.F.T.A. is very simple indeed. No

THE E.F.T.A.
COUNTRIES

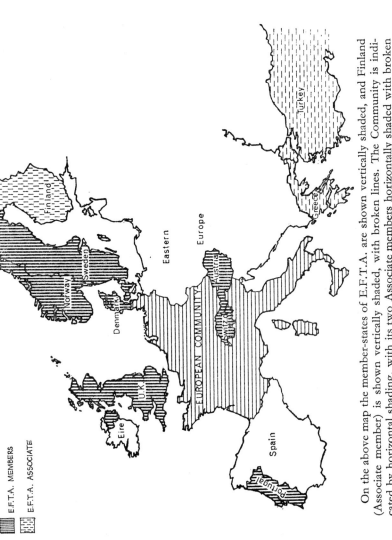

On the above map the member-states of E.F.T.A. are shown vertically shaded, and Finland (Associate member) is shown vertically shaded, with broken lines. The Community is indicated by horizontal shading, with its two Associate members horizontally shaded with broken lines. The peripheral situation of the E.F.T.A. countries locked round the Community and without many common frontiers, is clearly apparent.

attempt has been made to set up a supra-national system to rival that of the Communities. A decision made by the Council is binding upon the members. Policy matters require unanimity, but for routine work a simple majority (four votes or more) is sufficient. In the event of a dispute between members, the Council also acts (under Article 31 of the Convention) in an arbitral capacity to settle any matter referred to it by a member-state.

The Council presents an annnual Report of its activities to the Consultative Assembly of the Council of Europe.

E.F.T.A. ORGANIZATION (Geneva)

COUNCIL (two tiers): 7 Ministers (Occasional Conferences).
7 Permanent Representatives (Frequent Meetings).
(Finland, as an Associate member, is represented if necessary. Iceland has recently become an Associate member.)

FIVE ADMINISTRATIVE DEPARTMENTS: Trade Policy, General & Legal, Economic, Press & Information and Secretariat.

SIX STANDING COMMITTEES: Customs, Trade Experts, Consultative, Economic Development, Agricultural Review and Budget.

(The entire administrative staff numbers only about 100.)

CHAPTER X

Britain and the Community of Europe

(1) FROM PARIS TO STRASBOURG

In 1950 Britain had declined to join E.C.S.C. as a founder-member and in the following years she had stood aloof from the negotiations leading to the ill-starred E.D.C. Treaty as well as the later Treaties of Rome. In 1957 she had initiated the creation of E.F.T.A. and become its most powerful member. Then there was a change of mind. In October 1961, she opened negotiations with the Six with the intention of becoming a full member of the Community after all. Immediately most of the other E.F.T.A. countries followed suit: Denmark, Norway and Ireland applied for full membership, Austria, Sweden and Switzerland for association.

The talks between the Community representatives and Britain's delegation lasted throughout 1962. Edward Heath and his British team of experts, with nothing like a united country behind them as far as the desirability of Community member-ship was concerned, battled on and on. Matters of amazing detail were discussed, including such unusual commodities as kangaroo meat and dried seaweed. The British delegation was at pains to look after the interests not only of the United Kingdom, but also (in general terms) of their E.F.T.A. partners and of the Commonwealth. These interests not infrequently appeared to be somewhat divergent. In several instances the British government's concern later turned out to have been rather unwarranted, as alternative solutions were readily available. As regards E.F.T.A., it is now apparent that there was very little need to worry at all.

At any rate, towards the end of 1962 the interest of the British public which in the meantime had flagged very considerably, was gradually re-awakened by the appearance of 'anti-Market' candidates at by-elections (without any marked positive success), and by passionate speeches warning against the signing of the Treaty of Rome at the Labour Party's annual conference held at Brighton. In due course the Leader of the Opposition, Hugh Gaitskell, even flew over to France to put his party's negative attitude plainly to the French Foreign Minister. As an election was due to be fought in Britain in less than 2 years' time, when in all probability the Labour Party would have a good chance of winning and forming a government before Britain could possibly be firmly 'established' as a member-state, and while she could still opt out again without causing much hardship, the British domestic background was patently unstable.

The year 1962 closed with a resurgence of scepticism in Britain concerning the implications of her application for Community membership. It was widely feared that the Commonwealth might be placed in considerable danger of breaking up, the other E.F.T.A. countries were being let down, the 'special relationship' with the United States would have to be terminated, food prices would rise sky-high and armies of foreign workers would flood the labour market in the United Kingdom. In opposition to these rather alarming forecasts, a growing band of zealots now began to urge the British delegation to sign the Treaty of Rome and have done with the problem – it was simply another trade pact which would solve Britain's recurring economic problems once and for all.

Suddenly, in January 1963, General de Gaulle stated unequivocally that his representatives would not agree to Britain becoming a member at this stage. The British Prime Minister had just concluded an Agreement with the United States, at Nassau, arranging for the construction and supply of a number of 'Polaris' carrying submarines, an offer which had been tentatively extended to France, where it had been refused at once. Britain, said the General, was not part of the essential Europe, her ties were with the Commonwealth and the United

States. After some token resistance, the other five member-states acquiesced. France signed a special pact with her German partner in the Community. Britain's team returned home. The negotiations had been most ably conducted, perhaps too conscientiously and in too much detail. They had failed at a very late stage when – and possibly because – there was almost nothing left to argue about any more.

(2) ONWARD WITH E.F.T.A.

Very few people in Britain had troubled to inform themselves correctly about the 'Common Market' and what Edward Heath's negotiations had been about. They had confidently expected that Britain would eventually become a member, albeit to an accompanying chorus on the home front of grumbles and moans. Instead, General de Gaulle had slammed the door most unceremoniously. The popular reaction was simple: if this is the Continent's gratitude for Britain's stand during World War II, very well. We shall be able to get on fine with our partners in E.F.T.A., with the Commonwealth and with the United States. If you don't need us, we don't need you either. Many people lost interest in the Community altogether, and the percentage of 'Don't Know' replies to opinion poll queries as to what people thought of the Common Market showed a marked increase. For instance, in February 1963, the percentage ratio of pro-Market: anti-Market: 'Don't know' distribution, according to Gallup Poll Ltd., was 42: 37: 21. By March 1965 it was 65: 14: 21, and in March 1967, 57: 27: 16. But within one month the picture had changed again to 43: 30: 27! From 1963 to 1966, Britain's volume of trade with the developing Community rose very satisfactorily, in both directions, yet at two successive General Elections, in 1964 and 1966, the problem as to whether another attempt should be made by the United Kingdom to become a member, was not strongly canvassed and certainly had no material effect on how the votes were cast.

From 1964 onwards there were recurring financial crises which severely upset the British economy. The years of expansion were over, at any rate for the time being, borrowing was restricted, curbs were imposed on spending, and the entire economic machinery was slowed down most drastically. In view of the fact that the Community was regarded in Britain as little more than an organization to co-ordinate the economic policies of six countries, it is not surprising that among the cures prescribed for these sudden attacks of financial thrombosis, membership of E.E.C. was often mentioned. But would this really be an effective panacea? And was that really what it was all about? There are many indications to the effect that the British public in 1970 is almost as scantily informed about the new Europe as it was during the years of palaver from 1961 to 1963.

It is now useless to enquire as to who is to blame for this non- or misinformation. Certainly the politicians have not been helpful by dragging in many false and biased data to emphasize their respective arguments. The topic was altogether too complex for the daily newspapers to treat adequately. Talks, lectures and 'teach-ins' might have been useful, but not many people had either the time nor the patience nor the opportunity to attend. The years passed, until almost surreptitiously the 'Market' had once again become a high-priority topic, in buses and pubs, at work and at home. Britain's application, so ostentatiously left lying on the table in Brussels, will soon be listed on the Agenda once more. What would be the results of 'success at last', and what might follow if the talks fail again?

(3) SOME ECONOMIC FACTS OF LIFE

A situation has developed in which many of the industries which are of great importance to the British economy find that the home market is inadequate for their further development and, in some cases, even for their continued existence. In other words, their exports are not merely desirable for Exchequer purposes but essential for the very survival of the industry concerned. Outstanding examples of such industries are aircraft production, shipbuilding, construction of motor cars, computers and other machinery, and the manufacture of chemicals. In some instances even the Community cannot provide a sufficiently wide market. But in most cases, at any rate for a good many years to come, the substitution of a Greater Home

Market of about 350 million with a proportionately greater purchasing power, would enable these industries to plan more forcefully, expand more confidently and maintain a more even rate of production. In turn, this would permit the employment of a larger labour force, under steadier conditions, as well as additional capital expenditure on new plant and equipment.

Secondly, there is an increasing number of industries where it will soon be essential to resort to international co-operation either to reduce the number of models or types, or to enable production of particularly expensive items to go ahead at all. Only very large industrial units or consortia will be able to build the ships, the aircraft, the power stations, the factories and other sophisticated items which an industrially viable country must construct and export or erect abroad if it wants to stay in the front line of World Trade. The supertankers, the 'Concorde' aircraft, and many of the nuclear power stations of today are eloquent examples of these developments.

Thirdly, Britain's percentage share of World Trade has declined steadily for years. This has been happening notwithstanding almost full employment for many years, technological modernization and stimulation of exports by a variety of means. Over the same post-war period, ever since its inception in 1957, the percentage share in World Trade of E.E.C. has risen steadily. Supposing these trends were to continue – and the mere fact that there is at present some slowing down of the upward trend in trading conditions does not necessarily affect such a supposition – E.E.C. would soon, in a year or so, export twice as much as it did in 1958, whereas Britain would not achieve a similar result until the mid-seventies. In 1968, Britain was the Community's second-best customer (after the U.S. and just ahead of Switzerland), resulting in a trading loss of about £14 million.

Fourthly, Britain's exports to the Commonwealth are not increasing either by volume nor (if inflationary effects are discounted) by value. Her exports to the United States move rather erratically, as that market is fickle indeed due to its innate competitiveness and other specific factors. Britain's best export performances in recent years were achieved in dealings with E.E.C., and secondly, with E.F.T.A. As regards imports, the flow from the Commonwealth is gradually spreading elsewhere. The former dominions and colonies are trying to find new markets and they know that they must diversify their productive capacity. In 1968 Britain's imports from the Commonwealth fell gently to a new low of 30·1 per cent of her total imports, whereas her imports from the Community rose sharply by about one-third to 24·2 per cent of her total imports. In 1954, one half of Britain's exports were sold in the Commonwealth, but since 1962 her sales to the Community have been about three-quarters of those to the Commonwealth. In 1968, the United Kingdom's balance with the Community was negative: Exports, £1,196 m., and Imports, £1,567 m., a net loss of £371 m. With the Commonwealth, Britain had an even greater deficit: Exports, £1,404 m., Imports, £1,870 m., a net loss of £466 m.

Fifthly, the purchasing power of the Commonwealth and of the 'emergent' countries is still very limited – their principal needs are for basic machinery and 'simple' products and not for many of the sophisticated items of modern 'hardware'. Thus while Britain remains a vital market for Commonwealth goods, the Commonwealth is steadily and inexorably declining in value and capacity as a potential market for many of Britain's foremost exporting industries. Recent trade statistics tell this story in its stark reality: for a long time now Britain has incurred an annual loss of between £300 to £400 million as the result of adverse trading balances with the Commonwealth. Britain's trade balances with Canada, Nigeria, India, Ceylon, New Zealand, Ghana and Zambia were negative, the deficit with Canada in 1968 being nearly £214 million. There were positive balances with Australia, Malaysia, Pakistan and Kenya. Of course, the political and social features of Britain's very special relations and ties with some members of the Commonwealth transcend mere financial considerations and must be taken into consideration on a different basis. A considerable degree of stability exists as regards some of these markets. A safe supply line of cheap food stuffs has been created, in many cases as the result of the persistent and deliberate development of some former colonial possessions for that very purpose. There are lasting ties of kinship with the old Dominions, and a resultant feeling that Britain can depend on these countries in any emergency. There is a common language and in some cases, a shared history and common traditions. But there is also a recurring adverse trade balance of such magnitude that it cannot be corrected by normal commercial adjustments or by the gentle changes of the terms of trade. About one third of the entire National Health Service could be paid for out of the annual deficit arising out of Britain's trade with the Commonwealth. The ties of kinship and friendship must be kept alive but the financial burden on Britain may have to be lightened for the sake of all concerned. It is most improbable that membership of the Community will have any effect on the natural links of race, language and common heritage.

Finally, some important sectors of British industry seem to have made up their minds already as to where they must seek their principal markets in future. In spite of the frustrations of the past decade, an ever-increasing number of companies and firms proceeded to make trans-channel arrangements for themselves. As so many industrial ventures now require a complicated and elaborate organization and large viable combines or cartels to handle most of the crucially valuable industrial and commercial projects, there was a flood of mergers within the United Kingdom and many consortium agreements were made with congenial undertakings in the Community. Today nearly 400 major British companies are operating in the E.E.C. countries, through subsidiaries, holding companies, consortium contracts and by other means. Their experience seems to have been most encouraging, on the whole. The development of container transportation, the success of the 'drive-on, drive-off' system for lorries, and increased commercial carriage by air, together with a certain amount of Government support, have boosted British exports to the Community. They now amount to almost half as much again as the exports to her E.F.T.A. partners, in spite of the tariff advantages available within the Trade Association. Her exports to the Community (£1,105 million), are approaching in value her total sales to the entire Commonwealth (£1,404 million) and are more than 50 per cent in excess of her sales to the United States (£1,105 million and £2,055 million, respectively). This trend cannot be ignored.

What are the implications of these six economic facts of life? They may perhaps be summed up in this way:

(i) Most of Britain's earnings from 'visible' exports are derived from the sales of products which in all probability can soon only be manufactured or constructed economically and sold profitably by very large and extremely efficient organizations.

(ii) World trade is expanding but Britain's share is shrinking. Her trade with the Community is rising fast, in spite of increasingly adverse tariff restrictions.

(iii) The Commonwealth links must be maintained but the financial implications have become too difficult for the United Kingdom; many of the Commonwealth countries would in due course benefit from increased diversification of their industrial efforts which severance of some of their supply lines to the United Kingdom might make necessary.

(iv) The risk of loosening existing trade links must be assessed with due regard to the danger of growing commercial isolation of the United Kingdom from her Continental neighbours. Money is not everything, but a position entailing continuous loss cannot be maintained indefinitely.

(v) Membership of the Community is no temporary trading arrangement, and must not be contemplated primarily (if at all) as a cure for Britain's economic ills.

These are some of the principal considerations which must be borne in mind when the advantages and disadvantages of British membership are discussed.

In the Spring of 1967 the Labour Government of Britain engaged in a number of very brief exploratory talks with the governments of the six member-states. In spite of French reluctance to make any gesture in favour of British membership, the renewed application to join the Community was handed to the Brussels authorities on 2nd May, and Ireland, Denmark and Norway followed suit, while the Swedish Government stated its interest in the form of a governmental letter.

Further talks ensued at several levels, with the French authorities giving no sign of encouragement whatever. On the other hand, the British emissaries displayed greater enthusiasm than ever before, not only as far as economic integration was concerned, but even on the highly controversial issue of political unification. Of course, it had always been accepted that the true objective of the European Community is a political union of some kind, but it seemed odd that such fervent support for a Patrie Europe was now displayed by the same party in Britain which some 17 years earlier had refused to sign the comparatively 'harmless' E.C.S.C. Treaty because it appeared to be too 'supra-national'.

At any rate, the four essential conditions of British membership were seen to recede into the background as the talks progressed. The need for membership was clearly greater than the obligation of party-political undertakings given in the recent past. Britain's application failed again, and two more years passed. In early 1970 the parties agreed to try again. This time, at any rate, 'enlargement' as such will not be regarded as a deterrent factor.

Once more the problem of the implications of British membership is about to be paraded in front of the British public.

(4) 'WHAT HAPPENS IF WE JOIN?'

The winds of change have been blowing for a long time across the European Continent. The point of departure as far as the Community is concerned was the Schuman Declaration of 1950. Asia and Africa are persistently clamouring for increased shares of the world's riches, while the United States and Russia have taken over the political leadership among the nations. Europe is divided into two political sectors. The nations to the East of the Iron Curtain are only slowly finding their feet again after the agonies of the World War and its aftermath. The Western European nations are split into separate economical groups.

E.C.S.C. was a beginning, E.E.C. and Euratom have been established as a possible basis for a United Europe. What would happen if Britain joined this Community, taking with her several of her E.F.T.A. partners?

In 1950/1 Britain refused to join E.C.S.C. In 1961/2 Britain tried to join E.E.C. as a full member. In July 1961, the Prime Minister, Harold Macmillan, made it clear that 'no British government could join the E.E.C. without prior negotiations with a view to meeting the needs of the Commonwealth countries, of our E.F.T.A. partners, and of British agriculture'.

In October 1961, Edward Heath accepted 'without qualification the objectives laid down in Articles 2 and 3 of the Treaty of Rome'. Britain's special problems, he added, could be dealt with by means of protocols.

In October 1962, when the negotiations for British membership were entering their final stages, Hugh Gaitskell, the Leader of the British Labour Opposition, stated that 'if we could carry the Commonwealth with us, safeguarded, flourishing, prosperous; if we could safeguard our agriculture, and our E.F.T.A. friends were all in it, if we were secure in our employment policy, and if we were able to maintain our independent foreign policy, and yet have this wider, closer, association with Europe, it would indeed be a great ideal' (Brighton Speech). Gaitskell then flew to Paris and talked to Government officials. Then came the Nassau Agreement, and France's veto.

In 1970, on reflection, Gaitskell's conditions sound parochial, narrow, overcautious and not quite realistic. The Commonwealth required only minimal safeguards, with a few specific exceptions like New Zealand's exports of mutton and butter. Several of the E.F.T.A. countries were only too willing to join the enlarged Community. In 1962 the Mansholt Plan had not yet been consolidated to form the basis of the Common Agricultural Policy and if Britain had joined then she would have had a part to play in the implementation of that policy. There was no actual 'threat' to her agriculture at that time. Furthermore it was contrary to the fundamental objectives underlying the Treaties that the independence of foreign policies on the part of the member-states was to be preserved as a matter of principle and for ever. On the other hand nobody was desirous in 1962 to interfere deliberately with the member-states' foreign policies, but rather to harmonize them gradually and incidentally, as the Community developed.

Gaitskell had said in Brighton that 'we do not close the door'.

Yet his speech and the obviously widespread scepticism in Britain as to the desirability of joining had guided the hand which closed the door for him, and for the United Kingdom.

Four years later, the Labour Prime Minister Harold Wilson started new discussions 'with the clear intention and determination to enter E.E.C. if, as we hope, our essential British and Commonwealth interests can be safeguarded'. He stated that he meant business and would accept the Treaty of Rome 'provided we receive satisfaction on the points about which we see difficulty'. These points had been mentioned by General de Gaulle in the course of his 'veto' speech in January 1963: 'England is, in effect, insular, maritime, linked through its trade, markets and food supply to very diverse and often very distant countries . . .'. One day, he continued, it was possible that she would 'come round to transforming herself enough to belong to the European Community without restriction and without reservation and placing it ahead of anything else, and in that event the Six would open the door to her and France would place no obstacle in her path . . .'.

Edward Heath had gone to the limit of his mandate, and probably further than British public opinion would have wished in January 1963. Seven years have passed. Has Britain really 'transformed' herself, and do her people place the Community 'ahead of anything else'? To answer these questions, we must go beyond the economic issues. We must first of all establish with as much certainty as we can, what joining the Community in the early seventies would imply for Britain.

A. As regards the common tariff and customs policy, the common agricultural policy and all other policies and parts of policies which are operational at the time of joining, Britain will have to accept them as they are, in accordance with agreed plans and time-tables.

B. Britain will have to accept the Institutions, Committees and other bodies as they have been set up and established at the time of her accession to membership subject to the appropriate allocation of offices and votes to her represen tatives.

C. The Treaties, Rules, Regulations, Directives, etc. will have to remain as they are as regards everything except the allocation and weighting of votes and other administrative details (including financial contributions) depending on the number of member-states. The operative policies cannot be re-negotiated.

D. The position of the many countries and territories which have special relationships with Britain can and will have to be regularized by means of protocols to form part of the Treaty.

E. There are a number of British laws, measures, taxes etc., which have effects beyond her national borders and contravene Community Law in some respect. These will have to be amended, replaced, or allowed to lapse, as will also be the case as regards a number of Commonwealth trading agreements.

In the result, the Treaties and many measures passed in accordance with the provisions contained in them, are likely to be amended only as far as necessary to make allowance for the additional member-state or states and its or their voting rights, contributions, representation, etc. In this respect the advent of Britain, probably accompanied by at least three other countries, will upset the Community almost as much as membership will upset the British economy.

The Ottawa Agreement, some of Britain's G.A.T.T. obligations, the E.F.T.A. arrangements and certain bilateral involvements with the United States would require severe amendments. Fiscal arrangements such as S.E.T. and restrictions on the export of capital would have to be changed. Sterling as a world reserve currency might require extra protection from non-European convulsions and crises beyond the ability of the enlarged Community's financial strength. There would seem to be no general support for compliance with the erstwhile French demand that sterling must 'cease' to be a reserve currency. It may be that a further devaluation is considered necessary to achieve a situation where sterling would be sufficiently viable for Community purposes. The devaluation of 13th November 1967 (by $14\frac{1}{2}$ per cent) was possibly not sufficient to achieve the desired effect *vis-à-vis* the Six, particularly in view of the completion of the tariff removal inside the Community, in July 1968. The annual price review and the support given to British agriculture would have to be replaced by acceptance of the Community's common support system, and the prices of a number of food stuffs would rise in consequence. Britain's markets would have to be opened to the Community's exports without tariff protection; exports to the Community could no longer be subsidized. The British coal, steel and atomic energy industries (except for military installations) would have to be operated in accordance with the common policies in force in the Community. The British labour market would have to make vacancies available, without any reservations as to the availability of British applicants, to Community workers. Only for short periods of an 'employment emergency' could this 'Freedom of Establishment and the Free Movement of Workers' be impeded. There would have to be a good deal of 'harmonization' of laws, standardization and adjustment. Some £300 million will have to be paid annually into the 'Common Fund' of the Community, and another large contribution, possibly £200 to £250 million, will become due to the Agricultural Fund – the European Agricultural Guidance and Guarantee Fund (E.A.G.G.F.).

There would also be substantial savings, *e.g.*, smaller negative trade balances with the Commonwealth and a simplified system of administration. The national support given to agriculture – about £240 million – would cease in part. Balance of payment crises would probably be less severe and possibly less frequent. In due course the £ sterling might be fixed on a parity basis with the other Community currencies. Moreover, Britain could regard the entire Community as her new 'home market'. For every door she must open, some others would be opened for her across the channel. Yet she would never be the same again.

The City of London, the much underrated 'services' which for so long have accounted for the bridging of the trade gap by providing adequate 'invisible exports', the overseas interests of British commerce and industry – all these and many other vital institutions would have to fight harder for their lives in their wider arena of the Community. It is, however, an encouraging factor well worth mentioning that of late there has been very little apprehension in financial and industrial circles about the future. After all, it is said, we know that other people can build ships and aircraft, other insurers can underwrite policies, other banks are able to offer loans. But in all these circles, throughout the City of London and elsewhere in Britain, there is very considerable confidence in the ability of those concerned to face the future from within the Community.

Some policies would be decided in Brussels instead of in Whitehall. Parliament would lose control over the disposition of a considerable part of the national funds. Many planners would have to take into consideration measures under contemplation elsewhere.

There would undoubtedly be fatalities among the weaker units in British commerce. Exporters and importers would have to learn to muster greater resources and deploy their forces more advantageously. The British home market would become a happy selling ground for an eager army of Continental exporters. The casualty lists might be lengthy for a while.

Some social effects are probable in Britain if she joins. They need not happen, but they probably would. Changes would in most cases not occur as the result of the deliberate introduction of common policies, directly or indirectly, but by way of voluntary harmonization for the sake of convenience and general co-operation.

British wages would probably tend to rise over a wide range, but not excessively, to equal the Community average – a difference of no more than 1–3 per cent in most cases. The Community's Social Fund would extend its services to Britain where needed. The Community builds pro rata more houses than Britain, and this factor might provide a useful stimulus. The European social services are largely wage-related, as far as contributions and benefits are concerned, and the systems are not national but specific – dealing with specific sectors of employment and with other large groups within the Community. The comprehensive flat rate system introduced in Britain through the Beveridge Plan might well be gradually amended. But this, it must be stressed, would be largely a matter of controlled convenience rather than compliance with foreign law in accordance with a common policy. On the other hand, the

Community is likely to adopt to some extent such features as the British policy of funding most of the costs of the social services by general taxation, instead of by large-scale levies on individual employers and employees.

'Continentalization' would affect life in detail as well. In the wake of such adoptions of foreign creations as supermarkets, hamburgers and pop music, there might well rush in a flood of sausages, pasta, open air cafes, Sunday entertainments and the like. Of course, there might be a flow in the opposite direction as well, and the exportability of fish and chips, cricket and 'Speakers' Corner' might be put to the test.

On the whole, the Community and Britain have much more in common than General de Gaulle seems to have believed in 1963. There has been no noticeable 'transformation' in the British Isles since then, certainly no deliberate change of any kind. The average person's life, on both sides of the channel, is nowadays continually subjected to gradual changes. The tempo of these changes is quickening, and most changes now affect the whole of Western Europe, including Britain, more or less simultaneously.

Thus in the end this problem can be narrowed down to a single crucial question: what sort of transition periods would be granted to Britain if she joins? I believe that there would be several such periods, according to the severity and nature of the change involved. If preliminary negotiations can be concluded by the end of 1970, Britain might be able to join on either the 1st January or the 1st July 1972. The Common External Tariff and related measures could then be implemented in the United Kingdom within eighteen months. The Common Agricultural Policy can be fully enforced in two years. (Edward Heath, in 1961, suggested '12 to 15 years', but George Brown, when Foreign Secretary in 1967, stated that 'one year's standstill' would be adequate.) The newly agreed value-added tax could figure in the budget of 1972 shortly after Italy and Belgium. By 31st December 1973, Britain could be fully aligned with the other member-states, in all essential respects.

Spread over three or four years, it is doubtful whether these changes would be noticeable at all as far as anyone outside the Ministries and the statistical offices is concerned. The lives of people in the Six have changed since 1957, but whereas this transformation is discernible by a careful observer from the outside, it does not very noticeably affect the ordinary way of life. In the United Kingdom even the rise in the cost of meat, a popular issue in the course of discussions about the effect of joining the 'Market', is likely to be less drastic than, for instance, the constant effect of monetary erosion, effects of devaluation, or the after-effects of the major foot and mouth epidemic during the winter 1967/8. An increase of, say, 6/od. net per pound, over four years, amounts to a rise of 1/6d. per year. The normal seasonal price fluctuations and the gradual increase in cost due to the continuous erosion of the value of money, have caused greater changes in the past.

(5) IS IT THE RIGHT TIME?

Let us now make two assumptions: Firstly, that the British government and Parliament, on behalf of the people of the United Kingdom, are in principle prepared to accept the economic implications and also the political objectives of the three Treaties. Secondly, that it is accepted by the Government that Britain's accession to full membership would imply the acceptance of its Laws, Rules, Regulations, etc., as applicable at the time of accession and subject only to certain protocols, and, where agreed, to special arrangements in respect of a transition period or transition periods.

As far as the ordinary man or woman is concerned, it would seem that the overwhelming majority would accept a formal assurance by the government of the day to the effect that most economic changes as the result of accession to membership would be slight, gradual and hardly noticeable, if at all, and that in the event of specific hardship, special financial support would be given to alleviate damage and losses, or to bridge a difficult financial situation.

The British re-application for membership in 1967, left lying (dormant) 'on the table' in Brussels, and now about to be re-activated, prompts one to pose one or two questions.

Is the time right? The Community achieved a vital 'crystallization' stage on 1st July 1968, when the C.E.T. became fully operative. The common agricultural policy is in the course of implementation, in the matters of legal and fiscal harmonization definite progress is being made towards the achievement of certain targets in 1970. Two E.F.T.A. members have applied to join the Community together with Britain and Ireland as soon as possible. E.F.T.A. itself has achieved its principal objectives. The economic value to Britain of the fixed Commonwealth preferences is decreasing year by year. Many of the Commonwealth countries have realized the urgent need for economic diversification. Some of them have come to terms with the Community, others are considering such steps. The post-war economic boom has flattened out; there is every indication that severe tests lie ahead for all national economic systems.

On the political scene, the ideological estrangement between China and Russia is likely to cause a change in the alignment of the great powers. The voices of individual European nations may soon be heard no more due to the clamour of more powerful organs; such a situation would most probably underline the desirability of political integration in Europe. The settlement of the 'June War' between Israel and several Arab states, by the representatives of the U.S. and the U.S.S.R., to the exclusion of European negotiators, was a case in point. De Gaulle's concern as regards political unification is now merely of historical interest and more intimate connexions between the European nations on both sides of the Curtain may soon come within the realm of serious discussion.

On the British home front there have been curious changes since January 1963. The principal opposition at that time came from a very large section of the Labour Party, then in Opposition, and from the right wing of the Conservative Party. Such resistance as there was, consisted mostly of objections based on purely political/tactical reasons with an eye to the approaching General Election, mistrust of foreign liaisons on principle, and antagonism due to misinformation. The British application certainly did not fail because the negotiating team under Edward Heath were unwilling to accept the Treaties and the Community, but it was weakened because their attitude had clearly no nation-wide backing. There was then a distinct possibility that the governmental signature might either not be ratified by the House of Commons, or might even be dishonoured by a new Government in accordance with pledges to that effect given before the Election.

During the seven years which have passed into history since the termination of Britain's negotiations in Strasbourg, the Community has made progress in many ways. The Common Market of 1970 is a more integrated organization than it was in 1963, and it is more firmly established. Inside the United Kingdom, too, there have been many changes. The Labour Government of 1964 had been largely anti-Market and not only for reasons of political expediency. The majority of Harold Wilson's supporters in the Parliament elected in 1966 are pro-Market, albeit three of the old 'conditions' are still mentioned; safeguards for the Commonwealth, for E.F.T.A. and for British agriculture. The preservation of an 'independent' foreign policy, which had not been a realistic proposition even in 1964, has more or less gone by the board. All in all, the terms on which Edward Heath was negotiating at the end of 1962 have now been widely accepted as a practicable platform by most of the members of the House of Commons, by most organs of the national Press and by a certain sector of public opinion. Here there has been a curious swing. At the beginning of 1966 a British Gallup Poll showed that 60 per cent of those questioned were in favour of making another application to join, but by July this percentage had risen to no less than 71. The 'Don't Knows' had dropped from 25 to 17 per cent. Then, by May 1967, less than half of the replies remained favourable, with 34 per cent disapproving of membership. A number of factors may have contributed to this development: disappointment in 1966, concerning the failure of the Commonwealth to take any action to provide an alternative economic arrangement after Britain's failure to join the Community, the tendency of some E.F.T.A. countries to hanker after Community membership, desperation about the recurring balance of payment crises at home and the difficulties besetting manufacturers and other people concerned with exporting are a few outstanding examples. Then, in mid-1967, after the renewal of Britain's application, the public swayed in the reverse direction, possibly because of French hostility, the lukewarm support elsewhere, and out of a general dislike for foreign aid which suddenly seemed to be dictating all economic activities in Britain. Genuine enthusiasm is still rare; many people in Britain are merely 'pro-market' either because they can see no better alternative solution in the offing, or because their original misinformation has been replaced by other equally false data with a pro-European slant. The Opinion Polls continue to indicate that most people are against membership on the part of Britain. The United Kingdom is now the only anti-Market nation in Western Europe, according to the pollsters.

The economic ties between Britain and the Commonwealth are being loosened. The special relationship with the United States has weakened under strain.

Is the time right for New Zealand, and as far as the problem still affects her, for Australia? The Holyoake government has achieved a measure of success as regards diversification of industrial production at home. Given a reasonable transition period, the imperilled agricultural exports on which New Zealand's prosperity so largely depends, might be substantially diverted or replaced by the time zero hour approaches. Australia is finding it less difficult than anticipated to make alternative arrangements for the future. And on the other side of the Channel? President de Gaulle seemed at best non-committal and the German coalition government – fully conscious of the fact that if the French were to oppose Britain again they would not like to do so alone, and therefore might appreciate some German support – were intent on selling their backing of Britain's re-application dearly. The French President protested that the Market would never be the same again if Britain joined. There is a good deal of truth in this, and all the member-states are averse to amending the Treaties, re-negotiating any substantial part of the agreed common policies or changing any of the major Rules and Regulations. Now, with M. Pompidou at the helm, France is a good deal more conciliatory – at a price. In Germany the change of Government has served to emphasize support for Britain's early entry.

Britain is still in a position which differs greatly in many respects from that occupied by any of the Six. The remaining Commonwealth ties, her nuclear weapons, even her 'old-fashioned' Labour Party with nationalization, closed shops and the aims of the Socialist International still on display, all these things cumulatively tend to preserve the 'island' picture painted by General de Gaulle in 1963.

It is difficult to form a definite judgment. It is possible that it is still too early for the British people to join the Community for the real reasons, for ultimate political integration. Unlike Professor Hallstein, most people in Britain still regard membership of the Community as a business proposition, not as a stepping stone to political unification. It is the duty of the Government to lead – they must not shelve their responsibilities by passing them on to an inadequately informed electorate.

It is far too late for Britain to hold that kind of position in the Community for which her record in World War II had fitted her, and to which she would then have been entitled. For these reasons it could be that any further delay might well lead to Britain having to join one day a more or less fully fledged economic entity, with all its common policies in operation. Transition periods do not last for ever, and the more the Community organization becomes 'run in', the harder it will be for the economy of any new member-state to adjust itself appropriately within an acceptable and reasonable period.

It is a straightforward case of 'better late than never'. Britain's real problem concerning the Community remains political – all the other 'obstacles' arise out of 'non-problems' when the position is examined closely and without bias.

(6) THE SECOND APPLICATION, 1967

At any rate, on 16th May 1967, General de Gaulle in a lengthy statement, made it clear that although he would not prejudge 'what the negotiations, if they take place – I repeat if they take place – would be about', he was prepared to enunciate his general views on the subject. He felt that Britain's accession would destroy the equilibrium of the Community, that her ties to the Commonwealth were irreconcilable with membership, that the role of sterling as a reserve currency impeded her desire for integration, and that this was not the time for Britain to join.

'If Britain one day reached [the correct] stage, with what joy would France then greet this transformation'.

One would have thought that this was once again the signal for a cessation of the approach to the Six, but the then British Foreign Secretary, George Brown, on 4th July 1967 declared that this was a 'decisive moment in our history. The issue [membership of E.E.C.] will shape our future for generations to come'. There were few questions which remained to be settled. There should be a transitional period of one year's standstill, following upon formal accession. Thereafter Britain can prepare to join Euratom at once, unconditionally and as regards E.C.S.C. 'we seek only a limited period of transition'. Brown had come a long way since Clement Attlee's refusal to sign the E.C.S.C. Treaty. Could it be that under nationalization British coal and steel had been 'conditioned' for supra-nationalization? Or were their relative values to the British economy now so low as to warrant no further insistence on 'conditions'?

The agricultural review was to be modified, but special 'financial arrangements' will now be necessary. The Yaoundé Agreement might be made applicable to certain Commonwealth countries, freedom of capital movement would be introduced by stages', the C.E.T. would be accepted as fixed. 'In all other fields we accept the obligations of the treaty establishing the E.E.C. and the regulations, directives and other decisions taken under it, subject only to a transitional period . . .' He hoped that as soon as the Commission's opinion had been given, negotiations would be started.

Soon M. Couve de Murville, Brown's French counterpart, was heard to say that until Britain had solved her economic problems and the pound had been made 'a national and not an international currency', France would not agree even to start negotiations.

On 29th September 1967 the Commission published a lengthy preliminary Opinion. In 194 paragraphs, spread over 104 pages, it dealt with the various problems likely to arise as the result of membership on the part of the United Kingdom, Ireland, Denmark and Norway.

The Summary of its conclusion was as follows:

190. Analysis of the chief problems involved in the extension of the Community reveals that the accession of new members such as Great Britain, Ireland, Denmark and Norway, whose political and economic structures and level of development are very close to those of the present Member States, could both strengthen the Community and afford it an opportunity for further progress, provided the new members accept the provisions of the Treaties and the decisions taken subsequently – and this they have said they are disposed to do. Their accession, although it would bring great changes with it, would not then be likely to modify the fundamental objectives and individual features of the European Communities or the methods they use.

191. The Commission wishes to restate the conditions which would have to be fulfilled if extension is to take place in a satisfactory manner.

First, the new members would, as a general rule have to accept the arrangements adopted by the founder members before extension, subject to any exceptional adjustments that may be made. In particular, they would have to accept:

(i) The Community customs tariffs as they emerge from the recent multilateral negotiations in GATT, and their gradual application to all non-member countries, along with all the rules necessary for the proper functioning of the customs union.

(ii) The basic principles of the common policies with the provisions for their implementation, particularly in the economic, financial, social and agricultural fields, and their gradual application.

(iii) The contractual obligations of the Communities towards non-member countries (association agreements, trade agreements, etc.).

(iv) The institutional machinery of the Communities as established by the Treaties and the decisions taken in application of the Treaties, subject only to those adjustments rendered necessary by the accession of new States;

these adjustments will have to be designed so that the institutions shall continue to be sufficiently effective and that a suitable balance is maintained in the representation of the various Member States.

192. In addition, the new members, especially the main one, the United Kingdom, would have to agree with the founder members on the solution of a number of problems which would be of vital importance for the harmonious development of an enlarged Community:

(i) Restoration of lasting equilibrium in the British economy and its balance of payments, entailing concerted action between Great Britain and the member countries of the Community, and examination of ways and means of adjusting the present international role of sterling so that the pound could be fitted, together with the currencies of the other member countries, into a Community monetary system.

(ii) The principle of a common policy in the field of research and technology, including atomic energy, and the general lines such a policy should follow;

(iii) Financing of the Community's overall activities, including the agricultural policy.

(iv) The relations to be established with those European countries – notably any E.F.T.A. countries which do not join the Community – and with the less developed countries, particularly the Commonwealth countries (these are urgent problems which would assume new forms through the very fact of extension of the Community).

193. To sum up, the new membership applications are impelling the Community to tackle at one and the same time the problems involved in its development and those involved in its extension. Opinions differ as to the priority to be given to the one or the other of these objectives. The best way of overcoming the difficulty would be to try to attain them both simultaneously. But, if this difficult operation is to be successfully concluded, it is essential that extension should not

hamper the pursuit of the normal activities of the Communities and should not subsequently entail weakening of their cohesion or their dynamism, especially where the establishment of economic union, the requisite measures of harmonization and the functioning of the institutional machinery are concerned.

The Commission is well aware that the cohesion and dynamism of the Communities depend to a great extent on the convergence of national policies in the essential fields. If full advantage is to be taken of the opportunities which extension opens up for the Community, it is apparent that Member-States should within a reasonable period be in a position to make progress along the road to political union.

194. It follows from all the considerations set forth in this document that the Commission is not at present in possession of all the information needed to give in final form the Opinion requested by the Council under Article 98 of the Treaty of Paris and under Articles 237 and 205 of the Treaties of Rome. Choices of considerable importance for any appraisal of the impact which the new members would have on the Community are still to be made. The general conclusions which would enable the Commission to give a final Opinion cannot be drawn until it knows the position of the candidate States on a number of essential problems, the attitudes which will in consequence be adopted by the present Member States, and the solutions which may be adopted to the main problems discussed in this document.

It is the Commission's Opinion that, in order to dispel the uncertainty which still attaches in particular to certain fundamental points, negotiations should be opened in the most appropriate forms with the States which have applied for membership, in order to examine in more detail, as is indeed necessary, the problems brought out in this document and to see whether arrangements can be made under which the indispensable cohesion and dynamism will be maintained in an enlarged Community.

Within two months, the British government found itself in yet another economic crisis. The pound was devalued by about fourteen per cent, a huge stand-by loan was secured, and stringent cuts were promised to be applied to the various parts of the public and private sectors of the country's economy. France welcomed the devaluation and hoped that the cuts would materialize. There was a general feeling that this time Britain meant business – for a few days. Then the pound began to slide from its new level, a 'gold rush' was let loose upon the Western world, and it became apparent that once again either the medicine might have been too weak, or the diagnosis wrong, or both.

On 18th December, after a discussion lasting two days, the Ministerial Council in Brussels was unable to recommend the commencement of negotiations as suggested by the Commission. That Opinion (albeit preliminary) had been submitted to the Council under Article 237 of the E.E.C. Treaty, Article 205 of the Euratom Treaty and Article 98 of the E.C.S.C. Treaty.

It is the duty of the Council, upon receipt of such an Opinion, to 'act by means of unanimous vote'. It was agreed that in view of France's earlier reservation on the issue of unanimity, a majority decision to allow negotiations to commence was not possible. The French veto was ready to be administered when the other five members of the Council decided to resolve the embarrassing impasse by adjourning their meeting without a final decision. *Sine die?* Or until the removal of the single obstacle? In October, 1968, M. Pierre Harmel, the Belgian Foreign Minister, announced a programme for co-operation with Britain in matters of defence, technology, and monetary and foreign affairs, the 'Harmel Plan'.

In 1969, the Commission re-stated its views with much greater emphasis. The leaders of the Six agreed that after settling the financial aspects of the agricultural policy, they would be prepared to discuss 'enlargement'.

(7) ALTERNATIVES FOR BRITAIN, 1970

What viable alternatives are there in the Spring of 1970, in lieu of full membership?

In the first instance, there is the possibility of Associate Membership of E.E.C. This would amount to an economic arrangement without any controlling power or responsibility. The system of associate membership was never intended for a country like Great Britain, still one of the leading industrial and commercial countries in the world of today. Article 238 of the Treaty of Rome envisages nothing more than convenient economic arrangements with other countries or groups of countries or international organizations, for mutual benefit but wholly outside the sphere of action and the real life of the Community. Such arrangements are designed to assist countries with weak economies to 'catch up' in a decade or two; they are likely to further the development of newly independent ex-colonies, but as an alternative for the United Kingdom such an arrangement would be worse than useless. It would perpetuate Britain's economic and political isolation, impede the development of her established overseas ties and offer no more than purely economic advantages in return. There are few advantages to be found in such proposals for co-operation in specific fields (such as the Harmel Plan) or 'new Communities', e.g. a Technological Community. The consensus of opinion in Brussels clearly favours persistence by the applicants for membership on the basis of the existing Community.

Closer ties between Britain and her E.F.T.A. partners with the Commonwealth? This is hardly a realistic alternative. Several of the E.F.T.A. countries do not wish to perpetuate their precarious positions around the periphery of the Community with its compact tariff wall. The Commonwealth itself is far from unanimous as regards future economic planning. Some members, like Nigeria, have concluded, or are concluding special pacts of association with the Community. Others, like Australia or Canada, are well able to stand on their own feet within geographically rather more congenial Free Trade Areas –such as an Asian trading arrangement or agreements in respect of the American continent.

There is no real basis for any apprehension that the existing close human bonds with some parts of the Commonwealth would be cut. The 'old' Dominions would not sever their real ties with the mother country simply because the needs of their growing populations demand economic re-arrangements more suited to 20th century conditions. Even India, Pakistan and

Ceylon would most probably maintain their special relationships with Britain whether the latter is within the Community or not. Indeed, in this respect a stronger British economy might be to the advantage of several Commonwealth countries.

We have previously discussed the essential instability of E.F.T.A. as an international organization. This factor, together with the member-states' comparatively small volume of trade with the Commonwealth would not in all probability make an E.F.T.A.-C.W. link a happy alternative for Britain. The fixed terms of the Ottawa agreement and the abolition of tariffs within a geographically disconnected group of European nations could not by themselves form the basis of a lasting union.

A merger – or something like it – with the United States, *i.e.* a North Atlantic Free Trade Association (N.A.F.T.A.)? This proposition has been canvassed by some and cannot be dismissed out of hand. It might be accomplished by transforming the British Isles into, say, 15 to 17 additional 'States' with their own federal sub-government. It would not be impossible. The fundamental links between the old mother country and the vigorous United States are real and strong. American investments in British industry are formidable and exceed the percentage of that country's holdings in any other major country in the world. But even this aspect might be a good deal less terrifying and dramatic than many people think. Europe is subject to a certain amount of Americanization in any event. Much of it is harmless, and there is some compensatory flow in the reverse direction.

A serious flaw, however, may be this: a union with the United States would have few useful political effects and its economic objectives could be attained by a bilateral agreement. Such an agreement could be negotiated only at Britain's peril as long as she is not a member of the Community. Any feelers in this direction extended at the present time would rebuff the Six much more thoroughly than the Nassau Pact. On the other hand, a trading agreement between the Community and the United States is likely to be concluded sooner or later, and if Britain were a member-state at that time she would be able to achieve all the economic advantages which such a Treaty could produce without having to take the risk of the political and social consequences of a bilateral union or of a merger with her powerful transatlantic ally.

On the whole any sort of union with the United States should be considered as a feasible alternative to Community membership only if and when any possibility of achieving the latter in the foreseeable future is to be discarded entirely. Opponents of Britain's membership of the European Community also maintain that an Anglo-Saxon Free Trade Association might be conceivable, on a loose and largely economic basis. This, they say, should be open to all subscribers to the rules, including the European Community itself. This plan, the 'political idea of the century', according to the Canadian Professor Beaton, has not met with much acclaim so far.

Finally, what about 'going it alone'? The protagonists of such economic isolationism usually point to Japan, another island economy prospering without specific economic arrangements or ties. The comparison is probably fallacious. Britain's proximity to the Community and to the Eastern European states, her social and cultural links across the Channel and her quite exceptional need for stable trade relations with the rest of Europe place her in a different position from that of the Japanese islands. Moreover Japan herself will probably become part of a Far Eastern trading area before long.

The only indigenous raw materials which are available in Britain in large quantities are coal, and, apparently, natural gas. Most other raw materials, a large proportion of her food and many other essentials must be imported. Britain relies for her very existence on the profits derived from selling her manufactured goods abroad and from providing financial, transport and ancillary services all over the world. Membership of a single regional community is bound to have some adverse effects on these arrangements. It may be that the role of international shopkeeper and agent is best suited to a lone individual nation without firm ties. But this is not the case as far as essential exports are concerned; if a country can only live by making regular and increasing profits year by year, through her exports, very largely of manufactured goods, a large home market is vital as a basis and such a market cannot be procured by a comparatively small wholly independent nation except by joining a larger economic system. The obvious 'home market' for Britain is that provided by the Community.

In conclusion of this survey of alternative possibilities let us remind ourselves once again that membership of the European Community would not by any means be a panacea for all the causes of Britain's economic instability, although it would probably cure or alleviate some of the more alarming symptoms. When all the feasible alternatives to Community membership are compared, an Atlantic Partnership with the United States would appear to be the only economically defensible suggestion. One of the consequences of such a union would be a deliberate and final derogation from sovereignty and independence, as opposed to the process of incidental erosion likely to be brought about by membership of the European Community. Would Parliament and the British public stand for this? To find an answer to this question we must now investigate what is regarded by most people in Britain as the most important problem to be faced by the Government as well as by the ordinary people, now that the issue is once again under active discussion: the question of Sovereignty.

CHAPTER XI

"We can't go in, because . . ."

(1) THE FOUCHET PLAN

The development of the Schuman Plan in actual practice posed new problems. The original scheme had been to integrate Europe politically through economic and military unification. The way in which matters developed in reality was not so straightforward. After the successful integration of the coal and steel industries there followed the failure of the parallel plan for an integrated defence policy. After this setback, progress was resumed slowly towards carefully phased economic unification by stages, with financial, social and cultural harmonization being encouraged simultaneously, and in a way incidentally, not in accordance with any precise and detailed plan.

The alteration of the original scheme caused by the temporary abandonment of the idea of a common defence policy (involving a unified High Command and integration of the armed forces down to quite small units), did not at any stage cause the statesmen and planners behind the new Europe to abandon their ultimate objectives: the prevention of another 'European Civil War' and the creation of some sort of European Union in the political sense.

An energetic attempt to go ahead with a measure of political integration was made on 18th July 1961, when the Prime Ministers of the Six met at Bad Godesberg, a German spa which had attained some notoriety in 1938. They decided to set up a Committee to submit proposals 'on ways and means which would make it possible to give a statutory character within the shortest time to the unification of their peoples'. The European Parliament was to be requested to widen the scope of its work and to include debates of these projects on its agenda.

The Plan which eventually emerged from the work of this Committee has never been officially published. It was called the Fouchet Plan after Christian Fouchet, who some time later became Minister of Education in the French Government. Although its text was not formally given to the Press, the Fouchet Plan has been publicly discussed in Strasbourg by the Council of Europe and by the European Parliament.

Its principal recommendations were:

(i) A common foreign policy on all matters of common interest, a common defence policy (E.D.C. resuscitated!), co-operation on problems concerning human rights, as well as in respect of cultural and scientific matters, and the eventual creation of a 'Union of European States'. (This phrase was to give rise to much heated argument in due course.)

(ii) A Council of heads of state or prime ministers, with occasional meetings of foreign ministers. It was proposed that this Council should meet about three times a year, but it was not intended to develop into a supra-national government. Its decisions would have had to be unanimous to be effective (a return to the original E.E.C. rule). A member-state would, however, have been able to avoid compliance with any decision by abstaining. In other words, unanimity was required to make any Council decision binding, but it would not bind an abstaining member-state.

Then there was a scheme for a European Political Commission, in some ways similar to the E.E.C. Commission but apparently intended in the first instance to perform the functions of a Secretariat-General for the new Community. The Commission was to have been staffed by senior Civil Servants from all the member-states. It would have been located in Paris, and one of its important tasks would have been the preparation of decisions for promulgation by the Council and the supervision of the implementation of these decisions. The Parliament would have been included in the proposed system of political integration, but initially restricted as at present to debates and recommendations.

(iii) The E.P.C. Treaty was to have been revised after three years, so that amendments could have been made on the strength of past experience. Membership of the Community would have been available not only to the Six, but to all members of the Council of Europe (*i.e.*, including Britain), although only with the unanimous approval of the Council.

The European Parliament debated the Plan in December 1961, and criticized it as a retrograde step. In the meantime Federal Germany had made its own proposals – to set up a Union of Peoples, not of States. Other members objected to the adoption of the 'Commission' principle, which in their view, would unduly subject the Community to the control of the respective national Civil Services. An independent Secretary-General with powers to choose his own staff and to initiate measures himself was in some circles considered a preferable alternative.

In due course it was suggested in the Parliament that the 'unanimity' rule, to which many Europeans objected in principle, might to advantage be toned down by arranging for matters to be referred back to the Parliament if the Council were not unanimous. This, it was felt, might possibly resolve a good many difficulties amicably. Parliament used the opportunity to ask again for early implementation of the plans to institute direct elections and to merge the Executives.

In 1962 the French delegation presented an amended version of the original plan, which was, however, rejected by the Belgian and Dutch governments. As Edward Heath was at that time suggesting that Britain should participate in the proposed political discussions if her economic talks succeeded, several delegations decided to hold up the talks on the Fouchet Plan until after a decision had been reached on Britain's application. France's submission was in any event contrary to any supranational conception of political unification: the French proposal suggested that the Council of Ministers of the Political Union should gain control over economic matters also, with the result that the unanimity rule would be reintroduced even in respect of decisions concerning the common economic policy.

On 15th May 1962, Paul-Henri Spaak made it clear that he for one considered such a plan for a Political Union of States quite unacceptable, and he advised to wait until Britain had joined the Six. A counterblast came from Charles de Gaulle: supra-nationalism, said the General was 'a myth and a fiction' – a declaration which caused the immediate resignation of five of his ministers but no change of heart.

On 22nd January 1963, the French President and Konrad Adenauer signed a Treaty of Co-operation on behalf of their two countries, and in April of the following year the Assembly of the Council of Europe noted with regret 'that there is a lack of unity in the foreign policy of the European states'. The governments of several countries, including Britain, still expressed themselves in favour of political union as the ultimate objective, in accordance with the original Fouchet Plan.

In September 1964, Paul-Henri Spaak put forward an addendum to the Plan: there should be 'three wise men' in charge of the Political Organization, instead of a Commission, they should be politically independent leaders, and set themselves up as a true Community organ or institution. Further proposals issued from the German and Italian governments, and the latter in due course sent out invitations for a conference to be held at Venice in May 1965. The French authorities, however, refused to attend any conference until the talks on the agricultural policy had been concluded.

The debate on the subject of political unification was not resumed. Even within the Economic Community it was quite impossible to convince General de Gaulle of the virtue of relying on majority decisions, although a compromise *modus operandi* was ultimately agreed upon. Concerning political co-operation the General repeatedly indicated that he would not agree to any system which would permit the making of decisions to bind a sovereign member-state, unless such decisions were reached by the unanimous vote of all the members.

In the event the Fouchet Plan proved to have been prematurely launched. Like the project for direct elections to the

European Parliament it lies in the filing cabinets of the Brussels headquarters of E.E.C. The good intentions, however, remain. At Bonn, in May 1967, the six Heads of Government agreed 'to consider some gradual tightening of their political links' – a somewhat vague proposition. Yet it is almost certain, in the quaint manner of diplomatic negotiations, that the willingness of the 'candidate' nations, to agree in principle to political integration, all play a significant part in the forthcoming discussions.

(2) COMMUNITY VERSUS SOVEREIGNTY

It is not difficult to pinpoint the obstacle which prevented the implementation of each of these three Plans (E.D.C., E.P.C., Direct Parliamentary Elections): namely the determination of the former President of France, supported by a sizable section of public opinion in the Six, that unification had gone far enough for the time being and that the political independence of the six sovereign member-states should on no account be jeopardized.

The proposed European armed forces and the plan to elect European members of parliament by direct suffrage had been deliberately designed to consolidate the unification of the Six. Political integration would then have been more easily accomplished as a natural sequel.

Against these propositions, the followers of de Gaulle advanced the following arguments: Europe is perfectly capable of defending herself by reliance on the independent armed forces of the Six, through an ordinary type of multilateral military alliance. The parliaments of the Six and their respective governments must maintain their respective sovereignties and their independence; directly elected 'European' members would either be useless deputies in a non-sovereign Chamber or would oust the national deputies if the European Parliament were invested with comprehensive legislative powers. The Community should devote its efforts to widening its economic horizons (for instance by establishing closer relations with the nations of Eastern Europe), by absorbing suitable member-states of E.F.T.A. and by generally making itself economically and financially independent of American assistance and inter-ference.

Such propositions are not wholly reactionary. De Gaulle and his followers did not wish to destroy the existing European Community, but they wanted to call a halt to any further unification or integration, at any rate for the time being. Why?

The problem is easily stated but exceedingly hard to solve. The key words are national independence and sovereignty. The conflict between the seemingly incompatible conceptions of 'United Europe' and 'National Sovereignty' has given rise to heated controversies culminating for the present in the accep-tance of the European *status quo* as more or less unalterable. In the Twenties the argument had been expressed as 'Federation *versus* Confederation'. Today the conflict is even sharper: 'Europe des Patries' *versus* 'Patrie Europe'.

Many of the European nations have long histories and their independent existence in many cases was achieved as the result of wars and insurrections long ago. Of the Six, France is the most ancient state in its present territorial shape, but the Netherlands in the wider sense, including all of 'Benelux', Italy and Germany (in the form of numerous smaller states), all have independent national histories and individual traditions. Why are these countries and, for that matter, most other countries so jealous of their national independence and their sovereignty?

The origin of these strong sentiments is easily traced: a people which has been in any way suppressed or mistreated by another dominant nation will value its eventual liberation and its newly-found freedom most highly. In due course, its ruler's sovereign right to do as he pleases on the international scene (on behalf of his countrymen, and with or without the approval of the latter), will be jealously guarded as the visible expression of national freedom. Thus in the end sovereignty comes to be regarded as the symbol of the people's freedom and indepen-dence, as the very epitome of their standing within the family of 'free' nations.

Why are the Gaullists and their allies opposed to further European integration? What would the effect be on the 'sovereignty' of each of the Six? To answer these questions it is necessary to examine briefly what sovereignty entails in 1970 as far as the Six are concerned. The result of such an inquiry may surprise many people. Economically the Six are to a considerable degree interdependent, in consequence of their adherence to the Community system. Financially, they are similarly interdependent through being parties to numerous international arrangements. Militarily, they are all members of N.A.T.O. (although France has discarded most of her responsibilities and duties in that connexion), and as such they are not free agents in the accepted sense of that term. Politically, all six countries are members of the United Nations, the three smaller countries have signed the Benelux Agreement, France and Germany are bound by a mutual pact. . . . There is not much left of genuine sovereignty in the sense that a truly sovereign country can do what it likes. Sovereignty in 1970 therefore in actual fact implies little more than that a state is free to do what it likes internally, whereas externally it can only be fully sovereign if it breaks its obligations.

What, then, does such internal sovereignty mean today? It consists of an assortment of rights: the state's right to deploy its manpower as it likes, to use its funds as it likes, to run its administration as it likes, to make or revoke laws without having to obtain anyone's consent, to elect its government freely and without interference, and generally to be able to ensure that its people live in freedom within its borders. Few of these rights exist in their absolute form anywhere today, as the result of the growing inter-relationships between nations. But to some extent the sovereign states of Europe are able to provide many of these privileges for their citizens.

The fear of the Gaullists and their friends is that any kind of European political community, any system involving federation, unification or integration of the Six, would make severe inroads into these precious rights. These fears are to some extent justified. The creation of any type of European political community would result in a number of supra-national administrative, legislative and executive activities. The very exponents of sovereignty, the rulers, prime ministers and parliaments, would lose some of their rights and privileges, some part of their independent and supreme powers.

How much would be lost – or rather, transferred from the

individual states to the supra-national authorities – would of course depend on the type of supra-national administration adopted by the member-states. They would have a choice between several forms of supra-statehood. There is federalization, on the American or German principle, confederation, as in Switzerland, or intimate association under a Central Government, as in the Soviet Union. There are other variants. The Fouchet Plan envisaged a hybrid system of federalization, under which the individual national rulers would preserve their internal status while the national parliaments would be subordinated in many respects (such as Foreign Policy, Finance, Defence) to a supra-national Chamber. The heads of the Community's Ministerial Council, a kind of Supreme Council of Prime Ministers, would be empowered to speak with one voice, on behalf of all the member-states in negotiations with other nations or groups of nations.

There is no doubt that these or similar arrangements would eventually curtail even the internal sovereignty of the member-states. However, it had been planned to achieve political integration by the same gradual process as in the case of the Economic Community's common policies, so that the inevitable erosion of sovereignty would progress step by step, almost unnoticed. It has been argued that as far as any essential factors of national independence and their eventual elimination or curtailment are concerned, the entire process would amount to no more than a slight acceleration of the incidental loss of sovereignty experienced in Europe over the past few decades.

It is in this connexion that the issues between the Gaullists and the Federalists are most clearly apparent: the former would wish to bring any further erosion of national sovereignty to a halt, while the latter would be happy to accelerate the present tendency towards national interdependence.

Under the present Community laws, neither political integration nor any major measure leading to any other kind of unification can be adopted without the unanimous approval of the Council of Ministers. Thus the future of the sovereign states within the Community is still controlled by the national governments of the six member-states. For the time being, until there is a unanimous desire for political union, the only effects on national sovereignty will therefore most probably be those which are incidentally brought about through Community policies in actual operation.

As far as Britain is concerned there is thus no real reason to be apprehensive as regards the immediate future, as no major interference with her sovereignty could take place without her specific consent. She would continue to have the ultimate decision as to her own sovereign status. Any change in this position would be most unlikely, unless of course the entire Community wished to bring it about.

This 'sovereignty' problem arising out of Britain's possible membership, must obviously be considered with reference to the effects of the operational common policies and the laws of the Community in force at the time when she becomes a member.

Under the circumstances of present Community legislation and unification, there seems to be no reason to fear any radical effects on her sovereignty.

(3) WHAT PRICE INDEPENDENCE?

Even today, Britain is no longer fully independent. This is true in all respects, whether the reference is to political independence, or to independence in the military, economic, or any other field. No man is an island, and no island can afford to exist in isolation. The growth of interdependence between nations has made many aspects of sovereignty quite illusory.

And yet it is a fact that membership of the Community would whittle down the national freedom of action even further. The nation's agricultural plans would be subject to policy decisions in Brussels. No subsidies, trade restrictions or preferential tariff arrangements would be permissible except by agreement on the part of the Commission. The Community laws, as interpreted by the European Court, would take precedence over the decisions of the national courts in relevant disputes. Budgetary decisions, bank rate levels, proposals to devalue the currency – all such measures would have to be agreed by the Community as a whole, and in advance. The recent changes in the value of the D-Mark and the French franc, without prior authorization by

munity, must not necessarily be seen as precedents for
ence to Community law.
of the existing economic links would snap – parts of
wa Agreement, some of the E.F.T.A. arrangements,
:rms of bilateral and multilateral pacts. Arrangements
International Monetary Fund or borrowing on a
de scale would only be possible 'by arrangement' with
munity Authorities. The 'sterling area' might be in
jeopardy although possibly not for any very cogent reasons.
President de Gaulle made its 'dissolution' one of the prerequi-
sites to membership on the part of Britain. But this would
appear to be an untenable argument: in the first place the role
of reserve currency is not deliberately acquired but it develops
with world-wide trade. It cannot really be shed deliberately.
And in the second place, the part played by sterling in the world
would assist the Community greatly in many ways, not least by
obviating the need to create a Euro-currency. The former President's principal criticism that the international holdings and
liabilities of sterling would cause the Community to become
financially involved beyond its wishes and/or its capacities,
would surely apply to its own Euro-currency too, as soon as the
latter became internationally accepted. If it failed to do so, this
would imply a setback for all the member-states. Then came the
'decline' of the French currency, and the President's resignation, as the result of which much of the strength of the anti-
sterling and anti-reserve currency argument has evaporated.

On a lower plane, it would no longer be permissible to
refuse arbitrarily to issue a 'Community' national with a
working permit solely because he is an alien, or to stop the
import of Community goods to protect a competitive British
product.

The harmonization effects would be less pronounced. Contributions and benefits under the National Insurance and
National Health Schemes would probably be changed to accord
with the 'wage-related' systems in the Community. Prescrip-
tion charges might be permanently retained. New standards for
quality, safety, durability, etc., might be adopted. There are
many hundreds of such 'voluntary' changes, which would bring
Britain into line with the Community. Such changes would

reduce her independence of action, without of course affecting her sovereignty.

Apart from these two types of change – the essential compliance with existing Community policies and laws, and the voluntary harmonization in certain fields for the sake of convenience – no drastic effects are likely. The illusory independence enjoyed by any country which owes large debts to its neighbours and which is entangled in numerous international agreements, would by and large continue much as before.

There would be some shifting of dependence, rather than any noticeable and specific loss of independence. There would be some sharing of sovereignty, rather than any actual loss of sovereignty. Apart from the specialized fields covered by E.C.S.C. and Euratom, there would be no actual transfer of control from any British industry to a Community agency. Centralized European control may spread, but this is unlikely for some time yet. Even the T.V.A. would not now have to be in force before 1972, by which time Britain may either be near to becoming a member or, having failed once again, be engaged in re-shaping her affairs with a view to living outside the Market for a long time to come.

There is not much national independence nowadays as far as a country's trade, her financial obligations and her general economic arrangements are concerned. The international character of trade and finance has for years had a considerable effect on the economic inter-relations between states. As the Community already constitutes a close economic association of states, the immediate loss of sovereignty on the part of a new member-state would be quite small. This is one of the reasons why an economic Community was created as a first step, and also provides an explanation of E.E.C.'s successful performance so far: there was no reason to fear that the Treaties of Paris and Rome would by themselves lead to political integration. There would seem to be no greater cause for apprehension concerning any planned diminution of British sovereignty as the result of Community membership, nor would there be much incidental erosion. The only justifiable cause for concern would seem to arise in connexion with planned political integration at some future time. It is most improbable that such a policy will be discussed in Brussels until after the new members have themselves been economically integrated, and most of the Common Policies are at the very least in the course of implementation.

(4) BRITAIN AND THE PROBLEM OF E.P.C.

We have traced the story of the Fouchet Plan to its negative conclusion (for the time being) in the archives of the European Commission. (There were two Committees, the original Fouchet Committee, and the Cattani Committee, which tried to secure agreements in respect of two draft plans put forward by the French delegation.) At the present time no other plan exists for the deliberate reduction of the member-states' sovereignty and their political unification.

We have also analysed some of the incidental derogation from sovereignty which Britain would suffer as the result of becoming a member of the Community as it stands today.

It only remains to take a careful look into the future to estimate what a Political Union is likely to mean for Britain if she becomes a member of the Community.

It is practically certain that political integration would never be enforced against the wish of any member-state, but the degree of economic and social unification may become so considerable, that in practice it would be impossible for a country to opt out of the political plan. In the event of such compliance *faute de mieux*, there might, however, still be an opportunity for a compromise arrangement.

Jean Monnet has said that 'European unity is not a blueprint, it is not a theory, it is a process that has already begun, of bringing peoples and nations together to adapt themselves jointly to changing circumstances'.

The Treaty of Rome (Articles 235 and 236) contains provisions for making its own terms adaptable to new situations and circumstances within the Community.

Forecasts are difficult, and none more so than those made in the teeth of political contingencies. But it may be reasonably safe to assume that the Gaullist reservations will not prevail unless the entire Community system collapses. Organizations of this kind cannot be allowed to stand still – they either develop in harmony with the tempo of human progress generally, or they break up.

On the assumption that the Community will be preserved from failure by at least five of its members, it would follow that the Parliament will in due course achieve a status above that of the national parliaments of the member-states, in all matters concerning non-domestic affairs. Some kind of European 'Council of Government' is likely to be established at the same time, relieving the national governments of the burdens of office in respect of, for instance, Foreign Affairs, External Finance, Defence, Foreign Trade, and International Transport. There would be no effective interference with the British Crown, nor any change in governmental or parliamentary control over domestic matters. Nevertheless, the reduction of political control by the British Parliament would probably further encourage the demands for decentralization in Scotland, Wales and other distinct ethnic or geographical regions. These changes are not likely to be drastic, nor should they necessarily be deplored. It is probable that an ethnically or geographically reasonably homogeneous population would administer domestic matters within its comparatively small territory more successfully than the large nation-states of today. In the past, the fateful administrative blunders of the small states of Europe were invariably made in connexion with foreign affairs involving other small states. All such matters of external policy might well be allocated to the new European Council of Government – while the purely domestic affairs would revert to the control of those immediately concerned.

There would be a certain amount of 'Europeanization' – through migrant labour forces, increased trade, more travel, and other developments in the same direction. But this would amount to little more than a broadening of existing trends. The citizen of tomorrow's Britain might at one and the same time be more parochial as well as more international than his present counterpart. He may be governed from Cardiff instead of London in many respects, yet he may pay some of his taxes direct to Brussels. His social service benefits may be assessed in

Edinburgh, but he may be told what price to charge for his milk by a directive from Strasbourg. In the course of such developments it is probable that London will be firmly and by general agreement accepted as the financial capital of Europe.

A word about the 'military implications' of accession to the Community: it has been said by some political leaders in Britain that there are no such implications. This is not really correct. The idea of an E.D.C. has been shelved, but it has not been buried. In the field of nuclear research, transport and production generally, there are many instances where the civil and military uses of research and development overlap. A fully integrated *economic* Community, destined to develop at any rate into a politically harmonized entity, cannot in the long run avoid the integration of its armed forces, if for no other reason than that it would be cheaper and more rational to operate a single High Command with one Army, one Navy and one Air Force.

In rounding off this attempt to lift the veils shrouding Europe's future, one factor might usefully be stressed once again: no country should apply to become a member of the European Community unless eventual political unification is freely accepted by the majority of informed opinion among its people. Indeed, the Heads of Government of the Six have ordered their Foreign Ministers to prepare a Report on political unification by the end of July 1970.

This Report may well be backed up by the new plans for closer economic co-operation. A medium-term 'common economic plan' is now being prepared, including an agreement for mutual stand-by between the issuing banks and consultations between the relevant Ministries of the member-states, until a phased policy has been agreed.

'Economic Union' being planned for 1978, and a common currency for 1980, it does not seem unrealistic to aim at political union during the next decade.

ALTERNATIVES: DEMOGRAPHIC AND ECONOMIC STATISTICS

POPULATION and AREA totals, and figures concerning trade with the U.K. in 1968, in respect of (a) E.F.T.A. (plus Finland) and the Commonwealth, (b) U.S.A. and the U.K. (with the Republic of Ireland) and (c) the Community, with its Associate members, the Republic of Ireland and Norway, Denmark, Sweden, Austria, Portugal and Finland.

(a)	Population	Area in sq. miles	Imports from U.K.	Exports to U.K.
C.W.	800 m.	14 m.	£1,404 m. (excl. U.K.)	£1,870 m. (excl. U.K.)
E.F.T.A.	99 m.	493,000	£856 m.	£1,160 m.
Finland	5 m.	130,000	£79 m.	£161 m.
Total	904 m.	14·6 m.	£2,339 m.	£3,191 m.
			Net U.K. deficit, during 1968: £852 m.	

(b)	Population	Area in sq. miles	Imports from U.K.	Exports to U.K.
U.S.A.	203 m.	3·5 m.	£842 m.	£954 m.
U.K.	55 m.	94,000	—	—
Ireland	3 m.	27,000	£261 m.	£268 m.
Total	241 m.	3·6 m.	£1,103 m.	£1,222 m.
			Net U.K. deficit during 1968: £119 m.	

m. = million

(c)	Population	Area in sq. miles	Imports from U.K.	Exports to U.K.
E.E.C.	187 m.	487,000	£1,196 m.	£1,567 m.
U.K.	55 m.	94,000	—	—
Norway Denmark Ireland	11 m.	666,000	£547 m.	£660 m.
Portugal Finland Turkey Greece	56 m.	511,000	£212 m.	£265 m.
Total	309 m.	1,758,000	£1,955 m.	£2,492 m.
			Net U.K. deficit during 1968:	£537 m.

m. = million

(d)   Finally, it may be of interest to see how the Community's trade with the major nations, apart from the applicants, was distributed in 1967 (amounts in m. U.S. dollars):–

	Imports	*Exports*
U.S.:	28,745	31,147
Canada:	10,966	10,555
Japan:	11,664	10,441
Australia:	3,913	3,478
New Zealand:	955	993
S. Africa:	2,945	1,931
E. Europe:	22,132	23,150
Dev. countries:	41,700	39,600
Latin America:	10,290	11,030
Far East:	14,720	10,090
Middle East:	6,010	8,450

Note: All the above figures exclude the so-called 'invisible exports', which enable the United Kingdom to bridge her annual trade (deficit) gap.

CHAPTER XII

Whither Europe . . . ?

(1) THE NEXT THREE YEARS IN THE COMMUNITY

The Government of the United Kingdom, having made another formal application for full membership, proceeded to inform the British public of the implications of this step if it succeeded. On the day of the application, 2nd May 1967, the Prime Minister, Harold Wilson, made a formal explanatory Statement in the House of Commons (Cmnd. 3269).

Some weeks later, there were published two Governmental Papers, 'The Common Agricultural Policy and the E.E.C.' (Cmnd. 3274) and 'Legal and Constitutional Implications of U.K. membership of the European Communities' (Cmnd. 3301).

The Agricultural paper forecast a definite change in relative profitabilities, particularly because of 'the incentive of higher prices for cereals' and 'a reappraisal of livestock production'. This would 'necessitate a substantial redeployment of resources'. The cost of food to the consumer would rise, and the actual increase was considered to be 10 to 14 per cent (*i.e.* about $2\frac{1}{2}$ to $3\frac{1}{2}$ per cent in the overall cost of living). (This was of course before the devaluation of the pound, which in itself helped to produce a similar increase without any of the corresponding benefits of Community membership.) In conclusion, this Government estimate forecast a total net cost to the United Kingdom of £175 to £250 million annually as the result of adopting the common agricultural policy.

The Legal and Constitutional Paper accepted the automatic applicability of Community Law if Britain were to join, and its prevalence whenever a provision of English Law were to be at variance with a Community Directive or Regulation. It accepted the automatic jurisdiction of the Community Court in the instances specified under the Treaties. Suggestions were made as to how the Treaties and all enactments made thereunder would be made applicable to the United Kingdom. No difficulties were foreseen, either in respect of the administrative steps by which the Treaties would become law in the United Kingdom, nor in connexion with the working of Community legislation *vis-à-vis* the Civil Service, the Courts and any other bodies.

The restrictive effects on national sovereignty as regards freedom to conclude treaties with non-member states, dealing with public disturbances or carrying out international obligations were stressed, without comment.

More or less at the same time, the Government issued a pamphlet entitled 'Britain and the E.E.C. – The Economic Background', which briefly examined the economic conception of the E.E.C. in the context of British trading arrangements. No comment nor criticism was made, nor was it intended to discuss 'the possible advantages and disadvantages'.

Nothing was said on behalf of Britain when the Council was unable to begin formal negotiations on the issue of membership, except that the application on behalf of the United Kingdom would remain 'on the table'. It is therefore relevant to consider the procedure likely to be followed if it should become possible to proceed to detailed discussions as regards admitting the applicant states.

Even if Britain were to be eventually successful in her pertinacious although belated quest, it would still take some time before any effects would be felt either in the Community or in Britain. In the first instance there would have to be a period of preparation lasting some months, for the necessary legislation to be passed and preliminary arrangements to be made. After this preparatory stage, Britain might formally become a member, but in practice this would probably mean the beginning of transition periods of varying lengths. These periods are likely to differ according to the difficulties of adjustment in any particular field of activity. Industry, exporters, banks and transport undertakings would have to be given time to adjust themselves to new procedures, and the entire economic system of the nation would to some extent have to be geared to the changes involved.

These transition periods might well extend to 1 year in respect of tariffs, customs and restrictive practices, where there is now comparatively little difference between the British methods and procedures and those operative within the Community; $1\frac{1}{2}$–2 years in respect of taxation and the common agricultural policy where any change must be gradual to avoid hardship; or 2 years in respect of such well-established non-domestic arrangements as the agreements with the Commonwealth, the E.F.T.A. Convention or certain trading pacts. It is not likely that longer periods could be realistically considered except perhaps in connexion with certain unusual products or procedures where a complete break with tradition might have to be made necessitating radical alterations of procedure or totally new assessments and evaluations. In a speech to the W.E.U. at the Hague, on 4th April 1967, the British Foreign Secretary seemed to envisage that a period of a 'one year's standstill' would be adequate for Britain's adjustment.

By 1972, when Britain might (at the earliest) be in a position to sustain the full implementation of Community laws and regulations, the Six will have advanced considerably beyond their present stage of integration. The common agricultural policy will be operative in respect of all products. Many hundreds of new regulations will have been put into effect to carry out the detailed provisions in respect of the huge variety of products and processes which fall under the generic title of 'agriculture'. Modern agriculture is of great complexity and the application of uniform rules to six different national systems presents a legislative problem of some magnitude. Nevertheless it is confidently expected in Brussels that by 1972 practically all the Community's agricultural products will be available within the borders of the Community as if the latter were a single domestic market.

By that time the last customs barrier in the Community will

have disappeared and there should be neither internal tariffs nor duties in the way of the free flow of trade. The coloured booms will have disappeared from a large part of Europe.

As a new member-state Britain may have to cope almost at once with certain new aspects of taxation. However, this aspect should not cause any undue difficulties. The T.V.A. could conveniently replace P.T., and S.E.T. might form part of the ordinary National Insurance system. Further tax harmonization is planned for later years. Britain would thus be joining at a time when the old 'tax-frontiers' are about to disintegrate.

These schemes for economic integration and fiscal harmonization are designed to bring about a true economic union in Western Europe. In 1972 the Six may have advanced a good deal towards that goal, but Britain would find much still to be accomplished to achieve these lofty objectives. She would find the implementation of new common policies in full swing, a process inevitably involving a multitude of new laws, regulations and directives.

It had been confidently expected that the free movement of workers throughout the Community would be an accomplished fact by the summer of 1968. Yet although the regulations for setting up business or establishing an individual anywhere within the Community had been passed, it was not in fact possible to carry out this plan. Nor was financial backing through Community resources available for such permanent migration. However, it now appears probable that by 1972 it will be possible to move capital as well as people freely throughout the territories of the Six. The psychological value of this 'freedom' is probably greater than its material importance. It rates as high priority in Brussels.

The common transport policy has proved to be a difficult project and this may be to the advantage of new member-states. Air and sea transport were not included when the E.E.C. Treaty was signed, although it was left open for these aspects to be dealt with at a suitable time. Recently some arrangements concerning administration and flight-pooling were made between some of the state-owned airlines of the Six, and a 'Euro-Airways' system may well be set up one day. For the time being, the common transport policy is expected to deal with such matters as standard designs and measurements for containers, common road signs, standardization of commercial vehicles, uniformity of documentation for transport by road and rail and other schemes intended to facilitate and simplify commercial (and possibly private) transportation. The 'first stage' has now been completed, and six out of the seven 'basic' Regulations have been adopted by the Council.

Concerning foreign trade, the Community had set itself the task of agreeing a common policy by 1970. This proved too much. A good many conferences will have to thrash out the essential details, and it will not be easy to translate even the basic principles into generally acceptable Directives. There is agreement as to procedure, but not in respect of implementation. If Britain were by then engaged in joining the Community, she might well find herself embroiled right away in an argument, and possibly in a clash of opinions, over the method of deciding on short-term trading policies. The interplay of politics will always be present in the background: *i.e.* to what extent should trade with politically hostile countries be encouraged, and how much attention should be paid, for instance, to American 'advice' in this respect.

Apart from such considerations of economic strategy, complicated lists of products will have to be agreed to allow for the numerous exemptions, exceptions and concessions in this wide field, where standardization and uniformity cannot be achieved overnight.

The merger of the three Communities into a single European Community will in all probability lead to some administrative reorganization as regards fuel and power resources. In view of Britain's high technological standing in the field of nuclear energy production, and also because of her newly discovered potential supplies of natural gas, it would be useful to all concerned if she could be included in these developments from the beginning. It is likely that certain departments of Euratom and the coal mines now controlled by E.C.S.C. will be merged with the other 'energy' industries to form a single power and energy department of a new single Commission. The British nuclear energy industry and her state-owned mines might be directly integrated into the new arrangements.

Another important development formerly scheduled for completion by 1970 is the over-all co-ordination of the member-states' economic policies. Here again the object is to strengthen the Community's economic integration, because diversification during the early stages of planning at national levels would then be easily avoidable. This is a field which offers many opportunities for unification, and would be of particular interest to the City of London. A single capital market, Community assistance for industries beset by specific difficulties, special 'European companies' and other revolutionary proposals are among the many items on the Commission's agenda for the next three years. Some of them have already passed the 'blue-print' stage and are merely awaiting the right climate for implementation. Preliminary discussions have already taken place on the subject of a common Development Policy, another proposition which would offer much scope to Britain in connexion with her Commonwealth obligations. As to the harmonization of development procedure and planning within the member-states a very great deal remains to be done, and much national pride and prejudice will have to be overcome.

Whether or not Britain enters the Community within the next three years or not, it is quite probable that some additional European countries will sign Association agreements during that time.

It must be remembered that whereas 'association' between the Six and non-European countries is envisaged as a definite policy under the E.E.C. Treaty (Articles 131–6), no such provisions exist as regards Association with European countries, such as negotiated with Greece and Turkey. It is therefore perfectly possible, for instance, to negotiate a bilateral 'arrangement' with Austria without offending against the Yalta and Potsdam principles, or to conclude any kind of special or transient Association Treaty with any European applicant. When the Treaties are silent, the Six are only bound by the general principles underlying them. It was presumably such an Association arrangement between the Community and Britain which General de Gaulle had in mind when he hinted at 'something less than full membership' in 1967.

It may well be that Spain, Portugal and Sweden, and almost

certainly Austria, may persist with their attempts to achieve some special 'custom-built' Association arrangements, in spite of the temporary halt in the Community talks with Britain.

Further special arrangements with non-European countries, particularly in North Africa, are also in the pipe-line. The finalization of the 'Kennedy Round', although expectations have been reduced of late, was expected to stimulate trading generally, and to lead to an intensification of business with the United States. This in turn may well result in the conclusion of an economic Treaty between the Community and the U.S.A., after the tariffs throughout the G.A.T.T. area have been lowered further. (The Community's tariff policies are in accordance with the G.A.T.T. provisions, as the total of the Community tariffs is less than the total of the old tariffs individually maintained by the Six.)

The system of economic relationships between the nations of the World is in a state of flux. It is not only in Europe that 'Common Markets' are developing, where recently, apart from the Community and E.F.T.A., the four Nordic countries have begun to operate a customs union, 'Nordek'. In Central America, for instance, Guatemala, Honduras, Nicaragua, El Salvador and Costa Rica are co-operating towards similar ends. They signed a Treaty on Central American Economic Integration in 1960, at Managua, and a 'Common Market' was established between them in 1966. There has been some alignment of duties and abolition of discriminatory practices. This market embraces about 13 million people. On 14th April, 1967, by the 'Declaration of the Presidents of America', signed in Uruguay, 19 Latin-American states agreed to set up a Common Market in 1970, which is to be fully operative by 1985. A Latin American Free Trade Association, set up in 1960, embraces four major nations, Brazil, Argentina, Paraguay and Mexico. And there are other parts of the world where free trade areas and tariff harmonization is being discussed with a view to making similar arrangements, for instance, the Caribbean Free Trade Association of eleven states, established in 1968. There can be no doubt that modern conditions of trading require that companies should join together to form consortia, that consortia should co-operate with each other and that even sovereign states should combine their economic activities in many fields. It is against such a background that the present British application must be considered. Two failures in the recent past have left their marks in Britain. These failures have also affected the European spirit, the drive towards integration, within the Community. The will to introduce new common policies has grown weaker. Too much cold water dampens even ardent spirits. Yet as the recent statements and opinions show, the Schuman spirit is not quite dead.

(2) A COMMUNITY OF TEN?

We have assumed, on the basis of semi-official pronouncements and for economic considerations, that if Britain were to join within the next few years, *i.e.* sometime in 1972 or 1973, the Community would in fact be enlarged by the simultaneous admission of as many as four new member-states, namely Britain, the Republic of Ireland, Norway and Denmark, while Portugal would probably become an Associate member, possibly in conjunction with Spain. Austria, for reasons stated earlier, will almost certainly sign a special Treaty of quasi-Association with the Community in any event.

The population of the Community proper would thus rise to about 260 millions, with 60–100 millions in the associated countries in Europe. Technologically as well as financially the enlarged Community would be the equal of any other power or association of states in the world, except in the exploration of space and as a nuclear power from a military point of view. The geographical position and proximity to each other of the ten member-states and their associates, together with their gigantic manpower potential (particularly of skilled men and women), their massive industries and their highly developed agricultural productivity, would make the Community a most formidable competitor in the world markets and a well-balanced, self-supporting organization of peoples in many respects. For example, it would control more than half the maritime transport of the World.

Such strength in a world still plagued by starvation and

poverty could prove to be a mixed blessing if it provoked undue hatred and jealousy in the less fortunate countries. It would not be easy to prove to the satisfaction of the political leaders of those underfed and under-privileged millions that the advantages to be derived from the prosperity and the outward-looking efforts of the Community are likely to outweigh any objections based on allegations of unfair distribution of the world's wealth. Yet it is on the basis of such difficult considerations that any enlargement of the Community, particularly by the election of a powerful new member-state such as Britain, must to some extent be judged.

Because the enlarged Community would constitute such a glittering prize for an unscrupulous enemy, it must obviously have adequate means of defending itself. There would be little justification for total reliance on American military aid for a Community of nations of such great financial and commercial strength. Yet there would be much justification for co-ordination in some respects, as it would be exceedingly expensive and indeed wasteful to duplicate in full the highly sophisticated defence and warning system of the United States in respect of areas and contingencies in which it could be utilized on behalf and for the protection of the Community. But the larger Community may have to provide its own submarines, missile launchers and warning systems as well as some sort of 'force de frappe' if it is to survive safely. The British taxpayer would have to contribute his share towards the cost of this extremely expensive hardware, but presumably a good proportion would be designed and made within the United Kingdom. Thus British membership might well herald a period of prosperity for domestic steel and engineering interests.

What would happen inside Britain if she became a member of a Community of Ten, in 1972 or 1973? The new vast 'home market' would of course provide tremendous scope for all those who have both the heart and the mind to tackle a difficult proposition. Conversely, it would most certainly mean the end of the line for all those people who, having hitherto relied on protection against competition from abroad in the shape of tariffs, restrictive quotas and other safeguards, would find themselves by stages exposed more and more to the icy storms from overseas. Some companies and some individuals would no doubt be able to re-organize themselves in time. That is what the transition periods are intended to achieve – to provide sufficient time and opportunity for readjustment. As we mentioned earlier, the City of London, the banks and the finance houses are not worried about their prospects in a Community of Ten.

We have left to the last the much-discussed problem of the immediate effects of Community membership on British agriculture and food prices. The British farming community is smaller than that of the other major member-states and comprises barely 4 per cent of the working population. In the Community as a whole, nearly 25 per cent of the working population are employed in the agricultural industry. Their work accounts for about 10 per cent of the Community's G.N.P., while in the United Kingdom the contribution by the agricultural industry is merely 3.4 per cent. This comparatively small industry has in the past achieved a very high degree of efficiency. Considering the adversities of the British climate and the limitations of space, productivity is of a very high order. These levels were achieved behind a protective wall of tariffs and on a plateau of compulsory financial support by the taxpayers. If Britain joined the Community, the deficiency payments now made to British farmers would have to be replaced, over a period, by the Community system of price support out of a common fund. Contributions to this fund would be obligatory, and would have to be made by the agricultural industry itself, not by the British taxpayer.

It is probable that some £180 million per annum would be saved by limiting the Exchequer's deficiency payments to purely domestic products (about £100 million). The British farmers' contribution to the Common Agricultural Fund of the Community would initially amount to approximately £230 million per annum. On the other hand, the British Exchequer would be considerably better off as the result of major reductions in the annual trading deficits with the Commonwealth countries, some £450 million in an average year. Thus there would be a net saving of many millions per annum as the result of Community membership, but while the Exchequer would be handsomely in pocket, the consumer (*i.e.* the housewife and her husband) would have to pay higher prices for many goods, particularly food.

Those items which are at present 'supported' or subsidized, like for instance eggs, milk, poultry and fertilizers, would cost considerably more. Heavily subsidized domestic products and the cheap Commonwealth imports would gradually be replaced in the shops by more expensive Community goods. Yet this is not quite the whole story. At present imports from the Community are usually foodstuffs in the higher price ranges. Many cheaper varieties are available which would be worth exporting to Britain if the tariffs came down. Some of the Commonwealth goods would still be competitive and would remain available, and there are many domestic products which would remain within the reach of the average wage earner even without the national subsidies. British agriculture is much more resilient than is generally assumed.

In any event, it has become almost a routine matter for the index of food retail prices in Britain to rise by 4 per cent or more, year by year. In the 12 months to April 1969, it rose by about 7 per cent. These rises had nothing to do with imports from the Community – they were due to higher wages, increased taxation and the farmers' demand for higher standards of living for themselves. The increase in food prices after joining the Community would be gradual and by fixed stages. It would take place over a period of possibly four years, after which stability ought to be achieved. The erosion of the currency, *i.e.* the continuous decrease of the value of the pound, should slow down perceptibly thus preserving the 'real' value of earnings. On 18th November 1967, the pound was devalued by 14·3 per cent, to a parity of $2.40. This was rather less than expected in some circles, and it may yet be that a parity of $2.00 would be a prerequisite to viable membership.

Thus the net result, during the transition period, would be savings by the Exchequer and increased costs to the housewife. These increases would not, however, raise the costs of the staple foods noticeably more than has been the case during 'normal' years in the past. An egg might cost ½d. more, the price of a loaf of bread is likely to rise by ½d. or 1d. a year every year during the transition period, and pork would probably cost 10 per cent more to show a rise of about one third after three years. Butter might well cost 3d. or 4d. a pound more per annum for the same period. These are specimen rises estimated by computer with most of the likely contingencies taken into consideration. The net extra cost to an ordinary housewife is not likely to be more than what has been grudgingly accepted, annually, by wage earners and their wives in the past.

What could be done to soften the impact of such price increases on the poorer families? There may have to be transition period payments based on earnings and size of family, and special allowances for pensioners and others living on small fixed incomes. And, of course, the Exchequer is not likely to be allowed to 'sit' on all its savings. These 'windfalls' will not readily be handed out as subsidies by the Exchequer, but there is a case for some proportion to be distributed to assist the poorer members of the population as well as for the purpose of general tax reductions.

As to those countries which would lose part of their existing British markets, particularly some members of the Commonwealth, the position has improved greatly since President de Gaulle stopped Edward Heath on the last lap of the Great Race in January 1963. There is now little cause for worry. Canada, Australia, New Zealand and some of the new African nations, as well as India, Pakistan and Ceylon have made extensive alternative arrangements. Their home industries have been diversified, and new markets have been opened for some of the goods which hitherto had been almost entirely destined for the British market. As regards the British imports of mutton, wool and butter from New Zealand and Australia, specific transition arrangements would still have to be made to allow for a gradual change-over. Special protocols would also have to be annexed to the Treaties in respect of such territories as Gibraltar, Malta, Singapore and other small dependencies. But such arrangements are normal Community procedure and should not be regarded as 'entry conditions' in the normal sense.

And lastly, what would be the immediate effect of Britain's entry on the Community itself? General de Gaulle once said that it would never be the same again. It would be larger, stronger, more viable and stable. The larger Community would hold additional advantages for its present members and it would constitute a more attractive and realistic entity which might in due course form the basis of a United Europe embracing the Eastern countries as well as almost all the states to the West of the Curtain.

The smaller member-states would gain more than the three major powers among the Six. French apprehensions are to some extent justified, as her leading position would be undermined not only because of Britain's political record and her position as a financial world power, but also through essential alterations within the Community administration itself. This argument is best demonstrated by way of an example; figures in this case speak more eloquently than any words. At present, unless unanimity is required, the Council's weighted votes are distributed as follows: France, Italy, Germany: 4 each, Belgium and the Netherlands: 2 each, Luxembourg: 1. If the Community were to enrol Britain (probably 4 votes), the Republic of Ireland, Denmark and Norway (2 votes each), the combined total of possibly 27 votes would require a minimum of 18 votes to pass legislation or to take other positive action. At the present time, France only needs the support of 2 votes (*i.e.* of either Belgium or the Netherlands) to stop any measure from being passed. In the enlarged Community it would clearly be much more difficult to carry out the Gaullist policy of minimum supra-nationalism and slow economic integration, as France would always have to align herself with at least two other member-states if she wished to oppose effectively any measure on the agenda. The entire system may have to be altered.

This is one view as seen from the other side of the Channel. It has taken France a long time to get over her wartime experiences and her present position within the Community means a great deal to her. Her debt of gratitude to Britain makes her position even more complicated; what she wanted from the Community was the opportunity of a new beginning and the certainty of being able to live in peace with her neighbours. Britain's entry would necessarily mean a certain amount of going back over old records, as well as some re-negotiations of Treaties and Arrangements which it took France a long time to agree with her five partners. It is easy to understand her apprehensions, particularly when the basically sound French economy was rocked in late November, 1968, by a monetary crisis which led to the closing of the Exchanges and temporary measures reducing the free flow of capital from France and in the end to the devaluation of the franc.

(3) EUROPE 1970

The President of E.E.C. said years ago that 'we are not integrating economies, we are integrating policies'. The miracle of Europe must not be judged by the world, and least of all by Britain while she is contemplating the possibilities of membership, as a kind of European Supermarket. The men of Brussels and Luxembourg, with the exception of the Gaullists, are not envisaging an economic future for Europe as an end in itself. To these people, economic unification in fact *means* political union.

There is now world-wide interest in the impending development in Western Europe. If the Community is prepared to take the risk of adding new members and new problems to its existing difficulties, another irrevocable step will have been taken towards the realization of the ultimate target, United Europe, or towards breakdown. Will the Community be able to digest as rich a dish as these four new member-states one of which would be extensively garnished with many and varied international involvements?

A good deal will depend on Britain herself. Having declined the offer of coming in as one of the founder members, indeed of being their leader, she was prepared some years later to join during the formative stages of the Community. Having failed in this, she then resumed her independent economic way within the loose confines of E.F.T.A. At the end of the Second World War Britain had what was probably her last chance of participating in the rebuilding of Europe as the head of a multi-racial Commonwealth, a final opportunity of being a leader in two camps at the same time. Churchill's call from Zurich was in vain. Domestic social reappraisal was at that time regarded as the first priority. In 1962/3 the United Kingdom went to the conference tables of Strasbourg with two alternatives still available to her if she could not come to terms with the Six: an E.F.T.A./C.W. partnership on purely economic lines or closer association with the United States. The first of these is today no longer a realistic proposition and the second has not yet been sufficiently investigated to permit serious discussion.

It is now becoming evident that E.F.T.A. is nearing the end of its usefulness as a stopgap, and the mists are beginning to drift away from the intellectual battleground over which the coming fight for European unification may have to be decided. The forces of the Community are lined up, and 'popular' opinion is apparently everywhere in favour of enlarging the Community by the admission of new members, including Britain. The French Government, however, remains at best cautiously determined to sell the pass dearly. The price will have to be compensation for the French farming community. On the other hand, the German Social-Democrats appear to be less insistent on a political bargain than their predecessors.

Several of the E.F.T.A. countries are also in favour of climbing on the Community bandwagon themselves, even though the latter is merely jogging along for the time being. None of them were in outright opposition when Britain decided to reapply. The Commonwealth, too, has no longer any objections in principle to such a move, and few apprehensions regarding the economic results which might follow. The United States would much prefer a more self-supporting Europe, which would enable her further to cut down her foreign commitments, although in due course a stronger Community would mean increased economic competition. Soviet opposition amounts to little more than formal objections, while the New China for the present is bound to be implacably hostile to any activity which could be of benefit to the capitalist world.

Within Britain the major political parties remain split on the issue of what the country should do. Both the Government and the Opposition are in favour of applying again, the so-called 'four essential conditions' having been tactfully pushed into the background, without being formally jettisoned. The political implications of membership are stressed almost exclusively by the opponents of Community membership, while the protagonists of the 'pro-European' brigade remained careful to emphasize the purely economic advantages of membership. Britain at the time of her re-application, was 'pro-Market' for the wrong reasons, and now, at this crucial stage, some of her leaders and a majority of the voters appear to be hostile – again for irrelevant reasons.

If one tries fairly to assess the multitude of conflicting interests and problems, one is struck by the weight of British opinion which stubbornly refuses to recognize the finality of Community membership. All the Treaties and Pacts hitherto signed and ratified by the United Kingdom contained clauses under which she could contract out. The Treaties of Paris and Rome are not of this kind. They are not normal Treaties. They are irreversible – there is neither a way back nor a way out. It may be argued that there is no such word as 'never' in the vocabulary of a sovereign state and that an independent country in the last resort can act precisely as it pleases, albeit at its peril. But does this argument really stand up to the circumstances of the present time? The economic, financial and social involvements arising out of prolonged membership of the Community (say, three years or more) would surely be such that withdrawal by any country would be tantamount to its economic suicide. And joining for a 'trial period' of a year or two is totally unrealistic. All of which simply adds up to the brutal and unpalatable but unassailable truth, that after some three years membership would have to be regarded as virtually 'forever' unless the Community were itself to collapse as the result of some internal or extraneous catastrophe. It was not without good reason that the Treaties were 'concluded for an unlimited period' (E.E.C. Treaty, Art. 240).

Active and positive participation in the continual striving of Europe towards integration must be above party-political considerations. It is neither a game nor a bargain-hunting expedition. It is not even a case of 'In for a Penny, in for a Pound'. It is a decision as to whether to go along with Europe, for better or for worse – without a chance of a divorce. The Community is 'in politics', which means that its members must be determined to develop a new loyalty, a loyalty to the new Europe under construction, before all other loyalties in the international field. This does not mean the ending of old friendships or of special relationships, and certainly not the severance of ties of trans-oceanic kinship, but it does mean that Community loyalty will always have to come first.

It is interesting to speculate about the price of food if Britain were to become a member. The chance freely to trade, travel or simply to vegetate anywhere within the enlarged Community area may be attractive to some people in Britain, and of no interest to others. The ultimate result of enlarging the Community might be a federation, or government by some supra-national Board. These are fascinating conjectures but in the context of the advisability or inadvisability of British membership they are the wrong problems. The ultimate decision on behalf of the British nation must be made by the Government of the day. It cannot now be passed on to the electorate by way of a referendum. In 1967 it was apparently made on the basis of the government's assessment of Britain's political and economic future as an independent nation outside and close to a Community of 8 or 9 members, with 5 or more Associates in Europe. As against this prospect they had to consider the effects of membership, implying a permanent change of Britain's status in the world. It amounted to an evaluation of the prospects of continued independence against the risks of political integration with 'strange' countries.

The lodging of Britain's second application for membership must be seen as a definite decision that the Government for the time being wants to be linked with the Community in some way or other, preferably by full membership. If the Commons' overwhelming vote on 10th May 1967 in favour of full membership (488 to 62), the full support of the employers and the trade unions, and the assent of the three major political parties meant anything at all, the British people at any rate in 1967 had made up their mind to 'go in'.

The developments during the following years may justifiably have annoyed many of those who wanted to go ahead. They may console themselves with the thought that the British aloofness during the years when the foundations of the Community were laid, was equally irksome to her European friends.

Nevertheless, the road to membership was only temporarily barred by the veto of a single man. Like the customs-barriers within the Community, this impediment could not for ever stand in the way of a permanent British-European link in accordance with the wishes of the British people. In November 1968, a ray of hope pierced the cloudy horizon, when M. Debré, France's Foreign Minister, announced his country's willingness to co-operate 'beyond the Six' on 9 issues: customs, technical trade obstacles, technology, tax, industrial property, the 'European Company', mergers, transport and energy.

The resignation of President de Gaulle on 27th April 1969 was ostensibly the result of the rejection by the French electorate of his plan for devolution of power from Paris to the Regions. It may have been planned to avoid any association with a possible devaluation of the French franc. It was hailed by the protagonists of European integration as the first major chink in the armour of lethargic immobility behind which the work of the Community had to be carried out in 1968 and early 1969. It proved to be a turning point in this protracted affair, but the turning manœuvre was slow indeed.

In spite of economic unification, organizational reconciliation and incipient harmonization in many spheres, the Six are still very much in the 'nation state' stage as far as matters of finance, defence and foreign policy are concerned. It is the direct result of this preservation of national identities, deliberately encouraged by President de Gaulle during his long reign, that Europe now has no voice when major policy decisions are made to determine the future of mankind. The individual voices of France, Germany and Italy may ring out loud and clear at home, but they are hardly listened to on the World Stage, where the United States, Russia and increasingly, China, are writing the script and hogging the leading parts by mutual dissent.

Nor has Europe been able to find her way through the jungle of international finance. With their national currencies never in harmony, with capital periodically flowing out of the weaker partners of Community, the control of the world's funds has moved to Wall Street and Bahnhofstrasse, Zurich. In defence matters, Europe is still as dependent on its transatlantic props as it was before the formation of the Force de Frappe. The Six, it has been said, play the role of the 'O' in the figure 90 with the US supplying the '9': a lot with it, but nothing without it!

An invitation to Washington is still regarded as the Grand Prix by any European Prime Minister, but at least it would appear that President Nixon is fairly sympathetic towards the conception of European unification – on a limited scale.

Thus in early 1970, political integration remains a vision but probably not quite an illusion. The post-de Gaulle era is likely to be more positive. There is now no fundamental opposition to enlargement, nor to further integration. The elections in Federal Germany in September 1969 resulted in a change of Government. The minority party in charge will certainly do nothing to rock the European boat. In Italy the forces of extreme Socialism are being held in check by little more than the present prosperity which may not last much longer. It is high time for a positive 'happening' in Common Market matters. Associations with non-European powers cannot provide the required impetus which, in the view of Brussels, can only come from the accession of Britain and the other European candidates, and the definitive and universal acceptance of majority vote principle.

Unfortunately Britain's future remains obscure. The idea of Common Market membership is still liable to be exploited for party-political purposes by leaders whose enthusiasm originates from the brain, but not from the heart. They are apt to pay lip-service to the concept of 'One Europe' if the Opinion Polls show that such a policy may command additional votes, but the threat of dearer butter can at any moment reverse that trend. Even Mr Heath, who fought such a valiant battle in Brussels, may find if he were to succeed Mr Wilson some time in 1970 or 1971, that the weakened British economy would not allow him to accord much priority to thoughts of European integration. If the elections have not been held by the time negotiations get under way, declarations of intent may be demanded of the two larger parties. The bizarre situation of 1962/3 must not be allowed to occur again.

It is all very sad, yet much of the present dilemma is Britain's own fault. As the only genuinely victorious power in Europe in 1945, she threw away all her chances to win the peace. She could so easily have led Europe into unity in the early Fifties, and the Commonwealth would have benefited far more from such a shift of priorities than from the deliberate abdication from power which the people were persuaded to prefer. It is sad, but it is not too late. At the time of writing the conception of Europeanism is steadily gaining adherents in the United Kingdom. And it is amongst the younger people, who are beginning to realize that turning one's back on glory may lead to a slap in the face, that the new enthusiasm is most noticeable. It is a development very much along traditional lines: a ready-made Treaty, with fixed objectives and precise principles is not much to the liking of most British people, who prefer gradual, empirical development. Thus once again it has taken rather longer for a new conception to take root on this side of the Channel, but it is probable that in due course its roots will go all the deeper for this. There are now many more people who, while they regret the possibility of dearer food, consider this a worth-while sacrifice in the interest of peace. There are not many now who fear an invasion of workers from Southern Italy, having quite possibly been immunized by the influx of Commonwealth immigrants of many colours. At least, it is said, it will be easier for European migrant workers to return to their respective homes. And somewhat quaintly, many of the supporters of Scottish and Welsh independence are heard to applaud European sentiments, although it is hardly likely that Scotland or Wales will ever seek independent affiliation.

The change of heart in Britain, which ex-President de Gaulle made a condition sine qua non before permitting the consideration of British membership – in the belief that it could not be achieved for many years – may not have come about. It may occur in the hearts of the young instead. The people provide the votes which in turn confer political power and therefore it seems reasonable to expect that sooner or later the pursuit of genuine integration with Europe will be accorded a measure of priority in one of the main parties' election manifestos.

CHAPTER XIII

Decision on Europe

On 10th October, 1969, the Commission published its considered views about the possible accession of new member-states, the development of the Community in the recent past and the functioning of its Institutions. Rather more emphatically than in 1967, they emphasized that the 'strengthening and enlarging' of the Community should go hand in hand, but without sacrificing any of the objectives already attained.

The ball was now back in the Ministerial Council's court, which in effect meant that President Pompidou was left with most of the trump cards in his hand. In Germany, Herr Brandt had formed a Socialist coalition government; the D-Mark had been up-valued and the economic position generally remained strong. In Italy and Benelux there was a measure of dissatisfaction with the implementation in practice of the Mansholt Plan by way of the common agricultural policy.

In France, the devaluation of the franc had not by that time resulted in greater competitiveness either within or without the C.E.T. wall, and there was a good deal of impatience among the farming community concerning the promised 'improved terms of trading'. Quite clearly, M. Pompidou was in a much weaker position than his predecessor, who had twice rejected the four 'candidate' states, including Britain. Thus the time was relatively opportune for a change of policy: France had not quite maintained her 'leading' position within the Community, her economy needed a powerful fillip and the 'European spirit' was at a low ebb. Gently, without any formal indication of a change of heart, M. Pompidou proceeded to unlatch the gate through the tariff wall. The four candidate nations' applications would have to be considered together. They would have to accept the common agricultural policy. They must agree in principle to the need for strengthening the Community, and 'participate fully in the creation of a politically and economically united Europe'.

So the gate was just about ajar once again. The four applications were still lying on the table. In Britain, all the party leaders were committed to 'entry on reasonable terms' – but now the Opinion Polls proclaimed (perhaps not surprisingly), that a majority in the country was opposed to entry and a growing percentage had joined the 'Don't Knows'. Such views were a clear indication that most of the electorate were unwilling to back the party leaders' avowed intention to persevere with the application of 1967. Truly, the situation at the end of 1969 was bizarre indeed, and the underlying problems merit examination in some detail.

(1) THE COST OF LIVING

This problem, as far as British membership of the Community is concerned, is inextricably linked with the financial effects of the Common Agricultural Policy (C.A.P.). This policy, developed from Dr Mansholt's Plan, is fairly simple in essence: the agricultural markets of the Community are to be 'unified', and the member states are to be jointly responsible for the stabilization of their agricultural markets in the widest sense. Thus, within the Community, all agricultural produce must eventually be sold at fixed prices (generally above the world prices), and in such a way as to make any surplus flow to areas of need. Artificial 'support prices' will be established by levies on imports and subsidies of exports.

The whole scheme is intended to be jointly financed. Imports 'over the tariff wall' are intended always be a little more expensive than from member-states, while exports in the opposite direction or within the Community will be balanced by means of financial equalization arrangements. In practice, the target prices for the various commodities are fixed by taking the cost at Duisburg (the area of the greatest deficit) as a norm. Thus a 'threshold price' is established – *i.e.* a price worked out on the basis of the respective 'Duisburg plus' target price for any given area, but lower than that target price by the relevant transport cost from the point of entry. A variable levy then raises the import price to the 'threshold price'.

This plan should work in theory, but like all blue prints it is bound to be both rigid and complicated. It is the most elaborate and intricate system of Regulations so far devised within the Community administration. Perhaps it is ahead of its time. It was certainly in advance of the rest of the Community's legislation when it was introduced. The unauthorized up-valuation of the D-Mark, and the similarly 'unilateral' devaluation of the French franc certainly upset the planned equilibrium. As a result of these changes, French produce could temporarily be sold 'on the cheap' in Germany, while German products were 'dear' and often had to be placed in store. The Commission had not been consulted at all, and was only informed after the respective decisions had been taken.

In Britain, where the Press turned its spotlights on these difficulties across the Channel with some understandable glee, farmers asked themselves what would happen to them if the C.A.P. were introduced in this country. Predictions are hazardous, but one may expect that 'in due course' (*i.e.* after a period of transition), the probable effect may be a gain of between 10 and 12 per cent on grain farming revenue; in cereal and beef there would be lesser gains, while in pork, eggs and poultry incoming Community produce would score. The likely effect on milk profits is thought to be slight, while it is now apparent that as regards mutton, lamb and sugar everything will depend on the 'Conditions' to be formulated and on the phasing out of the present preferential trading agreements relating to these commodities.

What of the consumer in Britain? The artificial creation of a certain amount of additional competitiveness in some parts of the farming industry is likely to cost about £40 million, taking into account the cessation of 'inefficiency subsidies' at the same time.

The transfer to the Community authorities of excess payments for food and other agricultural produce, mostly from the Commonwealth, and by way of levies raised in conformity with the target and threshold price system, may cost as much as £200 million in the first year or two. Thus a family in Britain may, at the end of the main transition period, pay about 15s. (75p.) more for their food as the result of the United Kingdom having joined the Community, but it should be possible to lower income tax quite substantially perhaps by as much as 9d. (4p.) or 1s. (5p.) in the £. Some of these savings will have to be used to subsidize impecunious persons dependent on fixed incomes.

It is very probable that by the time the C.A.P. has been fully implemented in Britain, some prices of goods in the Community (including butter, of which there has recently been a persistent glut), will have fallen considerably, so that the effect on the British housewife may be less severe than commonly predicted.

By and large, taking into account such matters as further wage claims due to higher food prices, and other results of the cost-of-living spiral, as well as the heavy additional import costs (for feeding and soil improvement) to enable the British farmer to increase his output, the change-over may cost the Exchequer about £250 million a year. This is a substantial amount and a suitable weapon for 'frightfulness' propaganda. In fact, we are here concerned with only a small proportion of what is spent annually by the nation, for the net total amount spent by the people each year on food and other farming produce, is less than 1p. out of 100p. spent overall, as food consumption accounts for less than 1 per cent of the national G.N.P. As so often it is largely a matter of perspective or 'presentation', whether a set of figures 'frightens' or 'pleases'!

(2) EFFECTS ON COMMONWEALTH AND FRIENDLY NATIONS

Since the débâcle of 1963, the Commonwealth Governments have had seven years to appreciate the position and to come to terms with possible developments. They have not been slow. New markets have been opened for sugar and mutton, the principal commodities likely to be affected by Britain entering the Community and moving behind the protection of the C.E.T. wall. (Small communities like Fiji, depending on only one or two industries, will have to be dealt with by way of individual Annexes to the amended Treaty.) The strengthening of economic ties with the United States and Japan has gone hand in hand with attempts to establish marketing bases in Africa and South America. Some of the developing countries are acquiring sufficient financial strength to make purchases of bulk imports at competitive prices, and the advent of the super-bulk carrier of 100,000 tons or more will prove very helpful indeed in furtherance of those countries' attempts to seek new trading connexions with distant communities.

E.F.T.A. (which recently completed arrangements with Iceland to make her an Associate member), would lose its Nordic members. Denmark and Norway are co-candidates with Britain and Ireland for the talks scheduled for the summer of 1970. Denmark, Norway and Ireland, with a total population of about 11½ million, will add to the Community about 170,000 square miles of territory, and three trading deficits of varying severity. The departure of the two Scandinavian kingdoms into the Community, with Sweden and Finland in all probability applying for Association status, would herald the end of E.F.T.A. as a viable trading area. Switzerland, Portugal and Austria are not economically inter-connected in such a way as to make the continuance of an E.F.T.A. rump a desirable proposition. It is probable that Spain will join with Portugal in applying for an Association arrangement between the two Iberian nations and the Community, which could be based on the partial argument already reached between the E.E.C. and Spain in the course of prolonged negotiations. Switzerland, with her exceptional wealth and her financial world role, and as a traditional neutral, is not inclined to join the Community for obvious political and ethnic reasons. In the present tentative stage of supra-national development in Europe, her reasons are valid and realistic. Austria, as a 'new' neutral, financially less well endowed, may find it advantageous to adopt a position much like that of Switzerland, as far as her close trading links with Germany permit. Europe can afford an uncommitted heart for the time being.

It seems probable, at the time of writing, that the successful outcome of the proposed negotiations with the Community, on the part of Britain and her three co-applicants, would lead to the gradual phasing out of the Ottawa Treaty and the E.F.T.A. arrangements. It cannot be stressed too emphatically that the ending of any existing Agreement, however cogent the reasons, can be justified only if it is replaced by a better Agreement. There are too few links between nations to let any one be broken without replacement. In attempting to replace the Ottawa Agreement and its many sub-treaties, as well as the E.F.T.A. arrangement, within the framework of the Community, those concerned with the drafting of the Revised Rome Treaty will have their work cut out.

(3) SOVEREIGNTY AND INDEPENDENCE, 1970

The 'national' complications of Community membership remain ever-present in the background, whenever the 'Common Market' is discussed. These problems cannot be shrugged off, or refuted by statistics like the 'price of butter' argument. They cannot be countered by reference to facts and figures, relevant to the 'Commonwealth Trading Area' argument (in connexion with which one may also stress the certainty that the ethnic ties with the white Commonwealth, the ties of law, language, blood, friendship and alliance, will persevere quite unaffected by any Community arrangements). As regards British independence as a sovereign nation state, one is dealing with a wholly 'special' situation, evoking unique problems and considerations of emotions affecting the heart rather than the mind.

Only seventy years ago, Britain was the head of the most powerful colonial empire ever united by man. After two successful World Wars, her non-European dependencies have broken away completely, and the old settlers' colonies have become politically independent. After the diplomatic and military presence of the British Raj had departed, only the economic and cultural ties remained. The Treaty of Rome will inevitably tend to weaken the former, and membership will surely imply the gradual phasing out of many trading agreements.

It is easy to understand that in the traumatic aftermath of an

Imperial dusk, pipedreams such as N.A.F.T.A. or a Commonwealth Trading Area will appear more comforting and soothing to many than the 'remote' blue prints for Europe, made in Brussels. However, there has been no enthusiasm for the N.A.F.T.A. project in the United States, nor are there many protagonists of the 'Commonwealth before Europe' school of thought even in Australia, New Zealand or Canada. When he enters upon the resumed negotiations with the Six, the British Prime Minister of the day will have a much easier task than his predecessor Harold Macmillan: the millstones of Commonwealth responsibility will have dropped away. Negotiated transition agreements should not be unduly difficult to agree and to fulfil. And yet . . . and yet . . . One cannot easily whittle away any aspect of the supreme position of the Crown, the sovereignty of Parliament, and the traditional independence of the United Kingdom, unconquered for nine hundred years. To some extent the writing is indeed on the wall: the prospects of a European Parliament with real powers, a supreme Council of Prime Ministers, complete economic, military and political union in the Community – all these projects now form an integral part of future Community policy. It is certain that many a hard word will be spoken and written before a suitably amended Treaty of Rome becomes part of the Law of England.

In September 1969, only 26 per cent of a sample questioned by a reputable firm of Opinion Pollsters in Britain were in favour of joining the Community, while 57 per cent were opposed to the idea and 16 per cent 'did not know'. Yet at about the same time, sample opinions taken on the Continent of Europe were overwhelmingly (12 to 1) in favour of letting Britain in.

In 1963 the negotiations failed when Mr Heath had many of his country's leaders and all but one of the Community's leaders on his side. At this crucial stage, it may be rewarding to analyse three vital aspects of the European problem confronting Britain today: the kind of Community which has developed over the years and with which the candidate nations are now concerned, Britain's own opposition in front of the opening gate at Brussels and the type of procedure which may be followed to implement the suggested 'enlargement' of the Community.

(a) THE COMMUNITY OF EUROPE IN 1970

The policies laid down in the Treaties of Paris and Rome were originally agreed in outline only, except for the elimination of customs duties. Details were set out only concerning the establishment of a common tariff and the removal of certain quantitative restrictions within the Community. These objectives of the Treaty of Rome have been largely implemented, and the movement of goods between the member-states is more or less 'free'. Uniform customs laws are being drafted.

We have already dealt, in broad terms, with the Common Agricultural Policy, which provides the machinery for the implementation of a vital common policy, in accordance with Art. 38(4) of the Treaty of Rome.

Some progress has been made towards the free movement of persons, services and capital. But whereas impressive proposals are awaiting discussion to make it possible for members of the professions to work as freely anywhere in the Community area as the migrant workers, such retrogressive decisions by individual member-states as unilateral currency re-valuations and restrictions (albeit labelled 'temporary') on export of capital, constitute severe set-backs to the planned unification of Europe.

The common Transport Policy is still in its early phase of development. It now seems certain that at an early stage sea and air transport will be added to the sectors referred to in the Rome Treaty.

The special energy policies and the common production and utilization of coal and steel under the Euratom and E.C.S.C. Treaties have on the whole worked out better than anticipated. It was easier to create a *modus vivendi* concerning a definable range of products than in respect of a wide and ill-defined field of human activities. This supposition is corroborated by the sporadic and fitful progress in respect of the 'general' policies. Clearly, in the life of nations there is as much need for precision as in the life of individuals. Some progress has been made with legal and fiscal harmonization, particularly as regards unfair competition and restrictive practices. The value-added tax has proved more difficult to introduce than expected – and the

Commission had to agree to a delay of its introduction in Italy and Belgium.

Regarding the 'peripheral' spheres of 'harmonization', for instance in regard to municipal laws, economic trends and social provisions, there has been slow but steady progress. The innate convenience of universally applicable rules is proving attractive. The success or failure of a scheme in one of the six member states, the good sense of adopting similar rules for similar practices, and the advantages of increased efficiency or monetary savings as the direct result of harmonization, are proving the best inducements to make further changes and to adopt additional common usages. Cases in point are the introduction of family allowances in Germany, the gradual harmonization of social benefits throughout the Community, and the 'assimilation' of traffic regulations for the sake of general convenience.

The twelve-year transition period laid down in the Treaty of Rome ended on 31st December 1969. From that date, additional matters could be resolved by majority decision, instead of by unanimity, of the members. Now unanimity is only required for such fundamental steps as to extend the common transport policies to sea and air, to harmonize additional taxes and general national legislation, to admit new member states or new associates, or to achieve objectives not provided for in the Treaties.

It is becoming more difficult for a member-state to obtain authorization for even temporary measures in contravention of the Treaties. The member-states, of course, remain sovereign nations and cannot easily be forced to comply with any 'order', but as the Community is based so firmly on the 'voluntary compliance' principle, the basic requirement of authorization prior to any departures from the Rule of Community Law is not likely to be disregarded easily.

All in all, the 'Eurocrats' have managed to set up rather a formidable system of co-operation and co-ordination. The Community is the only supra-national system with institutions designed for political and administrative unification and has evolved a fairly detailed and effective system of laws and regulations, with viable sanctions.

Following the Commission's publication in October 1969 of

its revised 'Opinion' concerning the widening and strengthening of the Community, with particular reference to the effect on the implementation of the common policies, the Heads of Government of the Six and their Foreign Ministers were invited by the Dutch Government to assemble at The Hague on 1st December, 1969, at the request of the French Government. (This was not a meeting of the Council of Ministers.) On the second day of the meeting, the Commission itself was invited to participate.

The official Communiqué issued at the end of the Conference announced agreement concerning definitive financial arrangements in respect of the common agricultural policy, by the end of 1969. (This had been the fundamental issue raised by the French Government. Outline financial agreement was in fact achieved before the year ended.) The member-states' right to amend the details, but not the principles, of this policy by a unanimous decision was specifically reserved.

It was further resolved to strengthen the Community as an economic union. During 1970, a plan for the creation of economic and monetary union is to be worked out. A Common Reserve Fund of $2,000m, to counteract 'currency upheavals', was set up in January, 1970.

After stating such general aims as the desirability of close technological co-operation, further research by Euratom and the possible establishment of a European University, agreement as to the enlargement of the Community (under Article 237 of the Treaty of Rome) was 'reaffirmed': 'In so far as the applicant states accept the Treaties and their political finality, the decisions taken since the coming into force of the Treaties and the options made in the sphere of development, the heads of state or government have indicated their agreement to the opening of negotiations between the Community on the one hand and the applicant states on the other. They agreed that the essential preparatory work could be undertaken as soon as practically and conveniently possible. By common consent, the preparations would take place in a most positive spirit.' (Hague Communiqué, par. 13.)

Once the proposed talks were under way, it was further stated, negotiations with other interested E.F.T.A. members would be initiated.

A report by the Foreign Ministers of the Six on political unification was requested by the end of July 1970.

In effect, this announcement made it possible once again to start negotiations with Britain and the other three applicants, provided M. Pompidou managed to achieve the required adjustments of France's short-term financial liabilities under the common agricultural policy. Agreement *in principle* had been reached, in the nick of time, as usual. The plans for 1970 thus comprise a wide range of European projects – technological harmonization, uniform tax laws, higher education on a supranational basis, plans for political unification and the opening of discussions to admit new members.

It was generally expected that July, 1970, would be the earliest date for negotiations with the candidate nations to begin. There were demonstrations at The Hague by students and other young people in favour of a United Europe. All over the Community the opinion polls disclosed increasingly large majorities in favour of admitting the applicant nations, and in support of political union in Europe. In Britain, however, it rather seemed as if only the younger generation was any longer in favour of such changes.

(b) BRITAIN *vis-à-vis* EUROPE, 1970

In the Annex to its Opinion, the Commission expressed some general views about the likely effects of 'enlargement' on the Community itself. Dealing first with the *Customs* Union, it was felt that the four new members would bring about a considerable expansion in trade within the area of the Six and with other countries; in fact intra-Community trade (f.o.b. exports from each member-state to every other member-state) were expected to rise from about $28,400 million (1968) to about $41,200 million solely as the result of increased membership. The enlarged Community would then account for 25·6 per cent of the world's trade. In fact, the impetus is likely to be greater still, through indirect stimulation and 'spin-off' developments.

There was no reason, in the opinion of the Commission, why the introduction of a *common commercial policy* should be delayed by the 'enlargement' process, nor would the implementation of that policy raise major problems for the new members.

As regards *industrial harmonization*, at lower levels (European company, market unification for specific products, a Euro-patent system, etc.), much remains to be done, but the new members should find effective co-operation no more difficult than the Six founder members. As regards the British steel industry, the Commission added a special rider. The current price regulations would require alteration, and the dominant position of the nationalized British Steel Corporation might have to be adjudged in the light of the Community Regulations concerning undue industrial (monopolistic) strength (Articles 66 and 67 of the Treaty of Paris).

In the sphere of research the new members, particularly the United Kingdom, would obviously provide much new strength and drive. The nuclear power development in Britain by the U.K.A.E.A. would enable the Community to take a leading position in the world as far as this field of research is concerned. Some excellent theoretical work (with limited practical implementation), on the part of Norway and Denmark would further add to the Community's strength.

Dealing with the use of energy generally, the accession of Britain with her extensive and varied power and fuel networks, and of Norway with her hydro-electric power grid, would foster the project of a *common energy policy*.

Agriculture

Agricultural land in the enlarged Community would be increased by 30 per cent, but as farms in Britain and Denmark are on the whole larger than in the Six, the increase in the number of farms would only be about 20 per cent, and due to the greater efficiency rate in Britain, the number of agricultural workers would rise by only about 16 per cent.

There would be a reduction in the self-sufficiency rate of the enlarged Community as follows (1967/8 basis):

	Six Members %	*Ten Members* %
Wheat	112·5	97·6
Rice	100·8	85·9

	Six Members	Ten Members
	%	%
Sugar	104·6	83·0
Fruit	89·9	81·6
Vegetables	102·5	98·9
Mutton, Lamb, etc.	84·2	58·9
Butter	111·1 (provisional)	91·8 (provisional)
Cheese	102·7 (provisional)	99·9 (provisional)
Oils and fats	41·8	40·8

However sufficiency increases are expected as regards:

Feed Grain	78·6	79·6
Beef and veal	88·8	97·6
Poultry	97·8	100·0
Pork	100·0	103·9

Obviously, harvest and seasonal variations, changes of demand due to price as well as artificially induced trends might well upset this forecast. It is now accepted that Britain would be faced by special problems concerning sugar, butter and mutton. The United Kingdom imports nearly 70 per cent of her sugar from the Commonwealth, partly at a special price under the Commonwealth Sugar Agreement (about 1·8 million tons) and a further 4 million tons (also from the Commonwealth) at ordinary rates. All this sugar pays a low duty on entering Britain. In the face of a sugar surplus in the Community, it seems clear that on the expiry in 1974 of the Sugar Agreement, an entirely new arrangement will have to be made, gradually leading to some preferential conditions for Continental sugar.

Britain imports almost all the exportable butter produced by New Zealand (85 per cent). The Community for some years has had a huge butter surplus. Under the current trade agreement, Britain accepts 170,000 tons of butter per year from New Zealand. This agreement is due to end in September, 1972. As Britain's annual requirements amount to about 470,000 tons (her home production varying between 30,000 to 60,000 tons), the non-New Zealand imports are controlled by variable quota arrangements, including large imports from Australia (65,000 tons), France, Belgium and Netherlands (12,000 tons) and Norway, Denmark and Ireland (120,000 tons). It has been pointed out previously that the gradual switch to British absorption of the European butter surplus may initially force up the consumer price of this commodity.

In the view of the Commission, membership of the Community would have rather less drastic effects on Irish food prices. Most prices would rise, but sugar beet, potatoes and eggs would be cheaper.

Danish agriculture, which is exceedingly efficient, and often operates at lower price levels than the E.E.C., for instance as regards meat products, would benefit by increased trade, although consumer prices would tend to rise.

Norway, which depends on fishery and forestry (3·5 per cent of her G.N.P.) almost as much as on farming (4 per cent), and where farming in the northern areas has to be subsidized to overcome the climatic and territorial difficulties, would suffer a reduction in agricultural earnings. The removal of existing subsidies and the cost of imported food would lead to increased food prices generally as far as the consumer is concerned.

Finally the Commission added a few specific footnotes. *Freedom of exchange control* (Art. 67) would mean changes in British financial policy. The removal of almost all British travel exchange restrictions on 1st January, 1970 went some way towards achieving this objective.

Tax harmonization

Naturally enough, implementation of this policy is considered urgent. As not very much has been accomplished in this respect, the new members would start with almost the same handicap as the Six.

Competition

Here clearly the larger Community would generate additional internal competitiveness. No difficulties are foreseen. There is some danger that a Community of Ten may initiate a large wave of industrial mergers, thereby destroying the 'healthy' trend for greater competitiveness, and instead producing ever larger and more powerful industrial units, with the concomitant threat of monopolistic tendencies.

(c) HOW TO JOIN

We have dealt with some of the anticipated advantages and disadvantages of membership, and with the hazards inherent in some of the proposed changes. With due reservations in the face of all manner of contingencies, on the basis of what we have seen of the growth of the Community from its infancy to the present day, and in the light of some of the salutary experiences of the past, it may be that the actual process of 'Joining Europe' will proceed somewhat on the following lines:

By July, 1970, consultations between the Six, the Commission and the candidate states may be possible, and it is now most likely that the Commission will be allowed to participate directly in all the negotiations. There is no reason why these negotiations should not be concluded by November, 1970. (If a General Election has not been held in Britain by that date, and as it must be held by the spring of 1971, a 'declaration of intent' by both major parties would be desirable, perhaps on the occasion of their respective Annual Conferences in the autumn of 1970.)

It might then take about six months to draft a Revision or Supplementary Treaty to amend the three basic Treaties, which will then have to be presented to the Parliaments of the Six and the Four. Arguments are likely to be prolonged, particularly amongst the applicants' elected representatives. It is quite probable that the emphasis will shift, even in Britain, from the price of food via sovereignty to the status of the national Parliament. In this context the members of the Mother of Parliaments may well feel that the proposed strengthening of the European Parliament cannot be shrugged off lightly. The powers of the latter may well grow considerably and much faster than anticipated by many. Such is the habit of new Parliaments. It has been proposed that by 1974 the European Parliament should control the Community budget. By a two-thirds majority, the Parliament would then be able to pass the Community budget even against the wishes of the Council of Ministers, and the Community would be financially independent. In the first instance the money raised through the common tariff and customs charges would be retained by the Community, in addition to the present levies on coal and steel, which are comparatively small. It is proposed to carry out this process of 'weaning' the Community from the coffers of the Governments of the member-states, initially by adding revenue from the agricultural levy to the present national contributions to the Community funds. In accordance with the principle that he who pays the piper calls the tune, the Council would retain diminishing control up to 1973, but even during the interim period the economic independence of the Commission would be steadily strengthened.

After 1974 the European Parliament would be in control of the disposition of the Community's funds, and as these funds would include a considerable proportion of British revenue it is unlikely that such a transfer of control will be accepted with equanimity by the Commons. This financial maturity on the part of the Community is certain to lead to demands for greater administrative and political independence. Decisions taken in Brussels would then seriously affect the budgetary allocations in every member-state concerning taxation, social services and so on through all portfolios – a definite reduction of the freedom of the Ways and Means Committee to do as it pleases.

However, it may be anticipated that by mid-1971 the amended Treaties will have been ratified by all the Parliaments concerned, and the 'special' agreements with the neutrals and other European states will similarly have passed through the necessary stages. Thus the 'enlarged' Community could come into being, subject to specific transition periods, sometime during 1972 or early in 1973, in time for the beginning of the Community's fiscal independence.

The Euro-bus is a moving vehicle. It has been subjected to a number of break-downs and detours, but it is now slowly moving in the intended direction. Waiting to board it are four potential passengers, who are aware of the time-table and of the fare. They may not have agreed to the small print conditions, but the bus will not wait. A full load would benefit the prospects of the venture. Brussels, 1970, is a Request Stop. It may be the last within walking distance. We are all in the queue – whether we like it or not.

CHAPTER XIV

The Stage is Set

In February, 1970, the British Government published a White Paper on the 'Britain and the European Communities' series, entitled 'An Economic Assessment'. The official British view appeared to be that the cost of entry 'has been somewhat increased by devaluation, but on the other hand there has been a very substantial improvement in (the country's) balance of payments and the competitive strength of (her) economy'. Furthermore, there would have to be important re-assessments in view of several major steps taken within the Community since 1967: the new financing arrangements for the Community budget, the fact that only a unanimous decision can effectively change these arrangements, and the proposed extension of the budgetary powers of the European Parliament after 1974. Secondly, the costs likely to be incurred in connexion with the common agricultural policy. Thirdly, the decision taken at The Hague in December, 1969, to proceed with economic and monetary unification, and to consider the implementation of the common technological and social policies (Cmnd. 4289).

The White Paper deliberately omitted any references to the social and political implications of British membership and its comments were limited to evaluations of the economic consequences of Britain joining the Community during the early Seventies. The survey also dealt at some length with the economic effects on Agriculture and Food, Trade and Industry, and Capital Movements and Invisible Trade. These computations were based on the economic statistics for the recent past, an assessment of possible trends discernible from a study of the

figures available, a forecast of possible reactions and inter-
actions as the result of gradual implementations of the common
policies in Britain, and on a surmise of possible counter-
reactions as far as importers, exporters, financiers, banks and
(to some extent) the general public were concerned.

It was inevitable that any such forecast based on actual
statistics but subject to numerous incalculable estimates, would
produce minimum and maximum figures so wide apart that the
resulting 'brackets' cover almost uselessly wide ranges. The
change in the cost of British food imports, it was stated, might
range from a reduction of £85 million to an increase of £255
million per year. The maximum increase in food prices which
might result from such a change was also forecast as a bracket
figure: 18–26 per cent, over an unknown number of years (subject to the length of the agreed transition periods, if any).

Britain's estimated gross contribution to the Community
budget might be (according to the White Paper), between
£150 million to £670 million a year, while her receipts from
operating the agricultural policy were computed at between
£50 million to £100 million. The country's balance of trade
(excluding food) might be 'adversely affected to the extent of
£125 million to £275 million', but even this wide bracket 'is
based on over-simplification'. Thus 'the total effect of the
estimates of the costs of entry', in respect of the three main subjects covered by the White Paper, ranged from 'about £100
million to about £1,100 million', without making allowance for
certain 'dynamic effects', *i.e.* positive results due to membership
which it is impossible to predict at all. In conclusion it was
stated, with some emphasis, that 'the major uncertain factor is
still the balance of economic advantage particularly in the short
run', *i.e.* it was impossible to forecast with any useful degree of
accuracy what might happen during the first three or four years
of membership. Few people were likely to disagree with the
assertion that the 'White Paper demonstrates the need for
negotiations to determine the conditions' relating to entry.

The Heads of State of the Six, having declared their willingness to negotiate with the four candidates in December, 1969,
had since that date reiterated their desire to enlarge the Community if possible. The White Paper contained the British

Government's view of the present position and its thoughts about the possible future. The other three candidate nations were clearly determined to enter unless there were most serious economic obstacles, or, (possibly), unless Britain at some future stage decided to stay out after all.

Is this likely? The White Paper was anything but optimistic as regards future prospects. It was deliberately based on the least appetizing feature of joining, namely the short-term economic prospects, particularly such matters as rising food prices. It forecast a rise in the cost of living of between 4 and 5 per cent, but omitted to explain that this rise due specifically to membership would be spread over some four to five years, and would therefore amount to no more than a rise of about 1 per cent per year, compared with a 'normal' rise of about 3·5 per cent per year in Britain during the period 1965 to 1969.

Again the predicted rise of food prices was presented as an ominous burden on the housewife. On the assumption that these rises will be as steep as predicted, without any relieving features such as reductions in the cost of 'alternative' foods, the extra expenditure per year to the housewife during a transition period of, say, five years would be about 3–5 per cent per year. But annual rises of food prices in Britain during recent 'normal' years have been as high as 4–6 per cent per year, and while this was greeted with groans and criticism it did not 'break' many domestic budgets. The chances are that people will continue to chop and change, until they find goods which they like and can afford. It will continue to be a matter of supply and demand whether the Sunday joint is mutton, beef or pork. 'Public taste and preference' are not immutable; indeed, they have changed frequently from one decade to the next.

One final point with reference to the White Paper. There was almost no mention of wages. Yet it seemed as if in many sectors of the working community in Britain the rush for Community standards had already begun, albeit rather prematurely. The wages increases during 1968 and 1969 in the Community had been much greater than in Britain, and 'actual' incomes (based on the purchasing value of wages earned), had risen three and four times faster in the Six during those years than in the United Kingdom. The G.N.P.s of the Six had also risen faster than that of Britain during the 1958–1967 (see Table 14 of the White Paper, p. 30), but what was the reaction of the official commentators? They compared the Community with E.F.T.A., thereby obliterating the striking factor that Britain's comparatively slow growth was well behind that of every one of the Six during the period under review.

The Foreign Ministers of the Six met in Brussels on 6th March, 1970, to discuss enlargement of the Community, with particular reference to the transition periods, now to be known as 'exceptional periods'. It now seems probable that the Commission will suggest that the commencement date for these 'exceptional periods' (in respect of the new member-states), should be 1st January, 1973, and that the longest of these periods (presumably that contained in the protocols to cover the abatement and phasing out of certain Commonwealth preference agreements), would end in 1978.

Thus the stage was set, with the British Government clearly ready to go either way. For electoral reasons there was almost no indication for any preference. The people had been worried for years about the likelihood of rising prices. Particularly those who depend on fixed incomes and pensions were rightly afraid. As the outcome of the impending negotiations will largely depend on the British Government's readiness to accept a number of almost 'fixed' conditions (subject only to transitional arrangements over a few years), Members of Parliament will in the end be faced with the fateful question: 'Can the British people afford to join the Community?' It would be cruelly misleading to pose this problem in isolation, without the further question: 'Can the British Government afford to say "No"?' The answer may affect the fate of Europe, and therefore of the World, for a long time to come. It must not be based on economic considerations alone, however important these may be. There is more to the life of a nation than money.

Postscript

This book was written as the result of work done in the field of 'European politics', over many years. At most times, the conditions for building a better and stronger Europe were unfavourable. In a previous book, *What the Common Market Really Means*, from which the present volume was developed, I tried to explain the struggles for unity across the Channel. My self-imposed task, in these pages, was to confront the reader with a fair image of the European Community, to enable him (or her) to form a view in the coming period of decision-making.

The reading public of today, and particularly younger people such as students and other men and women engaged in all kinds of 'further education' usually prefer to be given the facts of a problem without propaganda. Of course, the background has to be painted in, and where there are alternative explanations of variable propositions or several ways of looking at a problem, those readers would wish to be informed fully, without omissions. 'The truth, the whole truth and nothing but the truth' would seem to be a good target to aim at. I trust the reader will forgive the deliberate repetition of certain basic facts. During innumerable discussions following talks about the new Europe, it has been my experience that a few important truths about the origin, the nature and the purpose of the Community are so little known that they should be stressed with particular emphasis.

In the case of the Common Market what emerges is a kaleidoscope of many hopes, many fears, many dreams and many misapprehensions. Having tried to tell the story impartially I feel that it would be less than frank not to add a few words of personal opinion. At the very least this will enable some readers to say that they 'felt all along that the writer was . . .'.

I believe that the method chosen for rebuilding Europe on the ruins left by the Second World War was the only practicable one. The artificial creation of a Pan-European state, which might have been achieved during the early days of painful awakening among the débris and rubble, would not have endured for very long. Such a 'rushed job' would have had to be accomplished in those days with American money, and I do not believe that the new Europe would have appreciated it if its reconstruction had been due to non-European charity, irrespective of motive. And so the work had to be done from the inside, slowly, first things first and step by step.

I also believe it was right to start with the pooling of coal and steel. The elimination of war risks provided the most cogent motive to lend force to the initial effort of bringing Europe closer together. It was a successful start. Thereafter a minority would have wished to leave things there. In my view, to call a halt at that stage would have doomed the entire project to failure, for sectoral integration is not likely to endure if national antagonisms are allowed to develop freely in all other fields.

For this reason I have no doubt that it was right to try to integrate the armed forces of the Six, and when that failed, to turn to economic unification. In this sphere the results were likely to become apparent rather quickly to ordinary people in their daily lives, possibly a reason why E.E.C. should have been 'initiated' before E.D.C. was put on the Agenda. The benefits of even an effective European Defence Force would not have been generally appreciated, if at all, except in time of war.

At this stage of integration many voices were raised against further unification. 'Let us have more cultural contact and let us get together socially, by all means, but enough is enough', they were saying. In my view these views are wrong, for this reason: the peoples of Europe are split and segregated into separate and clearly defined pseudo-ethnic groups in such a way that the mere pursuit of common economic policies, with some pleasant social and cultural harmonization added, would not survive the severe tests which undoubtedly lie ahead. For instance, what would happen to the Community if some but not all of the member-states were subjected to a threat of thermo-nuclear attack from outside the Six? Or if the political development in one of the member-states resulted in its being governed undemocratically and in accordance with dictatorial principles, *i.e.* if a member-state 'went Communist'?

If the vast sums of money, the concerted efforts and the massive idealism which were needed and which were made available to create the Community are not to be put at risk again, then the next step will have to be the creation of a Political Community. All those who planned the 'little Europe' of the Six (who did not then know that there would be only six members), were fully aware that some sort of political integration would have to be the end-product of their operations. Only when the foreign policies, the military planning and the financial dispositions of all the member-states of the Community are each handled in accordance with a single agreed policy, only when the Community speaks with a single voice at the conference tables of the world, can it be regarded as securely established.

It was never intended to build the mighty Community edifice merely to house a 'little Europe' of six nations, just because those countries happened to be the original members of the Coal and Steel Community. On the other hand the massive extension of the Community to take in the whole Continent from the Pyrenees to the Urals could not be justified at the present time. Such over-expansion would probably wreck the existing establishment.

However, the shelving as over-ambitious of ex-President de Gaulle's Grand Design does not imply that the figure '6' will have to be adopted as Europe's magic number for all time. I believe that the time has already arrived for those Scandinavian states which so desire to join the Community, and if Switzerland did not have grave political apprehensions (for obvious reasons) she, too, could now be enrolled as a useful member. Austria and Portugal will become valuable associates before long, in one way or another, and Spain and Finland may then join them. Closer to the 'Iron Curtain', I believe that Yugoslavia will in the not so distant future sign a special Treaty with the Community and this may set a precedent for similar special Trade and Culture Pacts with countries on the other side of the Curtain.

This brings me to the ultimate burning problem as far as the British reader is concerned: Should Britain join? If ever an opportunity was missed for bringing the benefits of Empire to bear upon the European problem, then 1946 was that time. There would then have been no need to talk of 'conditions' and 'safeguards' – Britain could have assisted Europe so much by her very preparedness to 'muck in', that she could have got anything she reasonably wanted, with thanks. Twenty-four years is a long time in an era when events move quickly, when new nations emerge in rapid succession, and when the balance of power is adjusted according to which country has the biggest thermo-nuclear bomb, complete with delivery device, at any given time.

The British decision whether to join or not must now be determined by the conditions agreed with the European Community in 1970 and the nation's intentions as to its future role in the world. Membership of the Community will imply equal status with France, Germany, and Italy for good, within a developing European Federation of some kind or other. (It is idle to speculate on what would result if the Community were to collapse after Britain had joined. In the ensuing free-for-all, anything might happen.)

Now the British application, together with those of the other applicants and the Swedish letter of intent, is about to be discussed in Brussels. What if it fails once more?

Continued isolation would probably bring with it a prolonged period of hard work, strict economic discipline and prolonged restraint in many spheres, with only an outside chance of regaining world power status. In my view these hardships and restraints are unnecessary. If it is intended to take such a chance with the lives of 50 million people, the Government and the Opposition must make their positions clear beyond any reasonable doubt. In that event it might be possible to rely on the Commonwealth and some independent nations in support of some kind of Economic Federation outside the European Community.

Almost certainly time is not on Britain's side as far as the solution of this problem is concerned. If membership of the Community is still the goal of both the major political parties, a good deal of immediate 'home work' ought to be done: there could be voluntary harmonization of many laws, regulations and procedures; alignment of economic arrangements; facilitation of the movement of workers, goods and capital to and from the Community; specific pacts concerning commodities or groups of commodities and increased 'cultural' exchanges. The pro-membership enthusiasm of 1967 has evaporated. A large sector of public opinion is against Britain joining the Community, for a variety of valid and invalid reasons. Only the young are mostly in favour of continuing with the negotiations.

The political gallantry involved in 'going it alone' hardly seems justifiable in view of the needless risks involved. On balance it would seem almost improper for a Government to take the political and economic risks involved in opting out of the new Europe.

I believe the development of destructive military hardware, sufficient to wipe out a large proportion of mankind in a few seconds at the push of a button, justifies the sacrifice of some sovereignty for the sake of survival, provided this means survival with dignity.

Therein I think lies the key to Britain's problem. Nothing she can now do would lend greater dignity to her great role in the world than the sacrifice of some of the trimmings of Commonwealth power and a measure of sovereignty. The objective would be sovereignty shared between all the member-states, not sovereignty lost by any individual country.

Membership by Britain now would not be the glorious entry of the deliverer into Europe that it would have been, had Churchill's call of 1946 been answered by action instead of silence. But in my view it would still be the next best thing: a firm step in the right direction. This step could be taken with much greater certainty if some of the preparatory work suggested above were undertaken without delay and with some measure of enthusiasm. The White Paper published on 10th February, 1970, contains many vague predictions and is devoid of any 'European' thought. It is but an estimate of costs to be incurred, and does not contain any reference to the spiritual values of a United Europe. It will not help the average man or woman to make up their minds about Europe.

It would seem fitting to conclude this book with the following words from the message by President Jean Rey on the
occasion of the abolition of all customs in the Community on
1st July 1968, 18 months ahead of the schedule laid down by
the Treaty of Rome: 'We must also unite Europe as a *political
entity* and enlarge our Community to include the other countries
of Europe which wish to join. The founders of the Community
never envisaged that it would be closed to other countries. They
believed that the six original members would be the *nucleus*
around which Great Britain and other European countries
could be united. The real aim of our endeavour is a *political and
spiritual reconciliation* of the countries of this continent in order
to achieve a *united, peaceful, socially progressive and free Europe.*'

My italics – but the words of a Belgian statesman and a
former prisoner of war in Germany, twenty-three years after
the end of World War II. It is high time for action in accordance with the sentiments expressed by the President of the
Commission, and later, much later, than we think. The objective,
in the last resort, is the provision of decent standards of living in
Europe, in conditions of security, peace and prosperity. The
heritage of Europe must be preserved if the achievements of its
nations are not to be jeopardized. In a world where 350 million
Europeans are only one-tenth of the world population, where in
one generation it is predicted that this earth will have to sustain
twice as many – over 7,000 million – people, the Community of
Europe is relatively only just adequate for survival. The planned
Europe would, proportionately, be no larger within the total
human population, than, say, Britain was a generation or so ago.

These large units – such as the United States, Soviet Russia,
China and Europe – may be able to preserve a precarious peace
better than the smaller 'nation states' of our days. The know-
ledge that a war between such giants might lead to their own
total destruction should have a salutary effect. Peace through
terror is not an attractive proposition. However, it is better
than the certainty of a truly 'total' war.

The ethnic communities, which may come to the fore a good
deal more if Europe unites politically, are not likely to go to
war. Their dignified survival in the centuries to come, safe-
guarding the survival of the European heritage (including that

of Britain), seems to hold out more desirable prospects for our future than a fight for survival in deliberate isolation (however justifiable for historical reasons), perpetually at risk.

Bibliography

(A list of books read while writing this book. Those recommended for *further general reading* are marked *.)

OFFICIAL PUBLICATIONS.
Journal officiel des Communautés européennes, from 1958.
Numerous publications by the Publications Departments of the European Communities, Brussels.
'European Community' and other publications by the European Community Information Service, London.
'General Statistical Bulletin', Statistical Office of the European Communities, Brussels and Luxembourg.

Albrecht-Carrie, R. *The Unity of Europe – an historical survey,** London, 1966.
Áraujo, De. *Le Plan Fouchet et l'Union Politique européenne,** Nancy, 1966.*
Bacino, E. *L'Europa cominciò oggi,* Florence, 1962.
Barach, A. B. *The new Europe and its Economic Future,* New York, 1964.
Barraclough, G. *European Unity in Thought and Action,* Oxford, 1963.
Bebr, G. *Judicial Control of the European Communities,* London, 1962.
Beddington-Behrens, Sir E. *Is there any choice?**, London, 1966.
Beloff, Max, *New Dimensions in Foreign Policy,* London, 1961.
Benoit, Emile. *Europe at Sixes and Sevens,* New York, 1961.
Bourely, M. G. *'Les Organisations européennes de co-opération en matière spatiale',* Revue française de Droit aérien, Paris, July 1964.
Caemmerer, E. von. *Probleme des Europäischen Rechts,* Frankfurt, 1966.
Calman, J. *Western Europe: A Handbook,* London 1967.
Campbell, A. *Restrictive Trading Agreements in the Common Market,* London 1964.
Camps, Miriam. *Britain and the European Community,** London, 1964.
— *European Unification in the Sixties,* London, 1967.
Cartou, Louis. *Organisations Européennes,* Bruges, 1965.

Catalano, N., and others. *Droit Communitaire et Droit National*, Bruges, 1965.

Catlin, G. E. G. *The Atlantic Commonwealth*, London, 1969.

Caves, R. E. *Britain's Economic Problems*, London, 1968.

Council of Europe. *Handbook of European Organizations*, Strasbourg (various editions).

Deniau, J.-F. *The Common Market – its structure and purpose,** London, 1967 (4th Edition).

Diebold, Jr., William. *The Schuman Plan*, New York, 1959.

E.C.A.C. *Annual Reports*, 1960–1966.

E.F.T.A. *The E.F.T.A. Convention – Summary and Explanation*, Stockholm, 1961.

Florinsky, Michael. *Integrated Europe?* New York, 1955.

Geusau, F. A. N. Alting von. *'European Political Integration – A Record of Confusion and Failure'*, European Year Book, Volume XI.

Gladwyn, Lord. *The European Idea,** London, 1966.

Graupner, Rudolf. *The Rules of Competition in the European Economic Community*, London, 1965.

Hallstein, Walter. *United Europe,** Cambridge, Mass., and London, 1962.

— *'Economic Integration and Political Unity in Europe'*. Community Topics, No. 2, London, 1961.

Heraud, Guy. *Federation Européenne*, Paris, 1968.

Hill, Samuel & Co. Ltd. *Britain and Europe*, London, 1965.

Jantzen, T. *The Operation of a Free Trade Area*, Geneva, 1964.

Jennings, W. Ivor. *A Federation of Western Europe*, London, 1940.

Junckerstorff, H. K. (ed.). *International Manual on the E.E.C.*, St. Louis, 1963.

Kitzinger, U. W. *The Challenge of the Common Market,** Oxford, 1961.

Krause, L. H. (ed.). *The Common Market*, Englewood Cliffs, N.J., 1964.

Ledré, Ch. *Robert Schuman, Pélerin de l'Europe*, Paris, 1954.

Malgrain, Y. *L'intégration agricole de l'Europe des Six*, Paris, 1966.

Manzanares, H. *Le Parlement Européen*, Paris, 1964.

Mayne, Richard. *The Community of Europe*, London, 1962.

Meynaud, J., and Dusan Sidjanski. *L'Europe des Affaires*, Paris, 1967.

Monnet, Jean. *Les Etats-unis d'Europe ont commencé,** Paris, 1955.

Morrison, Clovis C. Jr. *The Developing European Law of Human Rights*, Leyden, 1967.

N.A.T.O. *Facts about the North Atlantic Treaty Organization*, Paris, 1962.

Nijhoff, Martin. *La fusion des Communautés européennes,* The Hague, 1966.
Nutting, Anthony. *Europe will not wait,** London, 1960.
Okigbo, P.N.C. *Africa and the Common Market,* London, 1967.
O.E.C.D. *A Remodelled Economic Organization,* Report, Paris, 1960.
P.E.P. *European Organizations,* London, 1959.
— *The Parliament of the European Communities,* London, 1964.
Price, Roy. *The Political Future of the European Community,* London, 1962.
Rey, Jean. *L'Association de la Grèce et la Turquie à la C.E.E.,* European Yearbook, Vol. XI.
Robertson, A. H. 'The European Political Community',* *British Yearbook of International Law,* London, 1952.
— *The Law of International Institutions of Europe,* London, 1961.
— *European Institutions,* 2nd ed., London, 1966.
Robertson, B. C. *Regional Development in the European Economic Community,* London, 1962.
Sannwald, Rolf, and Jacques Stohler. *Wirtschaftliche Integration,* Basel and Tübingen, 1958.
Shonfield, A. 'The Common Market', *The Unheroic Phase,* Optima, March, 1969.
Shimm, M. G. (Ed.). Law and Contemporary Problems, *European Regional Communities,* Durham, N.C., 1961.
Sieger, H. *Dokumentation der Europäischen Integration,* Bonn, 1964.
Spaak, P.-H. *Pourquoi l'OTAN?,* Paris, 1959.
— *Strasbourg – the Second Year,* Oxford, 1952.
— *Combats inachevés,** Paris, 1969.
Speerenburg, D. P. *The European Coal and Steel Community.* Luxembourg, 1956.
Tinbergen, Jan. *International European Integration,* Amsterdam, 1965.
Trempont, Jacques. *L'Unification de l'Europe,* Amiens et Bruxelles, 1955.
Uri, P. (Ed.). *La Grande-Bretagne rejoint l'Europe,** Paris, 1967.
Valentine, D. G., and Donner, Judge A. M. *The Court of Justice of the European Communities,* London, 1965.
Various authors: *Europe and the Law,* London, 1968.
Wall, E. H. *The Court of Justice of the European Communities,* London, 1960.
Wohlfart, E., and others. *Die Europäische Wirtschaftsgemeinschaft,* Berlin, 1960.
Zurcher, A. J. *The Struggle to Unite Europe,** New York, 1958.

Index

Note: After names of officials and functionaries in the Institutions of the E.E.C. the respective Institutions are indicated as follows; C Council; CM Commission; CT European Court; PT European Parliament

Adenauer, K., concludes Treaty of Co-operation with France, Jan. 1963, 163; as 'new European', 96
African States, *see* Yaoundé Agreement, *and* Map, 86
Agricultural policies (*see also* C.A.P.), xix, 78–80; comparison between E.E.C. and E.F.T.A., 92; E.E.C. policy fully operative by 1972, 178; future of U.K. if a Member, in enlarged E.E.C., 112, 143, 176, 185–7, 207–9; system of levies in, 79–80; full implementation as present policy, 112, system of prices under C.A.P., 198; self-sufficiency rate, 207–8
Algeria, annexe concerning, under Treaty of Rome, 28
Anglo-Saxon Free Trade Association (plan) 158
Argentine: in treaty for mutual aid, with Euratom, 42; in trade talks with E.E.C., 88
Armengaud, M. (France) at Yaoundé Conference, 87
Arrangements of Association, *see* E.E.C.: Association

Arusha Agreement, October 1968, 87, 89
Association, *see* E.E.C.; Association Councils, 71, 73, 85; probable increase in, for European countries, 181–2; *see* diag., 89
Attlee, Clement; first Earl: as P.M., 119; and the E.C.S.C. Treaty, 151
Australia, U.K.'s trade with, 149; present freedom of choice, 156; *see also* Commonwealth
Austria: as E.F.T.A. Member, 121, 200; approach to, and trade talks with, E.E.C., 88, 128, 131
Austrian Empire, historic, 5, 8

Barre, Raymond (CM), 98, 100
Battaglia, Edoardo (PT), 102
Beaton, Professor, on proposed Anglo-Saxon Free Trade Association, 158
Bech, Joseph, 96
Belgium, 111; contribution of, to European Social Fund, 71; loans to, from European Investment Bank, 70; Senate's 'Three Wise Men', xviii, 163; *see* Maps, 33, 41, for coal and steel, nuclear research
Benelux Association, established October 1947, xvii, 166; in relation with Treaty of Rome, 29; Mansholt Plan of 1969 unsatisfactory to, 196
Bismarck, Prince von, 5, 6
Bergen, supranational school at, 108